D0937501

Spreadsheets for Librarians

Spreadsheets for Librarians

Getting Results with Excel and Google Sheets

Bruce White

LIBRARIES
UNLIMITED®

An Imprint of ABC-CLIO, LLC

Santa Barbara, California • Denver, Colorado

Library of Congress Cataloging-in-Publication Data

Names: White, Bruce, 1952- author.
Title: Spreadsheets for librarians : getting results with Excel and Google Sheets / Bruce White.
Description: Santa Barbara, California : Libraries Unlimited, [2021] | Includes bibliographical references and index.
Identifiers: LCCN 2020014189 (print) | LCCN 2020014190 (ebook) | ISBN 9781440869310 (paperback) | ISBN 9781440869327 (ebook)
Subjects: LCSH: Library administration—Computer programs. | Electronic spreadsheets. | Microsoft Excel (Computer file) | Google Sheets.
Classification: LCC Z678.93.E46 W48 2021 (print) | LCC Z678.93.E46 (ebook) | DDC 025.1—dc23
LC record available at https://lccn.loc.gov/2020014189
LC ebook record available at https://lccn.loc.gov/2020014190

ISBN: 978-1-4408-6931-0 (paperback)
    978-1-4408-6932-7 (ebook)

25 24 23 22 21   1 2 3 4 5

This book is also available as an eBook.

Libraries Unlimited
An Imprint of ABC-CLIO, LLC

ABC-CLIO, LLC
147 Castilian Drive
Santa Barbara, California 93117
www.abc-clio.com

This book is printed on acid-free paper ∞

Manufactured in the United States of America

Screenshots of Microsoft Excel are used with permission from Microsoft. Google and the Google logo are registered trademarks of Google LLC, used with permission.

Contents

Preface

I hope that you enjoy reading this book as much as I have enjoyed writing it but that it requires rather less effort. If you don't enjoy reading books about spreadsheets, which is a real possibility, then my next and more realistic hope is that you will find it useful, and that is its true purpose. Indeed "books are for use" was S. R. Ranganathan's first law of library science, while his second and third laws were "every person their book" and "every book its reader," so if you are a librarian wanting to know about spreadsheets, then this should be very much your book. But that will only be true if it is able to fulfil Ranganathan's fourth law, which is that it should "save the time of the reader"—a heavy responsibility indeed.

Time is never really wasted, however, and the many hours I have spent struggling over rows and columns and creating ornate formulas that still didn't tell me what I actually wanted to know has given me an extensive knowledge of how not to do it, of tricks that didn't produce magic results, and shortcuts that led at high speed in the wrong direction. Out of this I hope some practical knowledge of how to do it more or less right has been distilled that will make you a beneficiary of some of those otherwise unproductive hours.

While it may not be immediately obvious that the world needs another book on spreadsheets, it is becoming increasingly clear that the world does need librarians, and if this book helps them to do their work better while also saving time, then it will be playing its part in making it a better place. I don't claim to exceptional spreadsheet expertise, and some of you may have cause to shake your heads at times at some of the choices I have made, but I hope that what I do bring to the task is a store of practical experience of spreadsheet-based data analysis enlivened with a generous portion of enthusiasm and optimism. A key aspect of any skill is knowing when to use it and understanding its potential—and sometimes its limitations! Developing a spreadsheet imagination will require an investment of time but, providing you keep the end goal of saving time and improving the scope of your work in view, it will be worth it.

I have tried to keep my explanations simple and straightforward, and to avoid too much jargon, but there will be times when you are seized with an urge to hurl the book across the room and give up entirely. As librarians you should resist the former urge and instead put it aside to come back to in a few days' time. And remember, while it has been written to read as a journey, you don't all need to get to the end, or at least not right away. Some of the material *is* complex, and I defy anyone to describe a pivot table without resorting to showing, so if you are struggling and feeling that it's all rather beyond you, then that is normal too.

I have been fortunate in the help of a number of people and my dog. My partner Cynthia White told me in no uncertain terms that if I thought I could write a book, then I had no business in not doing so, as well as providing me with an outstanding example of application and hard work. Massey University Library provided me with a context in which to develop my skills as well as data, and my colleague Amanda Curnow read some of the chapters and tested many of the exercises. Jessica Gribble of Libraries Unlimited has been a continuing source of advice, encouragement, and positivity, and I am grateful to have had the opportunity to work with an established publisher in my professional field. And Jack, of course, has continued to remind me that nothing, but nothing, is as important as going for a walk.

"*Ko te manu e kai ana i te miro, nōna te ngahere. Engari, ko te manu e kai ana i te mātauranga, nōna te ao.*"
"The bird that eats the fruit of the miro tree has only the forest, but the bird that feeds on knowledge has the whole world."

—Māori proverb

"*The library is a growing organism.*"

—Ranganathan's fifth law

Bruce White
Palmerston North, New Zealand

CHAPTER ONE

Spreadsheets Are for You

Spreadsheets are for everyone. Or at least for every librarian and information specialist. You might think of spreadsheets as dark forests of data held together with impenetrable formulas that bring back your worst nightmares of high school algebra. You have maybe come across some IT expert who tells you that the spreadsheet you have been sent is really very simple and then switches to some apparently foreign language, performs a few magic clicks, and goes away leaving you none the wiser. You might think that the table function in your word processor is all that you need to keep lists of people or equipment and that your bibliographic management software will do every-thing you need to store details of publications. Or you might already be a competent spreadsheet user who suspects that you are really just scratching the surface or doing things the hard way and that you are ready to learn more. Whichever category you fall into, this book is for you, and I hope not only to convince you that spreadsheets really *are* for you but to get you well on your way to making productive use of them in your work as a librarian. For the sake of simplicity, this book will concentrate on Excel and Google Sheets, but what you learn here will be broadly applicable to other software packages that follow the same conventions.

Spreadsheets are tools and, like any tool, they are best described not by what they are but by what they do. A hammer may be an implement for embedding nails into wood, but this only makes sense when you see it used in building a house. Let's look at a few scenarios that show spreadsheets in use in libraries.

Everybody Loves Meetings

Every Thursday morning your department has a meeting at which you review how things are going in your corner of the library world, arrange your work for the following week or month, discuss any policy or planning documents that have come your way, and perhaps take a look at the big picture and do some future thinking. Ideally, some action resolutions will come out of the discussion, whether it is to change the telephone roster for Tuesday afternoon or to report back in a month's time on some new technology that could change the way your library operates next year.

Before the meeting, perhaps on Monday, the chair sends an email asking for agenda items, and the agenda is emailed out on Wednesday afternoon. It will include matters carried forward from the previous week—the action resolutions—and new subjects, and on Thursday morning the meeting will follow this format, first reviewing how last week's stuff went and then going on to look at this week's issues. In practice not all of last week's actions will have been completed, so some of them might be carried forward to next week or further into the future. During the meeting someone will take notes, and these will come out on Friday as formal minutes with the action statements highlighted and assigned to individual staff or groups, all ready for the cycle to begin again on the following Monday.

It's a familiar and comfortable routine, and everything is neatly documented for future reference. To make it easier to find the minutes, they are stored in a shared folder on the network that everyone in the group can access from their desktop computer and, because we are librarians, the file names are based on the meeting dates (year-month-day) so that they automatically file in date order. The folder can also be searched to find the last time the group discussed telephone rosters or book budgets.

This is all wonderful—or it would be if it worked. The problem really lies in the fact that life and work don't divide into neat and equal slices of one week's duration. In practice the telephone roster was changed immediately after the meeting, but the technology report took six weeks because there was so much reading to do, and then the person who had the notes took on another project and, well, everyone meant to get back to it but somehow it never happened—and by the time three months had passed no one was looking at the old action statements because everyone had too much to do, and then next year arrived. And . . .

But this is supposed to be a book on spreadsheets, right? How could a spreadsheet help with the problem of meeting actions not being carried out? Well, it's simple really, and the answer lies in the fact that everything in a spreadsheet has a space (known as a cell, but we'll get to that later), and that space may or may not contain information. If there's a space called *what happened to the new technology report?* and that space is blank, then the answer is that nothing happened (yet). In other words, the blank space actually tells us something, even if that something is "nothing." Think of it like calling the staff roll after an emergency evacuation of your library. You have a list of staff, you call out the names, put a tick next to each one as they answer, and then, when you've finished, the names without ticks are either still in the building or are not at work today. Calling out "who isn't here?" doesn't work nearly as well. In exactly the same way that asking a positive question about absent people is ineffective, you can't search for "things we didn't do" within the folder of minutes. The best you could do would be to go back over the past year's minutes and note the action statements and then the evidence that these actions were completed. Good luck with that.

Here's How It Works

Create a single (yes!) spreadsheet with the following columns:

A. Date of the meeting
B. Issue to be addressed
C. Action to be taken
D. Person primarily responsible (owner)
E. Others involved
F. Deadline (if needed)
G. Date completed
H. Action taken
I. Other notes or observations
J. Link to relevant documents

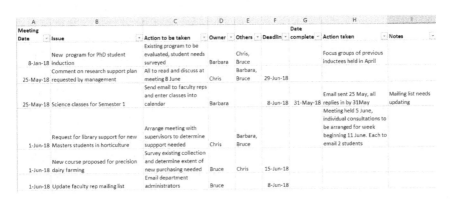

Meeting Date	Issue	Action to be taken	Owner	Others	Deadline	Date complete	Action taken	Notes
8-Jan-18	New program for PhD student induction	Existing program to be evaluated, student needs surveyed	Barbara	Chris, Bruce			Focus groups of previous inductees held in April	
25-May-18	Comment on research support plan requested by management	All to read and discuss at meeting 8 June	Chris	Barbara, Bruce	29-Jun-18			
25-May-18	Science classes for Semester 1	Send email to faculty reps and enter classes into calendar	Barbara		8-Jun-18	31-May-18	Email sent 25 May, all replies in by 31May	Mailing list needs updating
1-Jun-18	Request for library support for new Masters students in horticulture	Arrange meeting with supervisors to determine suppport needed	Chris	Barbara, Bruce			Meeting held 5 June, individual consultations to be arranged for week beginning 11 June. Each to email 2 students	
1-Jun-18	New course proposed for precision dairy farming	Survey existing collection and determine extent of new purchasing needed	Bruce	Chris	15-Jun-18			
1-Jun-18	Update faculty rep mailing list	Email department administrators	Bruce		8-Jun-18			

Anyone in the work group can place an item on the agenda ahead of time by filling in column A with the next meeting date and column B with a description of the issue. This should be reasonably brief, but column J can link to a discussion document if necessary. At the meeting each matter is discussed, and a brief statement of the proposed action (which could include "no action") is recorded in column C. The action is assigned to an owner (column D) and if necessary a working group (column E). It is the owner's responsibility to fill in column H (which could include progress reports later replaced by a final statement), but the action can only be marked as complete in column G (using the completion date) by a meeting of the whole group.

A busy department could add hundreds of lines to the spreadsheet every year, but most of these will be marked as complete within a relatively short time. What is now possible, however, is that once the meeting has begun a filter can be used on column G to remove all items that have been given a completion date, so that only *uncompleted* items are visible.

	A Meeting Date	B Issue	C Action to be taken	D Owner	E Others	F Deadlin	G Date complete	H Action taken	I Notes	J Link
2	8-Jan-18	New program for PhD student induction	Existing program to be evaluated, student needs surveyed	Barbara	Chris,			Focus groups of previous inductees held in April		
3	25-May-18	Comment on research support plan requested by management	All to read and discuss at meeting 8 June	Chris	Barbara, Bruce		29-Jun-18			
5	1-Jun-18	Request for library support for new Masters students in horticulture	Arrange meeting with supervisors to determine suppport needed	Chris	Barbara, Bruce			Meeting held 5 June, individual consultations to be arranged for week beginning 11 June. Each to email 2 students		
6	1-Jun-18	New course proposed for precision dairy farming	Survey existing collection and determine extent of new purchasing needed	Bruce	Chris	15-Jun-18				
7	1-Jun-18	Update faculty rep mailing list	Email department administrators	Bruce		8-Jun-18				

Any of these actions that have been finished can now be marked as complete at the beginning of the meeting before action statements and ownerships are assigned to the new items. By the end of the meeting the spreadsheet will accurately reflect the current state of progress. If an action was decided on in January and is still uncompleted in October, this will be immediately apparent, and if it is then decided to "retire" this action, that's fine too; this can be done by marking it complete with an appropriate annotation. This is important because the blank spaces in column F carry a piece of real information— *this hasn't been done*—in the same way that unticked names on the staff roll tell us something important—*this person isn't here.* One way to see it is that the blanks turn negative and invisible information (nothing happened) into positive and visible information (we *know* that nothing has happened yet, but we're still waiting). Once the action is marked complete, it is allowed to fall off the radar, although it can easily be uncovered again by removing the filter.

As well as ensuring that nothing gets overlooked, including the good intentions we had after the Christmas break, the spreadsheet gives us a permanent record of all the activity that goes through the weekly meetings, maybe over the course of several years. If one of the team is unexpectedly absent, the others can quickly look to see which tasks had been assigned to them, and it gives individual team members an easy view of what they are responsible for. But I would argue that it does more than this, that it subtly alters the way in which we approach tasks by making the blank spaces in column G visible. There's no longer a risk that we talk in January about renewing the induction program and then forget about it until the next round of students arrives in October. At the very least it's in front of the team's eyes once a week, and either the action gets done or the team decides not to proceed and marks it as complete with a note that they didn't have the time or that it turned out not to be necessary.

Maybe this seems like an excessive amount of effort for a simple checklist of actions, but it requires no special skills apart from the ability to type and the sort of rudimentary understanding of data fields that librarians can be expected to possess. It's just a matter of putting the right things in the right columns and remembering to click *Save*, and the only specific spreadsheet skill needed is filtering column G to hide or reveal the completed items. However, by the time you've finished this book, you'll realize that there's a lot more you could do with this list. You could count the number of activities that have gone through the meetings in a year, you could count the number of completions, and you could even calculate the average completion times (although that might be a bit obsessive). You could search the list to find out when you discussed mathematics ebooks a couple of years ago and what you decided to do, and link to the discussion paper that was written at that time. And, perhaps the best part, it's all on the one sheet, easy to find and always current. So, even if you stop reading now, try using a spreadsheet as a minute-keeping device or an action list, and you will have made a big step in the direction of being better organized.

What's in a Postcode?

Urban library systems worry about providing good service to the residents within their districts, but this can be really difficult to demonstrate, particularly when most of them might not have a library card or visit a library regularly. When we don't have data, it's tempting to fill in the blanks with guesses, and even more tempting to fill them with opinions that we already hold, but it's also a good idea to look at whatever data we do have to see if we can make anything of it. Let's take the City of Dulminster, population of 200,007 (2015). It has a central library (Central Dulminster) and four branches, North, South, East, and West. Central is located near the business district and has by far the largest collection of books, but the North and East branches are the busiest in terms of book borrowing per head of population. South Dulminster has a much lower borrowing rate, and over the years has tended to specialize in nonbook materials and outreach activities. South Dulminster Library is an important Internet access point for its community, and much of its space is devoted to computers and IT support. Many of the residents of Central Dulminster are students at Dulminster College in West Dulminster, who may use the college library rather than the public library.

Looking at the borrowing figures for the five libraries, the library manager might conclude that the people of South Dulminster read fewer books than the rest of the city, particularly the more affluent residents of East Dulminster. However, on its own this conclusion can't be allowed to stand without further investigation. Many of the residents of South Dulminster work in the central retail district or in East Dulminster, so they might use these rather better-stocked libraries rather than their "home" branch. It could also be that the time-rich retirees of North and East Dulminster read more books per month than the younger working population of the rest of the city but that a similar proportion of the actual populations borrows at least some books from the library. For the constantly busy person who is able to read only one book a month, this book may add as much value to her life as 10 books would do for someone else.

So what data does the manager have that might cast light on library use by their residents? The circulation system records the following information about each transaction:

- The barcode number of the book
- The ID number of the borrower
- The branch at which the book was lent

The system is able to take a "snapshot" of all books out on loan at any given time and output this data as a "comma-delimited" CSV file that can be opened by Sheets or Excel.

	A	B	C
	Barcode Number	Lending Branch	Borrower Number
1			
2	2095009571	East	4368
3	3617777997	Central	3751
4	6496938991	East	1856
5	1829733880	West	6184
6	5410260319	Central	4368
7	5261383263	South	3751
8	9590633665	East	4368
9	1089515500	East	3397
10	5926421139	North	2258
11	5255919712	Central	4368

The system also has a file of information about all of its registered borrowers that contains the following information about borrowers:

- ID numbers
- Names
- Addresses
- Postcodes

Now, the manager doesn't need to know names and addresses in order to find the information she is interested in—where the people borrowing the books live in relation to use of the five branch libraries—but the ID numbers and postcodes are enough to produce a pretty good picture of this if the postcodes can be mapped to the libraries. So first of all the ID numbers and postcodes are exported from the borrower file and imported into the spreadsheet:

A Borrower Number	B Postcode
1856	11514
3751	11522
4368	11517
3397	11520
2258	11525
6184	11512
4431	11518
5928	11519

Each library branch serves an area defined by three different postcodes, so a table is created that allows us to look up the postcode and assign the appropriate library to it for each borrower:

	A	B
1	Postcode	Branch
2	11511	Central
3	11512	Central
4	11513	Central
5	11514	North
6	11515	North
7	11516	North
8	11517	East
9	11518	East
10	11519	East
11	11520	South
12	11521	South
13	11522	South
14	11523	West
15	11524	West
16	11525	West

So when we match the postcodes in our list of borrowers to the libraries in the table, the list now looks like this:

	A	B	C
1	Borrower Number	Postcode	Branch
2	1856	11514	North
3	3751	11522	South
4	4368	11517	East
5	3397	11520	South
6	2258	11525	West
7	6184	11512	Central
8	4431	11518	East
9	5928	11519	East

Of course, the Branch column tells her where the borrowers *live* in relation to the nearest library—for example, borrower 4368 lives in postcode 11517, which is assigned to East—not which libraries they *borrow from*, so to find this out she needs to go back to the snapshot of transactions:

	A	B	C
1	Barcode Number	Lending Branch	Borrower Number
2	9590633665	East	4368
3	1089515500	East	3397
4	6116293860	East	1856
5	5926421139	North	2258
6	4889092566	East	1856
7	5814673452	East	6184
8	130736345	South	3751
9	4286222619	Central	6184
10	2186837314	North	4368
11	7994111133	Central	4368

Lines 2 and 11 tell the manager that borrower 4368 borrowed books from both East and Central, and she can now put this together with her knowledge that 4368 lives in East Dulminster to build a picture of library use across the city. When all this data is put together it looks like this:

26	North Library	South Library	East Library	West Library	Central Library	Total
27 North Residents	7	0	1	0	1	9
28 South Residents	0	2	1	0	2	5
29 East Residents	1	0	7	0	3	11
30 West Residents	1	0	0	2	0	3
31 Central Residents	0	0	2	2	1	5
32 Total	9	2	11	4	7	33

The row labels at the left show the locations of the borrowers, and the labels across the top show the libraries from which they borrowed books. For example, of the total of nine books borrowed from the North library, seven were borrowed by local residents, and one each by residents of East and West.

26	North Library
27 North Residents	7
28 South Residents	0
29 East Residents	1
30 West Residents	1
31 Central Residents	0
32 Total	9

Now, on the horizontal, here's the borrowing by residents of South Dulminster.

	North Library	South Library	East Library	West Library	Central Library	Total
South Residents	0	2	1	0	2	5

Less than half of the books they borrowed came from their local branch library.

From this admittedly small sample, data has been turned into information, and the manager now has quite a nuanced view of library-borrowing activity within the city. As expected, East and North are the two busiest libraries because of borrowing by their own residents. Central is the third busiest, but not from borrowing by local residents who borrow instead from East and West. South is the least busy library, but South residents borrow extensively from Central and East. Of course, the manager still has some difficult decisions to make, but she now knows that in order to improve library services to the people of South Dulminster, she might need to look at improvements to the Central library as well as the South library, while spending on the North library is largely going to benefit local residents.

It could be argued, of course, that it would be difficult in real life to assign branch libraries to postcodes in such a neat fashion, and this is absolutely true. Someone living at the northwest corner of 11520 might actually be closer to both East and Central libraries than to South library, which could explain our result. But most people in postcodes 11520, 11521, and 11522 *don't* live in the northwest corner, and when the transaction file records many thousands of book borrowings, then these anomalies will recede in importance. On top of that, the data could be further refined to reflect on-the-ground complexity; a data analyst might override some of the postcode allocations so that addresses in Long Avenue higher than 1500 were assigned to West rather than Central. But, however sophisticated we make it, what the spreadsheet gives us is a *model* of reality, deliberately stripped of much of its complexity, rather than reality itself. In any given instance a library book may be read cover to cover or used to prop open a window, but we can be fairly confident overall that the residents of East Dulminster read more library books than their fellow citizens in the west. And of course as well as number crunching, the library manager would do well to get out of the office and visit the libraries, malls, secondhand bookstores, parks, and workplaces and talk to some of the people who are represented by the numbers.

What the spreadsheet has done, though, is to give the library manager some new information. It was already known that some libraries were busier than others, so an assumption could have been made that people in some parts of the city just read more books than their fellow citizens. This view would not have been entirely wrong, either, but it also was based on a model—that there was a one-to-one correlation between the library that a person used and where they lived. Now, the circulation data by itself is not particularly helpful in this regard—it only tells us that borrower 4368 borrowed book 5410260319 from Central Dulminster Library—but when this simple fact is combined with the other simple fact that 4368 lives in East Dulminster, we see that the assumption that people always use their local library breaks down and we need to take cross-city borrowing patterns into account. The spreadsheet has allowed us to do this by taking one set of data—book number, borrower number, and library—and combining it with another set—borrower number and "home library" and then aggregating it over a number of transactions. The common element in both sets was the borrower number, which allowed us to cross-match residential locations with borrowing activity.

Now that our curiosity is piqued, there's no end to the questions we can start asking—and answering. Does the relatively high number of borrowings from people in some areas mean that there are more readers in those areas, or is it simply that a small set of individual heavy borrowers, residents of a retirement home, for example, push those figures up, while there may be as many library users in other parts of the city who just happen to borrow fewer books? Are there more inactive library members in some areas than others? Do users of the Central library also use their home libraries? And that's just from the two simple data files shown above, which contain the absolute minimum of personal data and no information about the books at all. If we wanted to, we could add bibliographic information about the books (using barcode numbers as the common data element) to find out if the residents of South Dulminster who use the Central library borrow a different type of book from those who use the local library. At this point we would need to make absolutely certain that there was no personal identifying information in the spreadsheet.

Linkedout

A good way of deciding which books to remove from your library collection is to look at how often and how recently they have been borrowed. Generally, this works pretty well—nobody wanted this book over the past 10 years, so it's a fair bet that no one will want it over the next 10 years either—but if you work in a research library this strategy can come badly unstuck, and you might find, through being told, that the dusty unloved tome you just ditched was in fact a landmark work in its field that no credible research institution could be without, and that only a total ignoramus would not know this. These are not interactions you want to have. Unfortunately, it's a well-known fact that you can't judge a book by its cover, or by its title, and unless you know the subject area really well, a book is a book is a book. You can try asking your researchers directly, but they generally don't have time and, in any case, incline toward wanting to keep everything. What you really need is some means of independently gauging a book's reputation, and one way of doing this is to find out if it has been cited by other books, and who cited it, and what they said about it.

Here's a record from our library management system for a well-regarded book you have probably never heard of. It has been imported into a spreadsheet.

	A	B	C	D	E	F
1	BIB-ID	CALL NO.	AUTHOR	TITLE	PUBLISHER	YEAR
2	b11280864	591.5 Wyn	Wynne-Edwards, Vero Copner, 1906-	Animal dispersion in relation to social behaviour	Oliver and Boyd	1962

We can search this on Google Books by copying and pasting the title and author into the search box:

"Animal dispersion in relation to social behaviour" Wynne-Edwards 　　　🔍

Google Books comes back with a rather fanciful number of results (it's a search engine, not a database), but where it finds the title and author on the same page it highlights them in its snippets:

books.google.com › books

Did Darwin Get It Right?: Essays on Games, Sex and Evolution

John Maynard Smith - 2012

FOUND INSIDE – PAGE 54

It is convenient to start with the publication, in 1962, of an influential book by V. C. **Wynne-Edwards**, of the University of Aberdeen, called **Animal Dispersion in Relation to Social Behaviour. Wynne-Edwards'** thesis was as follows. **Animal** ...

📖 Preview　　≣ More editions

Immediately, without counting any numbers, we have the answer to our question about whether or not to keep this book. It's influential, a starting point for later research, and exactly the sort of title we want to retain in the collection if our weeding exercise is to remain credible. We can even click on the link to see exactly what John Maynard Smith had to say about it.

I shall discuss the takeover bid later, but first, what were the new ideas about the evolution of animal societies? The problem is clear; if evolution occurs by the natural selection of properties that ensure individual survival and reproduction, how can we account for cooperative, and even self-sacrificing, behaviour? It is convenient to start with the publication, in 1962, of an influential book by V. C. Wynne-Edwards, of the University of Aberdeen, called *Animal Dispersion in Relation to Social Behaviour*. Wynne-Edwards' thesis was as follows. Animal populations rarely outrun their food supply and starve, because their numbers are usually regulated behaviourally; animals refrain from breeding before their numbers rise too high. To bring this about, special 'epideictic' displays have evolved that signal to individuals the density of the population. These displays form the basis of social evolution. Wynne-Edwards' great merit was that he saw that, if his argument was to hold, natural selection must be acting so as to favour some *populations* at the expense of others, rather than some *individuals* at the expense of others,

So far I have used the spreadsheet to capture the bibliographic data from the library management system, and I have copied and pasted the title and author into Google Books, putting quotes around the title and shortening the author's name to a citation style, last name only. I can now add a column to the spreadsheet and mark it "Keep," but I have over a thousand books to look at, and that's a lot of copying and pasting, so is there any way the spreadsheet can help with this?

Unsurprisingly, the answer is "yes."

When I search the title and author in Google Books, I notice that the address bar looks like this:

And I can copy this address to use for subsequent searches:

https://www.google.com/search?tbm=bks&q="Animal+dispersion+in+relation+to+social+behaviour"+Wynne-Edwards

Now a little experimentation quickly shows me that any title (in quotes) and author combination will run the appropriate search, and I don't even need to use the *plus* symbols (+) for the spaces:

https://www.google.com/search?tbm=bks&q="Feedback mechanisms in animal behaviour"+mcfarland

Once again I find a very relevant title:

An Introduction to Animal Behaviour - Page 421
https://books.google.co.nz/books?isbn=1107000165
Aubrey Manning, Marian Stamp Dawkins - 2012 - Preview - More editions
McFarland, DJ. (1971). **Feedback Mechanisms in Animal Behaviour**. New York:
Academic Press. **McFarland**, DJ. (1974). Time-sharing as a behavioural phenomenon.
Advances in the Study of Animal Behaviour 5: 201-25. **McFarland**, DJ.

So all I have to do is to tell the spreadsheet to take the title and slap quotes around it, add on the author's last name, and send it off to the Internet preceded by https://www.google.com/search?tbm=bks&q=.

It's much easier to click a thousand times than it is to copy and paste.

But there's a problem. If you look at the author's name in the spreadsheet, you'll see that we get a really librarianish version—Wynne-Edwards, Vero Copner, 1906–.

Now as it happens we can use this in our search:

https://www.google.com/search?tbm=bks&q="Animal+dispersion+in+relation+to+social+behaviour"+Wynne-Edwards +Vero+Copner +1906-

but we get a very truncated set of results as most citing authors don't use full names like this. Instead we get a reference book:

The Cambridge Dictionary of Scientists - Page 385
https://books.google.co.nz/books?isbn=052180602X
David Millar, Ian Millar, John Millar - 2002 - Preview - More editions
Wynne-Edwards, Vero Copner (**1906**–97) British biologist: proposed animal altruism as basis for population ... began to gather the results that were to be fully developed in his book **Animal Dispersion in Relation to Social Behaviour** (1962).

The Life of David Lack: Father of Evolutionary Ecology - Page 202
https://books.google.co.nz/books?isbn=0199922659
Ted R. Anderson - 2013 - Preview - More editions
V. C. **Wynne-Edwards** Vero Copner Wynne-Edwards was born In Leeds on July 4, **1906**. ... He published his magnum opus, **Animal Dispersion in Relation to Social Behaviour**, in 1962, and the ensuing debate between Lack and ...

To get it right, we have to tell the spreadsheet to give us the author's name up to, but not including, the comma. There's no direct "command" for this, but we can find out the position number of the comma within the string of characters that make up the name, and then use this to mark the end of the information fragment we want. In the string "Wynne-Edwards, Vero Copner, 1906–" the letter "W" is at position 1, "y" at position 2 and so on, and the comma is at position 14. We then use this knowledge to stipulate that we want only the first 13 characters of the string, and we have the author's last name, "Wynne-Edwards." (If that sounds confusing, it's because cataloguing rules and most citation styles mandate that for personal names the last shall be first.)

The final step is to put all of this together and send it off to the Internet. Here's the formula that allows us to do this:

=HYPERLINK("https://www.google.com/search?tbm=bks&q=%22"&TITLE &"%22+"&LEFT(AUTHOR,FIND(",",AUTHOR)-1))

Don't feel daunted by this at the moment; it will all be crystal clear by the time you are halfway through this book. The "=" symbol tells the spreadsheet that what is coming up is a formula (an instruction to do something), HYPERLINK says "send all this off somewhere," then we have the bit I got from Google Books, then a bunch of ampersands (&) and "%22" symbols, which you don't need to worry about just yet, then the title and then some fancy footwork to get the author's last name.

I'm not going to say at this point that it's all really simple and can be done in a minute, because it's not and it can't, at least not by me. This took me maybe 10 minutes, with a bit of puzzling over the parentheses and quotes and the %22s, but once it's done it's done. A file with thousands of entries can now be downloaded from the LMS and dropped into the spreadsheet, and the formula will work for every line. No more copy and paste, 10 minutes well spent and some well-informed choices made in your weeding program.

Data and Information

Each of these scenarios involves turning data—facts about the world—into information—connected and organized facts that yield insights into how the world operates and what is really going on out there. In our first scenario the meeting action list recorded each issue the group handled and then provided a structure that allowed all relevant aspects to be recorded—when the issue was first raised, what the issue was, what action was decided on, who was responsible, what was done, and when it was done. Out of this the group was able to answer important questions about its activities—what actions had they completed, which were still outstanding, which actions had each team member been responsible for?. The spreadsheet had done this by filtering alone, but the spreadsheet's structure itself encouraged the team to think of each issue in terms of all the essential elements so that there was less risk of deciding to do something without specifying who was to do it.

In the second scenario the library manager was able to bring disparate pieces of data together to see something that might not have been immediately obvious to anyone. A librarian working in a particular branch might think that "only local people use this library," but his definition of who is "local" could well include "I see them in the library every week." By using the borrower-ID number to pivot between two sets of data—books borrowed and borrower residential locations—the spreadsheet brought to light a phenomenon that was perhaps only dimly perceived before—the gap between residential address and the location of library use. Sometimes we see things quite anecdotally—crime is getting worse, the summers were hotter when I was a kid, the people of South Dulminster don't borrow books from libraries—when a full look at how the data fit together might tell quite a different story.

The third scenario gave us a glimpse at our spreadsheet's way with words, which are pretty much the librarian's stock-in-trade. We were able to take text data—authors and titles—from our library system, clean it up, and repackage it as part of an Internet search that produced useful results. When we think of spreadsheets, we tend to think of numbers—averages, medians, percentages, rates of return, and demographic trends—but spreadsheets have some interesting and powerful text functions that may not be as well known. Generally, we end up with numbers at some point—count the number of books with "conspiracy" in the title—but in this case they are numbers about words. The study of bibliometrics specifically deals with this area and has produced some remarkable insights into how research and scholarly publishing can be measured and analyzed.

Spreadsheets for Librarians

Spreadsheets are a great fit for librarians because they are really data organizers and metadata tools. If we look again at our meeting spreadsheet, we can see how this works.

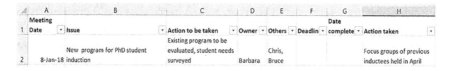

The top row (line 1) contains the headings for the columns A to J, and in doing so it defines the contents of all the lines below. Columns A, F, and G can only contain dates, columns D and E personal names, and so on. The problem, challenge, or opportunity goes into column B, the proposed solution or action into column C, and the action eventually taken into column H. The headings are a set of rules (i.e., metadata) that each row has to follow, and each column is a field defined by that metadata. I won't go into the exact differences between spreadsheets and databases, but you'll get the point that they are pretty similar creatures, both of them organizing and storing data by fields. This similarity makes it easy to take data from our library systems and slot it neatly into a spreadsheet for further processing.

In fact, many of the electronic systems we use allow us to export bibliographic data in the form of CSV files that can then be imported into spreadsheets for further manipulation. At least one major database exports a ready-made bibliometric analysis of the results of any search in spreadsheet format, although it also allows you to customize the output data (by selecting the fields to export) in order to create your own analysis—which is much more fun! Then, as well as our well-known bibliographic tools, in recent years research assessment and learning management systems have seen a proliferation of electronic utilities that produce CSV files. There is, in other words, no shortage of data for librarians with spreadsheet skills to work on, and as librarians begin to lay their claim to the field of data management, there is good reason for us to be acquiring and developing these skills.

This book cannot teach you everything you will ever need to know about spreadsheets. I have a massive volume on my desk of the "bible" variety, and even that disappoints me at times, so there's a lot to learn, and I have possibly missed out on whole areas that I simply know nothing of. I'm pretty much self-taught and sometimes blush at the time I must have wasted (so *that's* why you name ranges of cells!) over the years doing things the hard (dumb) way. What I hope this book will be is the sort of knowledge base I wish I had had 20 years ago, telling me what Excel or Sheets could do for me as a librarian. So, expect lots of tips and tricks as well as a basic toolkit of numerical, statistical, textual, and logical functions. More than that, however, I would like this book to work on your *imagination*, to open up possibilities and suggest new ways of seeing and describing the world (or at least the operations of your library). I'm not suggesting that you use spreadsheets to write poetry (please don't!) but that you begin to think like an engineer or an architect, somebody who applies science, technology, and information to solve problems or create new structures or services. As you assemble the tools, materials, and techniques you need to solve the specific problem in front of you, part of your mind will already be asking "and what else can I use this for?" When you get to the stage of meeting new problems with columns and rows containing data and formulas and trying this, and then that, and tweaking it a few times until the answer emerges, then you will have made it as an applied information scientist.

Spreadsheets are by no means perfect, nor are they always intuitive or easy to use. Like most computer applications they can be maddeningly literal, so that rather than saying "get up at 7 o'clock and have breakfast" you instead have to say "if it's 7 o'clock, get out of bed, put on your clothes, go to the kitchen, cook breakfast, eat breakfast, but if it isn't 7 o'clock stay in bed" only to find that your plate is empty because you didn't specify that the breakfast had to consist of actual food. In fact, it's worse than this because spreadsheets doesn't really carry out sequences—instead everything has to be "nested" so that eating your breakfast egg becomes "eat the egg that was boiled in the water that was contained in the saucepan that was placed on the stove. . . ." until you are about 10 layers deep (each layer a set of parentheses), and you still have to say that if there aren't any eggs, then don't do this at all. Error messages can be hard to interpret, so you can't be sure whether #N/A means that there aren't any eggs or that the water has been cut off or that your apartment doesn't actually have a kitchen. You should also be aware that bad results can be indistinguishable from good ones, so they need to be tested against reality in some way. An unboiled egg (which is what you get if you don't tell the cook to apply heat) looks pretty much like a boiled one, so maybe you should check that it's hot before you serve it to a guest. In particular, you need to be suspicious of any dramatic revelations that spring out from your spreadsheet. If the Dulminster library manager finds that 80% of the library users of East Dulminster are borrowing books from the West Dulminster Library, she should probably check that the postcodes have been correctly assigned before reporting this surprising fact to the mayor and council.

These are words of caution, but I don't want to put you off the spreadsheet journey because I believe it's an important one for librarians to make and that libraries of all types can benefit from good management and use of their data. A careful reading of this book should give you most of the basics plus, I hope, some good ideas of how to apply them, but as I said it can't be a comprehensive reference to everything Excel and Sheets. I will try to explain things in reasonably nontechnical language (no more eggs, I promise), but there will be times when you need a fuller explanation, so access to a good up-to-date reference work could save you a lot of time. The Internet is another really useful and quick way of answering questions and learning new techniques, and I have had regular recourse to it myself. Be aware, however, that Google searches often return quite dated results for searches on spreadsheet topics and that the most popular answer to your question won't necessarily be the best one. And before you cut and paste a formula, make sure you *understand* it and know exactly what it is doing with your data—an impressive result isn't necessarily a true or valid one. There is a list of useful books and websites in Suggested Readings at the end of the book.

CHAPTER TWO

The Basics

This chapter will cover the basics from the ground up. If you are already a user of Excel or Google Sheets, you might want to skip the chapter entirely, but I suggest that you at least skim it because it can be surprising to find out the really elementary things you didn't know—a bit like reading a guidebook to your hometown and discovering that before it was called Dulminster its original name was Hicksville. If you are a newbie, on the other hand, the relevance of some of this stuff may seem a little difficult to understand, and you might be inclined to say "but I'll never need to do that!" Trust me, you will. If you are already using Excel or Sheets, it will be useful to try out some of these ideas and techniques as we go along, but please keep reading too.

Spreadsheets, Workbooks, Worksheets, Cells, Rows, Columns, and Ranges: The Building Blocks

An Excel spreadsheet, more properly known as a workbook, is a file with an .xlsx or .xls extension, while in Google the spreadsheet is stored on your Google Drive and doesn't need a file extension. Either way, Excel and Sheets look and act very much the same. The spreadsheet is all made up of one or more *worksheets* in separate tabs (more on this later), and each worksheet is made up of rectangular *cells* arranged in horizontal *rows* and vertical *columns*. The cell is the fundamental element of the spreadsheet, and each cell has an *address* defined by its column letter and row number.

A1		×	✓	f_x	Barcode Number	

	A	B	C	D	E
1	Barcode Number	Lending Branch	Borrower Number	Date Borrowed	Date Due
2	2095009571	East	4368	05/12/2018	06/12/2018
3	3617777997	Central	3751	05/12/2018	06/12/2018
4	6496938991	East	1856	05/12/2018	06/12/2018
5	1829733880	West	6184	05/12/2018	06/12/2018
6	5410260319	Central	4368	05/12/2018	06/12/2018
7	5261383263	South	3751	05/12/2018	06/12/2018

Here the active cell (where the cursor is placed) is A1—column A, row 1—and in Excel we see this address spelled out in the *Name Box* at top left. Cell A1 contains the words *Barcode Number,* and this is echoed in the slightly misnamed *Formula Bar* at top right. (In fact, this space will show whatever is in the cell, which in this case is just text and not a formula, but later on we will find that it is really useful for entering and editing formulas.) As we saw in the last chapter, each column in this worksheet has a clearly defined purpose, in this case a piece of essential data stored about each lending transaction, and each row represents a single transaction made up of these data elements, so cell C4 is the borrower number (1856) relating to the other data in row 4 (barcode, branch, date borrowed, and date due). However, nothing about the spreadsheet forces the right data elements to go into the right slots, so if I had accidentally entered the borrower number into B4 and the lending branch into C4, the spreadsheet wouldn't object or try to warn me—but any resulting count of the number of books lent by East Library or taken out by borrower 1856 would be wrong!

Cells on their own don't do a lot, but organized into rows and columns like this they begin to turn the individual data building blocks into structured information. Cells A4, B4, C4, D4, and E4 record the entire transaction, and we call this a *range,* which has an address consisting of the first and last cells joined by a colon—*A4:E4.* Each column is a range in its own right, and their description is simply the column letter joined by a colon to itself, so that column B is simply *B:B.* However, the range doesn't have to be the whole column or row. If the transactions for May 12, 2018, took up the first 400 rows of the sheet we could count the occurrences of the word *West* in the range *B2:B401* to find the number of transactions for that date, while for all dates the range would be simply *B:B.* But ranges don't need to be confined to single rows or columns; they can cover any adjacent set of cells, which will always be a rectangle defined by the top left and bottom right cells. The screenshot above, for example, is the range *A1:E7,* and we could use a formula to count the number of cells in that range that contained data to make sure we hadn't left any gaps.

Ranges and rows aren't fixed units; they can be deleted or new ones inserted if we have a new idea or if our requirements change. If we wanted to add a column between columns A and B to record book titles, this would be done by clicking on the *B* at the top of column B to highlight the column, and then right-clicking on the mouse and selecting *Insert*. To remove a range, simply highlight it and then right-click and select *Delete*. If the deleted range (or its contents) has been referenced in any formulas, these will now show as errors, for reasons that will shortly be clear.

In most spreadsheets the columns will consist of separate data elements, and the rows will each constitute a set of data, such as a lending transaction or the bibliographic details of the book. The top row is known as the *Header Row,* and each entry will describe the type of data held in that column—for example, author, title, place of publication, year, and so on. It is really important to use descriptive headers as these will help you, and others, to understand what your spreadsheet is doing and how it works.

When a new worksheet is created, the columns come in fixed widths, but these can readily be changed by placing the cursor to the right-hand side of the column in the Header Row and stretching or contracting the column to a more suitable size. This can also be done with the fixed row heights, but to change the rows in this way would be a very cumbersome procedure. If the data in a particular cell is overflowing at the right, the best thing to do is to highlight the cell or the row and use "text wrapping." This is found on the *Home* tab in Excel and the Format tab in Sheets:

In this example we see that text wrapping has allowed us to keep the publisher and title columns at a manageable width.

Publisher	Place	MajorTitle
Palgrave Macmillan	Basingstoke	Strategy and human resource management
Thomson	Mason Ohio	Cost accounting: Foundations & evolutions
South-Western Cengage Learning	Masin OH	Investment analysis and portfolio management
World Bank	Washington (D.C.)	Analyzing banking risk: A framework for assessing corporate governance and risk management

You can select a single row to be wrapped, but it's a good idea to select the whole worksheet (by pressing *Ctrl-A*) and then using the wrapping procedure which will be applied to any rows that need it.

Careful use of column widths and text wrapping will make your worksheet easier to follow and will become critical whenever you wish to print any of the data in your spreadsheet. Another useful option can be to "hide" columns that contain important information but that you do not need to regularly consult.

Workbooks and Worksheets

We might think that this set of rows and columns we are looking at on the screen is a spreadsheet, but it's actually a *worksheet,* and a spreadsheet or workbook is a collection of worksheets. At the bottom of the screen we can see four tabs that indicate that this spreadsheet is made up of four worksheets—each with its own function.

1092	1946489438	West		2258	05/19/2018	06/19/2018
1093	1003004258	East		4368	05/19/2018	06/19/2018
1094	168642774	North		1856	05/19/2018	06/19/2018
1095	746341252	North		1856	05/19/2018	06/19/2018
1096	8934063787	North		1856	05/19/2018	06/19/2018
1097	855350774	East		5141	05/19/2018	06/19/2018

Transactions | Postcodes | Borrowers | Summary | (+)

We are currently in the *Transactions* worksheet that records all the borrowing transactions, while the next one (Postcodes) contains the table that maps postcodes to areas served by libraries, the next (Borrowers) is the table of borrower-IDs and postcodes, and the final worksheet (Summary) contains the formulas that generate information out of the data held on the other three sheets. Then at the right there is a *plus* symbol (+) that allows you to create a new worksheet. When you click on this, a new tab will appear with a system-assigned name—Sheet1, Sheet2, etc.

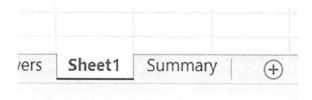

If you right-click on this, you can rename it:

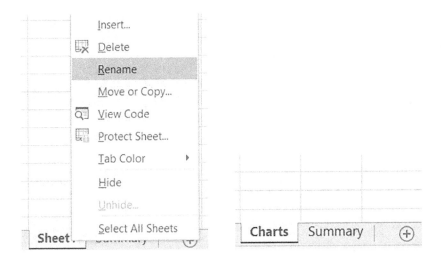

It's a very good idea to do this, rather than leaving your worksheets named simply by their sheet numbers. When you first create Sheet1 and Sheet2, it's obvious (to you) that they hold the transactions and postcodes, but when you come back to the spreadsheet in six months' time that's not going to be at all clear. Using descriptive names also makes writing and understanding formulas much easier. Make sure also that each worksheet has its own function and is used only for that purpose. For example, I could have put the "map" of postcodes and libraries (actually just two columns, the first with postcodes, the second with library names) in the empty columns on the right side of the *Transactions* worksheet, but if I do this I can't then delete a transaction without deleting part of this map. I would also have broken my rule that each column and row must contain only one type of data, because some of the transaction rows would have had postcode data tacked onto the end. It's not very elegant, which also means that it's not good practice. As we saw in Chapter 1, the ability of a spreadsheet to identify tasks that have not been done relies on the lack of ambiguity in its structure—each row a transaction and each column a data element—which in turn relies on your own clarity of thought in designing it. While it might seem a lot of effort, or even "wasteful," to open a whole new worksheet just to store a few pieces of data like the map of postcodes (and sometimes only a single parameter), these are critical items of information and need their own place in the overall structure, not just a few random cells borrowed from the transaction rows and at risk of deletion.

Sorting

Sometimes, although not as often as you might think, it can be useful to sort the rows in your worksheet. For example, our worksheet of lending transactions is sorted by the dates of the transactions, but if we re-sorted it by borrower number we could see how many books each person has out on loan. (There is a better way of doing this that we will come to later, but this is a simple example of how sorting is done and the results it can produce.)

In Excel, the best way to sort is to select the whole worksheet by highlighting all the columns or by pressing *Ctrl-A*—this avoids any risk of sorting a single column only. Now click on the *Data* tab and select *Sort* to see the options:

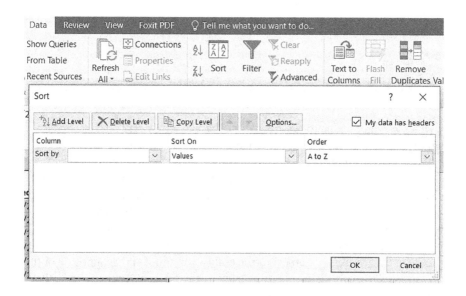

We see that *My data has headers* has been selected—this already shows the usefulness of descriptive headings along the top row to make sorting easier and more transparent.

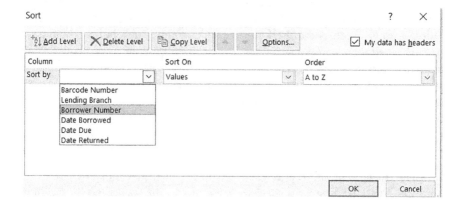

We will choose to sort by Borrower Number.

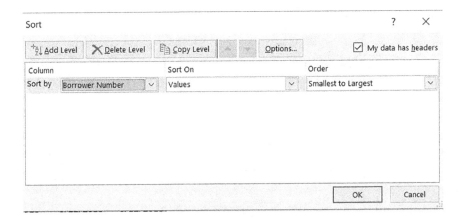

Because this column contains numbers, we are offered the choices *Smallest to Largest* or *Largest to Smallest*. If we had chosen to sort by Lending Branch, the choices would be *A to Z* or *Z to A*. The worksheet was originally sorted by Date Borrowed, so this order is maintained in column D:

	A	B	C	D
	Barcode Number	**Lending Branch**	**Borrower Number**	**Date Borrowed**
	6496938991	East	1856	05/13/2018
	4889092566	North	1856	05/13/2018
	6116293860	North	1856	05/14/2018
	9381762514	North	1856	05/16/2018
	6961924774	Central	1856	05/17/2018
	745156686	North	1856	05/18/2018
	168642774	North	1856	05/19/2018
	746341252	North	1856	05/19/2018

If we wish to, we could add a secondary sort level such as Lending Branch:

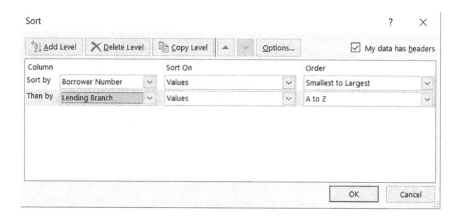

A word of warning about sorting in Excel—if you are not careful, you can end up accidentally leaving some of your columns out of the sorting procedure, so that, for example, column A and column B are sorted while column C retains its original order. Because the data for each row represents a single borrowing transaction, all the elements must be kept together; if this does not happen, then your data no longer corresponds with reality. If you select a single column, Excel comes back with a handy warning when you attempt to sort:

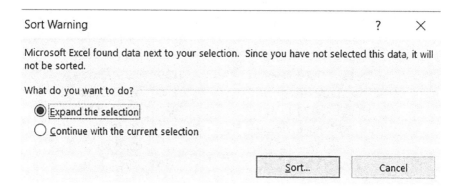

However, if you have selected more than one column but not all columns, then this warning does not appear and the unselected columns will not be part of the sorting process. Always exercise caution when sorting, and be aware that there may be better alternatives such as filtering.

The process is very similar with Sheets. Select the entire worksheet, or at least all the columns containing data, and click on the *Data* tab.

Data	Tools	Add-ons	Help	All change
	Sort sheet by **column F**, A → Z			
	Sort sheet by **column F**, Z → A			
	Sort range by **column F**, A → Z			
	Sort range by **column F**, Z → A			
	Sort range...			

You'll notice that Sheets starts with the suggestion that you sort the entire worksheet by the right-hand column. If you wish to change this, click on *Sort range* and choose your option. If you specify that there is a Header Row, then you will be given the appropriate options:

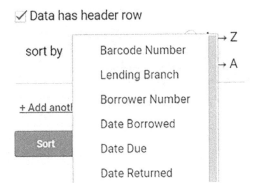

Sheets has a second option for sorting using the SORT function, which we will look at in the next chapter. This does not sort the range directly but creates a new sorted version of the range at another location.

Linking Between Cells and Worksheets to Create Simple Formulas

So far our data is just sitting in the cells where we put it, which is not terribly useful unless we can get the cells talking to one another and coming together in new combinations. To do this, we're going to create our first formula, which is a really simple one that takes whatever is in one cell and copies it into another. All formulas begin with an equals sign, so to copy the contents of cell A2 into cell C2 we simply type =A2 into that cell.

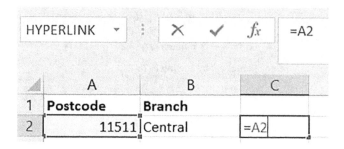

Before I hit Enter, note that cell A2 has been highlighted to indicate that it is the cell being linked to, while the formula itself appears in the Formula Bar at top right. Then when I press Enter, the formula does its work and the contents of A2 now appear in C2.

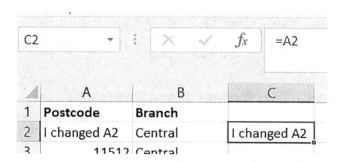

As long as this formula remains in place, whatever appears in A2 will also appear in C2.

The only exception to the rule that whatever is in A2 will appear in C2 is that if A2 is empty C2 will contain the number zero. (As Shakespeare might have put it, "Zero will come of nothing.")

C2		⋮	✕	✓	*fx*	=A2

	A	B	C
1	**Postcode**	**Branch**	
2		Central	0

This is really useful if you are dealing with numbers, but pretty unhelpful if column A normally contains text.

However, this is a one-way process and a change to C2 can't change A2. The *actual contents* of C2 are the formula, but what *appears* in C2 is the value from A2, either text or a number. Another way of seeing this is that the formula in C2 takes input from A2 and returns it as *output*. This isn't just an appearance thing though, because the output is real and can have real consequences if it in turn becomes input for another formula.

To get started with formulas, let's try a simple example using addition and subtraction.

B1		⋮	✕	✓	*fx*	=A1+4

	A	B	C	D
1	5	9		

This time the content of cell A1 is the number 5 and the content of B1 is the formula =*A1+4* (you can see it in the Formula Bar), so what appears in B1 is the number 9, which is the result of the sum 5+4. Now I'm going to add a second formula in C1, which will subtract 3 from whatever appears in B1.

C1		⋮	✕	✓	*fx*	=B1-3

	A	B	C	D
1	5	9	6	

What we really have here are two simple sums, 5+4=9 and 9-3=6, but the 9 in the second sum is the *result* of the first sum. If we change A1 from 5 to 6,

the result in B1 will become *10* and the result in C1 will become *7*. If you've
got Excel or Sheets handy, try it for yourself.

And now try this. Once you've started to create a formula with an equals
sign (=), there's no absolute need to type the cell address for A1—instead you
can just click on the cell itself. If you want to use cell D1 to add *100* to the
result in C1, you can enter this sequence in D1:

$$=[click\ on\ C1]+100$$

Then to add C1 and D1 in E1 enter

$$=[click\ on\ C1]+[click\ on\ D1]$$

You'll see the relevant cells highlight when you do this.

In referencing cells you are not confined to the current worksheet, so you
can copy data from a cell in another worksheet or incorporate it into a formula. Here is a spreadsheet with bibliographic and price data about some
books that we could order, contained in a worksheet called *Books*.

	A	B	C	D	E	F
1	Title	Publisher	ISBN	GBP	Quantity	Cost
2	Book1	Publisher12	2556591977	14.95		
3	Book2	Publisher11	7237339378	82.00		
4	Book3	Publisher10	9381762514	74.55		
5	Book4	Publisher9	3684189788	35.00		
6	Book5	Publisher8	6961924774	99.95		
7	Book6	Publisher7	3983532110	44.00		
8	Book7	Publisher6	5455991514	24.95		
9	Book8	Publisher5	745156686	66.30		

Books | Orders | Exchange rate | ⊕

The prices are in British pounds (GBP), but what we want is the total cost
in United States dollars (USD) using the current exchange rate for the quantity ordered. Columns A to D have come from the publisher, and column E
has been added so we can enter the number of copies wanted. Column F will
contain a formula that multiplies the GBP price by the quantity and by the
GBP to USD exchange rate. This formula will express the equation *USD
COST = GBP PRICE x QUANTITY x GBP EXCHANGE RATE,* and to perform
multiplication we will use the * (asterisk or star) character.

We'll build this formula in steps so you can see the operation in slow
motion. Let's say we want two copies of Book1—we enter the number 2 into
cell E2, and then cell F2 will use this to multiply the GBP price by two to
return the GBP cost of two copies. As you will see in the formula bar, the
formula for F2 is *=D2*E2*.

F2			×	✓	f_x	=D2*E2

◢	A	B	C	D	E	F
1	Title	Publisher	ISBN	GBP	Quantity	Cost
2	Book1	Publisher12	2556591977	14.95	2	29.90
3	Book2	Publisher11	7237339378	82.00		
4	Book3	Publisher10	9381762514	74.55		

If the quantity changes the cost will change, so we can start entering quantities into column E, but the formula in F3 will be =D3*E3 and so on. Having entered a quantity into E3, we place the cursor in F2 and press *Ctrl-C* (or use the *Copy* icon) to copy the formula, and then place it in F3 and press *Ctrl-V* (or use the *Paste* icon) to paste it.

F3			×	✓	f_x	=D3*E3

◢	A	B	C	D	E	F
1	Title	Publisher	ISBN	GBP	Quantity	Cost
2	Book1	Publisher12	2556591977	14.95	2	29.90
3	Book2	Publisher11	7237339378	82.00	3	246.00

Cell F3 now contains the correct formula, and the broken line around F2 signifies that the formula in F3 has come from that cell. This is called a *relative reference,* and because we pasted the formula one row down the row number in the formula increased by one. If we had pasted the formula in row 5, it would have read =D5*E5.

The next step is to copy the formula down a whole lot of rows rather than just one at a time, and this is easily done with the mouse. Rather than just pasting the formula into F3, we place the cursor in that cell and drag it down to F9 before releasing it:

E	F
Quantity	Cost
2	29.90
3	

When we press *Ctrl-V*, it copies into the selected cells, giving each of them the correct relative reference.

| F9 | | | ✕ | ✓ | *fx* | =D9*E9 | |

◢	A	B	C	D	E	F
1	Title	Publisher	ISBN	GBP	Quantity	Cost
2	Book1	Publisher12	2556591977	14.95	2	29.90
3	Book2	Publisher11	7237339378	82.00	3	246.00
4	Book3	Publisher10	9381762514	74.55		0.00
5	Book4	Publisher9	3684189788	35.00	1	35.00
6	Book5	Publisher8	6961924774	99.95		0.00
7	Book6	Publisher7	3983532110	44.00		0.00
8	Book7	Publisher6	5455991514	24.95	4	99.80
9	Book8	Publisher5	745156686	66.30	6	397.80

You'll notice that, as we would have expected, where there is no entry in column E the cost is shown as zero, which happens to be the correct result.

The next step is to multiply the results in column F by the current GBP to USD exchange rate, which happens to be *1.33* on the day I am writing this. Now I could just change the formula in F2 to read =E2*F2*1.33 and then copy it down the rows below, but I would have to remember to do this for every formula in the spreadsheet that used the exchange rate every time it changed (which is going to happen quite regularly). A better solution is to create a place where I can store the exchange rate and update it as required, and that is why I added a worksheet called *Exchange_rate*. At the moment this worksheet contains only one currency, so it's pretty simple:

◢	A	B
1	Currency	Rate (USD)
2	GBP	1.33
3		
4		
5		

It's really important, however, because in cell B2 is the critical number we need in order to calculate the cost of our books, so the equation for the cost of our books is *GBP x QUANTITY x WHATEVER'S IN CELL B2 OF THE EXCHANGE_RATE WORKSHEET*. As it happens, it's fairly easy to make this happen.

Going back to the *Books* worksheet, we select cell F2 and place the cursor in the Formula Bar, right at the end of the formula:

| HYPERLINK | ▾ | ⋮ | ✕ | ✓ | *fx* | =D2*E2| |

◢	A	B	C	D	E	F
1	Title	Publisher	ISBN	GBP	Quantity	Cost
2	Book1	Publisher12	2556591977|	14.95|	2|	*E2

The worksheet lights up to show that F2 is already linking to output from D2 and E2, and we are now going to add another link. First we enter * to signify multiplication, and then at the bottom of the screen we click on the *Exchange_rate* tab, which will take us to that worksheet, and then on cell B2. When we press Enter we return to the *Books* worksheet, and our formula now looks like this:

| F2 | ▾ | ⋮ | ✕ | ✓ | *fx* | =D2*E2*Exchange_rate!B2 |

◢	A	B	C	D	E	F
1	Title	Publisher	ISBN	GBP	Quantity	Cost
2	Book1	Publisher12	2556591977	14.95	2	39.77|

Because we are referencing a cell on another worksheet, the formula includes the name of that worksheet followed by an exclamation mark and the cell address—*Exchange_rate!B2* in this case.

The formula is now complete. It multiplies the GBP price of the book by the number of copies needed and the current exchange rate. When the exchange rate changes, the appropriate cell (*Exchange_rate!B2*) is updated and the cost in F2 changes accordingly. If the GBP goes down in relation to USD, we could decide to order more copies, or if it rises we could reduce the number.

The next step is to copy the formula to all the cells in column F—changing F2 won't do anything to F3 until we do this. Here's where it gets tricky. Copying F2 and pasting it into the cells below produces this result:

| F3 | ▾ | ⋮ | ✕ | ✓ | *fx* | =D3*E3*Exchange_rate!B3 |

◢	A	B	C	D	E	F
1	Title	Publisher	ISBN	GBP	Quantity	Cost
2	Book1	Publisher12	2556591977	14.95	2	39.77
3	Book2	Publisher11	7237339378	82.00	3	0.00|
4	Book3	Publisher10	9381762514	74.55		0.00
5	Book4	Publisher9	3684189788	35.00	1	0.00
6	Book5	Publisher8	6961924774	99.95		0.00
7	Book6	Publisher7	3983532110	44.00		0.00

All the values apart from F2 return a zero result, which is clearly wrong. A glance at the formula tells us why this has happened—relative referencing has (correctly) changed *D2* and *E2* to *D3* and *E3*, but it has also changed *Exchange _rate!B2* to *Exchange_rate!B3*. Now because this is an empty cell the value zero has been returned so that the formula now means *GBP x QUANTITY x ZERO*. What we need is some way of turning the relative reference for *Exchange _rate!B2* into an *absolute reference*, which does not change when it is copied into other cells. This is done by putting a dollar symbol ($) in front of the element that must remain unchanged, in this case the 2 in *B2* so that it becomes *B$2*. The change is made in the first instance of the formula and then copied to the others so that the formula in F9 is now *=D9*E9*Exchange_rate!B$2*.

F9	▾	⋮	✕	✓	*fx*	=D9*E9*Exchange_rate!B$2

	A	B	C	D	E	F
1	Title	Publisher	ISBN	GBP	Quantity	Cost
2	Book1	Publisher12	2556591977	14.95	2	39.77
3	Book2	Publisher11	7237339378	82.00	3	327.18
4	Book3	Publisher10	9381762514	74.55		0.00
5	Book4	Publisher9	3684189788	35.00	1	46.55
6	Book5	Publisher8	6961924774	99.95		0.00
7	Book6	Publisher7	3983532110	44.00		0.00
8	Book7	Publisher6	5455991514	24.95	4	132.73
9	Book8	Publisher5	745156686	66.30	6	529.07

What's in a Name?

We've already seen how useful it has been to name worksheets. If this hadn't been done, the worksheet *Exchange_rate* would have been called *Sheet3* so the formula in F2 would have read *D2*E2*Sheet3!B$2* rather than *D2*E2*Exchange_rate!B$2*, which is much more descriptive. When I come back to the spreadsheet six months later I'm not having to try to totally guess what the content in *Sheet2!B$2* really is and what role it is playing in my formula, as I will know it has something to do with rates of exchange. But remember that the idea behind my formula is *USD COST = GBP PRICE x QUANTITY x GBP EXCHANGE RATE*, which is really transparent. Can we make the formula look more like this? What if the cell *Exchange_rate!B$2* was actually called *GBP EXCHANGE RATE*? Excel and Sheets do this and in rather different ways.

Let's start with Excel first.

There are a couple of ways of naming cells and ranges, but right-clicking on the cell or range you want to name is probably the simplest. Just right-click and then click on *Define Name:*

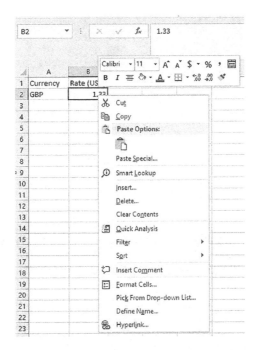

Now give it the desired name:

This now becomes the address of cell B2.

Unfortunately, Excel doesn't update the formula referencing B2 by replacing the cell address with the name, so we have to go back and edit it in cell F2 of the *Books* worksheet. A good way to insert the name into the formula is through the *Formula ribbon,* which can be found by clicking on the Formula tab at the top of the spreadsheet. Place the cursor in the correct position in the formula, and click on *Use in Formula:*

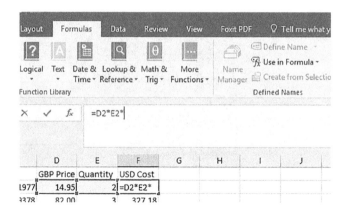

You will then be prompted to select the Named cell or range.

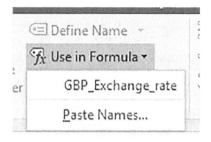

Our formula now looks like this—*D2*E2*GBP_Exchange_Rate*.
To copy it down the rest of the column, we can use another technique:

=D2*E2*GBP_Exchange_Rate

	D	E	F
	GBP Price	Quantity	USD Cost
7	14.95	2	39.77
8	82.00	3	327.18

The bottom right of cell F2 is highlighted; rather than copying F2 and then using the mouse to select the other cells and pasting the formula to these cells, just double-click this highlight and it's done! (Note that this trick only works if there is content in the column to the left.)

The process with Sheets is very similar. At the beginning of the process our formula looks like this:

$$=D13*E13*Exchange\_rate!B\$2$$

If we go to the worksheet *Exchange_rate* and right-click on cell B2, one of the options is to *Define named range,* which in this case will be a single cell.

Clicking on *Define named range,* we are given the choice to accept a suggested range name:

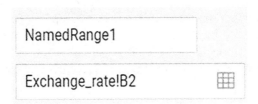

Instead we are going to give it our own more descriptive name:

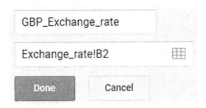

Once again it's necessary to update the formula where the cell is referenced:

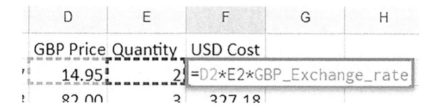

Don't forget to copy the new formula down the whole column!

The next step is to replace the other two cell references in the formula with names, and to do this we are going to name the ranges in which they occur. Once again, right-clicking is the simplest way of doing this. Just select the range, right-click it, and give it a name. Column D becomes *GBP_Price* and column E becomes *Quantity*, so that the updated formula in column F now looks like this:

$$=GBP\_Price*Quantity*GBP\_Exchange\_rate$$

Now, there is one expectation that this formula makes, which is that it occurs in a row on a worksheet that contains columns called *GBP_price* and *Quantity*. If this is the case, then it will choose the same-row cells from each of those columns to calculate the result, otherwise the formula will return an error message.

There are a number of advantages to using names rather than cell addresses. First, the meaning of our formula is fully transparent; if the column heading is the same as the name range, then the intention of the formula is obvious. For each row the number representing the British price is multiplied by the quantity ordered and by the exchange rate to give the U.S. dollar cost. The names not only help us to create logical formulas, they insist that we do so. Compare this with another perfectly correct formula that could produce the same result:

$$=D9*E9*Sheet3!B\$2$$

Looking at this formula there is no way of knowing exactly what it means or was intended to mean. Sheet 3 cell B2 could contain the exchange rate, or it could contain yesterday's temperature in Boston—it's all a mystery!

The second big advantage is that we don't have to go hunting around the spreadsheet to find the required values when we come to write formulas. Both Excel and Sheets have Name Managers that make it very easy to find where the required data or parameters are stored in the spreadsheet. In Excel this can be found on the Formula ribbon:

All the named ranges and cells are displayed here, and you can edit individual names if necessary.

In Sheets the name manager is accessed through the *Data* tab.

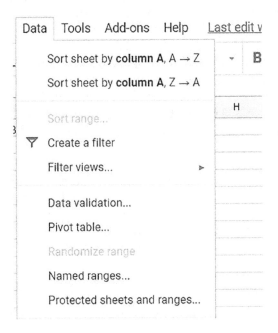

The Named ranges appear to the right of the screen and can similarly be edited:

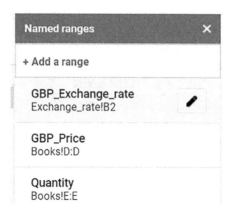

More on Copying and Pasting

The main thing to remember when we copy the contents of one cell or range to another position is the difference between cells that contain data and those that contain formulas. Where a cell contains a number or a piece of text, then it's perfectly straightforward—you just highlight the cell, click on *Ctrl-C*, move to where you wish to copy, and click *Ctrl-V*. Similarly, if you wish to move the contents from one cell to another so that they disappear from the original position, you cut and paste by clicking *Ctrl-X* and then *Ctrl-V* in the new position. Whole ranges can be copied or moved in this fashion. It's not quite so simple, though, when the original cell or range contains a formula—is it the formula itself that we wish to copy or is it the *results* of the formula, the output?

We've already seen the difference between absolute and relative cell references in formulas—if cell B2 contains the formula =A2, then if we can copy this to cell F2 it will change to =E2 unless we put a dollar symbol before the A, in which case it will read =$A2 no matter which cell it is copied to. Sometimes, however, we would just want to copy the results of the formula rather than the formula itself. Let's say, for example, we want column A to contain a list of the numbers from 1 to 50. An easy way of doing this is to type the number 1 into cell A2 and then in cell A3 enter the formula =A2+1—the result of this will be the number 2. If we can copy this formula down to row 51, then we will have our list of numbers. Once we've done this there is really no need to keep the formula underlying the list, so we can copy it and then paste the values rather than the formulas. There are similar ways of doing this in both Excel and Sheets.

In Excel the *Copy* and *Paste* icons are found on the *Home* tab. The easiest way to copy is to simply highlight the cell or range and press *Ctrl-C*, although you can use the *Copy* icon. However, if you want to paste values rather than formulas, you will need to click on the formula icon and choose the *Paste Values* option:

Don't worry about the different formatting options at the moment—the icon on the left will work just fine. Alternatively, you can use *Ctrl-Alt+V* to access the various pasting options.

Here is the same thing in Sheets. We use the Edit tab and choose the *Paste special* option to *Paste values only*. Sheets gives us the option of *Ctrl+Shift+V* to perform this operation.

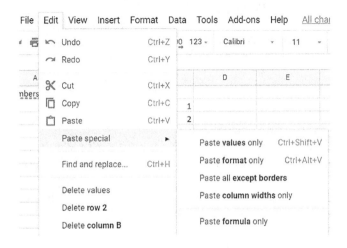

Freezing Rows and Columns

As we've already noted, the Header Row contains vital information about the data in each column, but once our worksheet holds more than about 30 rows this row will disappear from the screen as we scroll down. A useful trick is to "freeze" this row so that it will remain visible no matter how far down the sheet we go. In both Excel and Sheets this is done through the View tab.

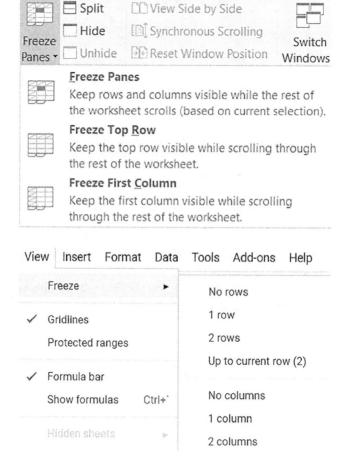

You will notice that it's also possible to freeze multiple rows from the top or columns from the left, but freezing the top row to keep track of the meaning of your data fields is by far the most useful application. Excel also has some sophisticated tools under the View tab that allow you to look at multiple worksheets at the same time.

Fun with Filters

Once you've got a lot of data in a worksheet, you will find that you want to start digging into it. We've already seen that it would be possible to sort the *Transactions* worksheet by borrower and then by branch to see how many books a borrower 6184 had checked out from the West Library:

855350774	East	5141	05/19/2018	06/19/2018
855350774	East	5141	05/19/2018	06/19/2018
4286222619	Central	6184	05/14/2018	06/14/2018
5814673452	East	6184	05/14/2018	06/14/2018
3684189788	East	6184	05/17/2018	06/17/2018
1829733880	West	6184	05/12/2018	06/12/2018
3983532110	West	6184	05/17/2018	06/17/2018

However, this is a cumbersome process and involves an actual change to the layout of the worksheet—we would need to change it back again to preserve the integrity of our data. A preferable method is to use filtering to give us the same information. To do this we make use of our Header Row, and in both Excel and Sheets this functionality is found on the *Data* tab (as well as the *Home* tab).

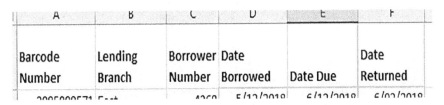

When we click on *Filter,* drop-down arrows will appear by each of the column headings:

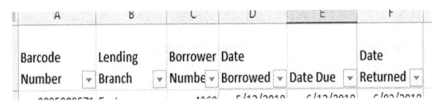

We see that there are some sort options here as well, but instead of using these we are going to use the checkboxes to select borrower 6184. To do this "unclick" *Select All,* and then choose the option that you want, in this case *6184,* and click *OK.*

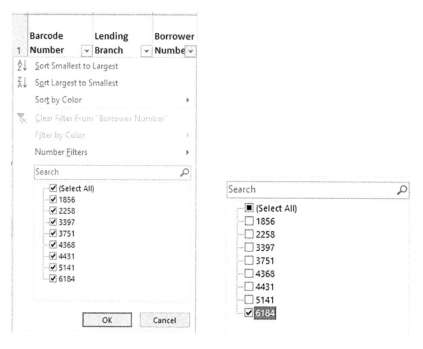

Now we see that the only entries in the Borrower Number column are for 6184, and then we filter the Lending Branch column to show entries for West only. The two columns by which we have filtered now show the distinctive Filter icon next to the drop-down arrows.

Barcode Number	Lending Branch	Borrower Number	Date Borrowed	Date Due
1829733880	West	6184	5/12/2018	6/12/2018
5814673452	East	6184	05/14/2018	06/14/2018
4286222619	Central	6184	05/14/2018	06/14/2018
3684189788	East	6184	05/17/2018	06/17/2018
3983532110	West	6184	05/17/2018	06/17/2018

Barcode Number	Lending Branch	Borrower Number	Date Borrowed	Date Due
1829733880	West	6184	5/12/2018	6/12/2018
3983532110	West	6184	05/17/2018	06/17/2018

The process is very similar for Sheets. Rather than unclicking *Select all*, click on *Clear* to remove the ticks and then click on the value you wish to filter by:

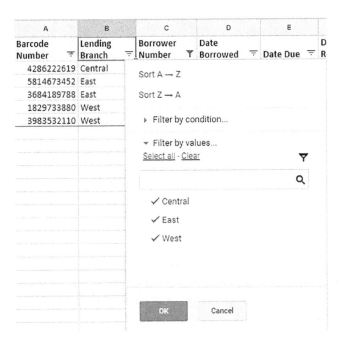

Effectively, this is a Boolean search of the data to find rows corresponding to borrower 6184 AND branch West and to hide all other rows.

Make sure that you have cleared all filters after using them. This is particularly important if you are copying formulas, which will only copy into "visible" cells; as some cells have been hidden as a result of a filter, the formula will not copy into them. To clear a filter from Sheets, click on *Select all*. In Excel use the *Clear* function:

Yes, this is a little confusing. The *Clear* function in Sheets is used to deselect all rows prior to making a selection rather than to remove a filter.

Conditional filtering is particularly useful. Rather than selecting criteria values from the list, you can create them yourself using either numerical values or text. If we have a worksheet containing details of books provided by a library vendor and we wish to exclude titles costing more than $50, we could simply set a filter for less than that amount by using a Number filter set to *Less Than*:

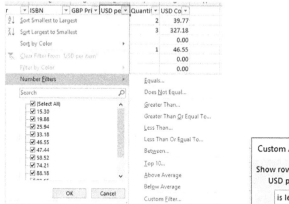
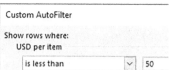

For librarians, conditional filtering by text is really powerful. Let's say that one of the columns of our worksheet contains the names of publishers, and we wanted to identify those items published by Wiley. Unfortunately, there are a number of variations of this name—Wiley, John Wiley, John Wiley & Sons, Wiley Australia, John Wiley Australia, and so on. Choosing these names from a list of hundreds of publishers would be not only burdensome but probably inaccurate as well, so instead we use a text filter to find all rows that contain the name *Wiley*:

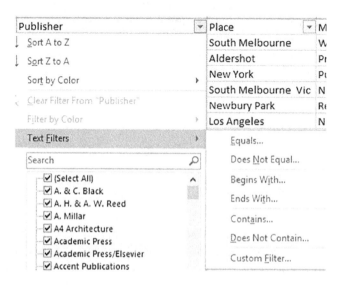

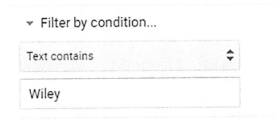

Here it is in Sheets:

And here is the filtered list:

	A	B	C
1	Publisher ▼	Place ▼	MajorTitle ≡
23	John Wiley & Sons	Hoboken	International financial statement analysis
28	Wiley-Blackwell	Chichester	Property valuation
43	Wiley	Chichester U.K.	Marketing communications: A brand narrative approach
81	Wiley	Chichester	Psychology and law: Truthfulness, accuracy and credibility
169	Wiley Blackwell	Chichester	Research methods in sociolinguistics: A practical guide
180	Wiley Blackwell	Malden, MA	Women and poverty: Psychology, public policy, and social justice
200	John Wiley & Sons	New York	Architectural acoustics: Principles and practice
202	John Wiley & Sons, Inc	Hoboken NJ	Fundamentals of microelectronics
207	Wiley	New York	Project management in practice
208	John Wiley	Hoboken N.J.	Forensic accounting and fraud examination

We will take a closer look at filtering in Chapter 8.

Printing

Occasionally, you will want to print a worksheet or a portion of it. Before you do this, make sure that you have text wrapped any rows in which data is overflowing into adjacent cells or is partially hidden by other data in these cells.

In Excel, you will need to create borders around the cells or the resulting print will be difficult to read. On the *Home* tab click on the Borders icon and select *All Borders*.

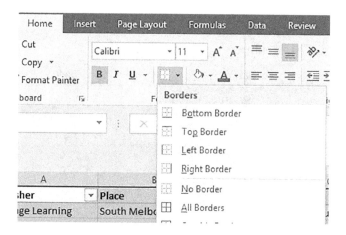

On the Page Layout tab use this selection to set the print area:

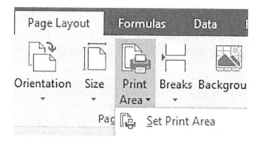

Now go to the File tab and click on *Print*. You will be given a preview, and you may need to change the orientation or size of the paper if your selection will not fit onto a standard sheet.

The procedure is very similar for Sheets, but there is no need to set the borders unless you have chosen not to display gridlines. Select the area you wish to print, then click on the File tab and choose *Print*. Sheets will default to printing the whole worksheet, which could be many pages long, so rather than printing the *Current sheet* choose instead *Selected cells*.

As a spreadsheet is a screen rather than a print medium, translating what you see into a paper output can sometimes be tricky. If a column does not fit on the page, it will be printed onto a separate page, so some adjustment may be necessary. Always check the previews carefully to make sure that what you see is what you really want to get.

Files and Saving

A useful, if rather oversimplified, way of looking at the distinction between the two spreadsheet packages is that Excel is a desktop-based system while

Sheets is web-based. What does this mean? One way of answering this question is to examine where the software controlling the spreadsheet is situated and whether it would operate if your computer was not connected to the Internet. To run Excel in desktop mode, you need to have installed the program on your computer, either purchasing it directly or as part of the Microsoft Office package. The spreadsheets it works with are files located within whatever file storage system you are using, either on your computer's hard drive, within a local area network, or within a cloud storage system like Dropbox. It is beyond the scope of this book to instruct you on file storage practice, but needless to say it is something that you should develop fluency with and follow good practice in matters like version control and backing up. Like other Office products, such as Word, Excel may require you to save your file from time to time in order to permanently store it—if you have made changes since the last time you saved and you attempt to close Excel, you will receive a warning about "unsaved changes," but if your system crashes then there is a risk that these changes will be lost.

Sheets, on the other hand, is cloud-based, and there is no need to install software on your computer. You need a Google account in order to use Sheets, and spreadsheet files are stored on your Google Drive. Just like Windows, Google Drive has a folder structure that you should become familiar with so that you can perform operations like renaming and moving files. Unlike Excel, however, it does not require you to save your work so that any changes that you make to a spreadsheet are permanent. Occasionally, you will make changes that you do not wish to keep, in which case there is an *Undo* button that will allow you to take your spreadsheet back to a previous state. In Chapter 10 we will look at using Excel files in Sheets and saving Sheets files in Excel format.

Conclusion

This chapter will have given you most of the important basic concepts, tools, and techniques of spreadsheeting, and you should now be in a position to move forward and learn some of the more powerful functions that will begin to save you time and bring positive results. Inevitably, there will be other basic functions that have not been covered here and that you will discover for yourself as you progress. Even for experienced users there can be the occasional embarrassing moment of realizing that some complicated trick they were using could have been done by clicking on an icon or looking at a tab they had previously ignored.

In the following chapters you will be working with practice spreadsheets, so you can use these to come back to this chapter and practice naming ranges, filtering and copying and experimenting with formats. Working on practice sheets is probably preferable to messing around with "real" ones—trial and error is a great way to learn, but there may be circumstances in which errors can have real consequences. As you work your way through this book, you can accumulate a store of spreadsheets containing all sorts of data, so keep them as digital sandboxes and add to them with your own examples. As with any learning experience, fluency comes with time, experience, and thought, and what may have appeared tricky in this chapter will soon become second nature.

In Chapter 3 we will begin creating formulas and transforming data into information. If you haven't tried spreadsheeting before, this is where the excitement should begin to kick in and some of the potential uses should start to emerge. If at all possible work through the examples as you read, or set aside time to come back to the book and carry out the exercises.

Starting With Formulas

Numbers and Operators

We've already seen that one of the uses of a spreadsheet is to carry out basic arithmetic. As Excel and Sheets both follow very similar terminology, we won't have to keep switching back and forth between them for this section. Arithmetic consists of four basic "operations"—*addition, subtraction, multiplication,* and *division*—on which all other mathematical techniques are built. Unfortunately, a standard computer keyboard includes the standard symbols for addition (the plus sign or +) and subtraction (the minus sign or -), but when written down multiplication is generally signified by the letter *x* which would be rather confusing while the division symbol (÷) is simply absent.

If you've studied algebra, you'll already be familiar with the idea of using letters or other symbols to stand for numbers in producing a generalized formula that allows you to carry out a series of calculations. If *x* stands for your hourly rate of pay and *y* for the number of hours worked, then your weekly pay before tax (*z*) is calculated using the algebraic formula

$$xy = z$$

In standard algebra we don't need to use a multiplication sign because running two letters together like this automatically means that they are multiplied, but because spreadsheets manipulate text as well as numbers it's necessary to make it clear when a mathematical function is being used.

The symbol * (asterisk or star) signifies multiplication, so that if we enter the formula

$$=2*3 \text{ (two times three or } 2×3)$$

into cell A2, the number 6 is displayed. (The correct word for a symbol used in this way is an "operator" because it performs an operation.) The advantage of using a spreadsheet rather than a desk calculator is that we can perform multiple calculations very easily and fast, so that if column A consists of a set of numbers representing whole years and the formulas in column C multiply these numbers by 12, then the results would be the number of months in those years. The formulas in C2 and C3 would be =A2*12 and =A3*12 or, if we had given column A the range Name *Years*

$$= Years*12$$

The operator for addition, not surprisingly, is + (plus) so that the formula =3+2 will return the result 5. Now, let's say we used column B to show the number of additional months in the time period over and above the number of years, so that in row 2 the total time period would be 3 years and 6 months, with the number 3 in cell A2 and the number 6 in cell B2. To calculate the total number of months, the formula in C2 will be

$$=A2*12+B2$$

which produces the correct answer of 42. Using descriptive Names the formula is

$$=Years*12+Months$$

You might notice that the spreadsheet has used the standard mathematical "order of operations" so that multiplication was processed before addition. If the number of months had been added to the number 12 and the result multiplied by the number of years, then our result would have been wrong. The order of operations is often summarized as PEMDAS (Parentheses, Exponents, Multiplication/Division, Addition/Subtraction), and it's a good idea to keep this handy if it wasn't thoroughly drilled into your brain at school! Our formula would have been clearer if we had added parentheses around the first calculation in the formula

$$=(Years*12)+Months$$

Subtraction is similarly obvious, using the minus operator, so that the formula for a simple profit/loss or surplus/deficit calculation would be

$$=Income-Costs$$

or more realistically

$$=Income-Costs-Tax$$

Another way of expressing this would be

$$=Income-(Costs+Tax)$$

which adds *Costs* and *Taxes* together first and then subtracts the result from *Income*.

The division operator is / (forward slash) so that 20÷5 is expressed as the formula

$$=20/5$$

Here's a typical division problem of the sort you might remember from elementary school. Let's say we have a mobile library with a carrying capacity of 1 ton of books. We do some research and discover that the average weight of a book in our library is 1 pound 10 ounces—how many books will our mobile library be able to carry? In order to solve the problem, we need to convert everything to a common unit which, for the sake of simplicity, will be ounces. There are 16 ounces in a pound, so therefore the weight of the average book is 26 ounces, as there are 2000 pounds in a ton, an easy way of expressing our calculation is

$$=(2000*16)/26$$

which divides total capacity by average weight (both in ounces) to show that we can carry 1454.545455 books in our mobile library, but in real life let's call it 1400. Of course, we could have used Names to generalize the equation

$$=(Carrying\_capacity\_in\_pounds*16)/Average\_book\_weight\_in\_ounces$$

This way we could adjust our parameters to find out how many extra books we could carry by varying the vehicle's capacity or the average book weight, by choosing to carry more paperbacks, for example.

The final mathematical operator is the exponent or "power," which represents the number of times a number is multiplied by itself. We are familiar with exponents as squares and cubes of numbers in equations like $2^2=4$ (two squared equals four) or $2^3=8$ (two to the power of three equals eight). The spreadsheet symbol for this is ^ (caret) so that our formula becomes =2^2 or =2^3. Exponents can be used to calculate areas and volumes, but another common use relates to compound interest and depreciation. There are some very sophisticated financial and actuarial spreadsheet functions, but here we will keep it simple and big picture.

Let's say we have a current materials budget of $100,000, and we wish to calculate what it will cost to maintain its purchasing value in the face of costs increasing at the rate of 5% per year. A good way of expressing a 5% increase of a number is to multiply it by 1.05, so that after one year (i.e., Year 1) the required budget could be expressed by the formula =100,000*1.05, which would return the result $105,000. Now the following year we need to multiply this amount by 1.05 again, so theoretically this formula would become =100,000*1.05*1.05, but this is really clumsy, so instead we multiply 1.05 by itself (in other words we "square" it) with the formula =100,000*1.05^2 to find the value in Year 2. The value in Year 3 is =100,000*1.05^3 and so on— for each year the previous result is multiplied by 1.05.

Once again, rather than hardwiring the values for initial budget and the annual rate of increase into the formula, it's a good idea to place them in separate named cells so that we can alter them easily. If we add a further Named range for the Year number, then this is what the formula looks like:

$$=Initial\_budget*Annual\_increase^Year$$

In this formula the exponent is calculated before the multiplication is carried out even though the multiplication operator appears first. Now we see that after three years our initial budget needs to have grown by an additional $15,000 to keep up with materials costs increases:

Year	Budget
0	$100,000.00
1	$105,000.00
2	$110,250.00
3	$115,762.50

Of course, annual budget increases can be difficult to argue for, so another way of expressing the question would be to show the results in terms of purchasing power of *not* increasing the budget in the face of materials cost increases. This can be done by changing the name *Annual_increase* to *Annual_change* and setting its value to 0.95, to show a 5% *decrease* in purchasing power each year from a fixed budget. Our formula now reads

$$=Initial\_budget*Annual\_change^{Year}$$

The results show a decline in value of almost $15,000 after three years:

Year	Value
0	$100,000.00
1	$95,000.00
2	$90,250.00
3	$85,737.50

Virtually any mathematical operation you might want to perform could be expressed in terms of these five operators: + - * / ^. For example, if we wanted to know the average value of the three numbers in the cells A2 to A4, we could calculate this through the formula =(A2+A3+A4)/3. Obviously, this becomes cumbersome if there are more than a few numbers to average, which is why we would use a formula instead (using the AVERAGE function, which we will come to in Chapter 4), but it's useful to bear in mind that all calculations are based on this simple arithmetic.

Working the Percentages

Spreadsheets have some other mathematical functions built in, the most frequently used of which are the ability to express numbers as percentages and to round decimal numbers to a set number of places. If we wanted to know what the number *20* was as a percentage of *40*, we can calculate this by dividing the first number by the second. The formula for this is =20/40, which returns the answer *0.5* which is correct but doesn't look very elegant. If, however, we click on the percentage icon on the toolbar, our answer becomes 50%. The usefulness of this becomes more apparent if we change the formula to =20/41, in which case *49%* is more expressive than *0.487805*. In Excel numbers are automatically rounded to the nearest full percentage value, whereas in Sheets they are rounded to two decimal points so the answer here is 48.78%. In either case it is possible to increase or decrease the number of decimal places by using the adjacent icons:

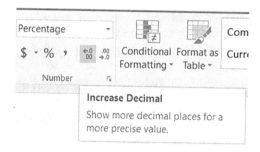

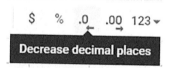

This can be done with any decimal number, not just with those formatted as percentages.

As well as calculating one number as a percentage of another, spreadsheets can calculate the difference between two numbers as a percentage to show, for example, an increase or decrease in library visits between two years. Here is a formula that does this using cell names to make the values transparent:

$$=(visits\_2018 - visits\_2017)/visits\_2017$$

The formula first calculates the difference between the two years (which could be positive or negative depending on whether activity increased or decreased) and then divides them by the value of the earlier year. Let's say there were 50,926 visits in 2017 and 54,302 in 2018; then the "true" formula would read:

$$=(54302-50926)/50926$$

which returns the result 0.066292267. By formatting it as a percentage to two decimal places we learn that visits increased by 6.63% between 2017 and 2018. Unpacking it a little further, there were 3,376 (i.e., 54302–50926) more visits in 2018 than in 2017, which is 6.63% of the 2017 total of 50,926. If there had been fewer visits in 2018, the formula would have produced a negative percentage.

EXERCISE

Open a copy of the spreadsheet for this exercise here:

http://bit.ly/30Zh9yv

Examine the Named ranges. In cell D2 enter the formula =(visits _2018 - visits_2017)/visits_2017, and copy it down the range. It will show the monthly comparisons between visits in 2017 and 2018.

For the year 2018 you are going to use column E to calculate the monthly visitor numbers as a percentage of the annual total.

Cell C14 contains this total, so you will give it the Name *total_2018*. In Sheets this is done by placing the cursor in that cell and clicking on *Data/Named ranges,* while in the Excel you click on *Formula/Define Name.*

In cell E2 enter the formula that will show the January visits as a percentage of the annual total. Copy it down the whole range.

Format column E to show the numbers as percentages. In Sheets this is on the toolbar; in Excel you will need to return to the *Home* tab.

Ways with Words

So far we have looked at spreadsheets as if they are all about numbers, but for librarians a really useful feature is their ability to deal with and manipulate text.

	A	B	C	D	E	F
1	Author	Year	Title	Subtitle	Place	Publisher
2	Armitage	2014	Pacific histories	Ocean, land, people	Basingstoke	Palgrave Macmillan
3	Flynn	2002	Studies in Pacific history	Economics, politics, and migration	Aldershot	Ashgate
4	Banner	2017	Possessing the Pacific	Land, settlers, and indigenous people from Australia to Alaska	Cambridge	Harvard University Press

Just as a number in one cell can be referenced from another cell, the same is true of words. If the words *Pacific histories* appear in cell C2 and the formula =C2 appears in cell G2, then the same words will appear in that cell. In itself this is not especially impressive, but in fact *Pacific histories* is the main title of a book whose subtitle is *Ocean, land, people,* which appears in cell D2. They have been exported from our library management system as separate fields, but now we want to join them up again to create a full title for a reading list.

To join these two text strings into a single one, the *ampersand* (&) symbol is used, and if you like correct technical terms, this is known as the "concatenation operator." It works just like the other operators so that the formula in G2 to join the title and subtitle would read

$$=C2\&D2$$

Unfortunately, though, the spreadsheet will interpret this rather literally. You asked for whatever was in A2 followed by the contents of B2, so here you are:

Pacific histories Ocean, land, people

The vital space between the words is missing so it is necessary to write it into the formula

$$=C2\&" "\&D2$$

Two ampersands have been used because we have to tell the spreadsheet that after the contents of C2 something else is coming, which is a space enclosed in double quotes. These quotes are used whenever literal text is included in a formula, even if it is only single space as in this example. Then the second ampersand indicates that another cell address is coming up. The result looks a lot better than our first effort:

Pacific histories Ocean, land, people

No one would guess that the innocuous little space between the third and fourth words would have required so much effort, but it's not perfect yet as the main title and the subtitle really need to be separated by a colon to reach our exacting bibliographic standards. This is easily done:

$$=C2\&": "\&D2$$

Pacific histories: Ocean, land, people

There's really no limit to what we can do with this. If Place of publication is in column E, Publisher in column F, and Year of publication in column B, and then if all of the spaces and punctuation are added in, we can place the following formula in F2:

$$=C2\&": "\&D2\&". "\&E2\&": "\&F2\&", "\&B2\&"."$$

And the result would be

Pacific histories: Ocean, land, people. Basingstoke:
Palgrave Macmillan, 2014.

Perfect! Right down to the final period. Except we forgot the author.

$$=A2\&". "\&C2\&": "\&D2\&". "\&E2\&": "\&F2\&", "\&B2\&"."$$

Armitage. Pacific histories: Ocean, land, people.
Basingstoke: Palgrave Macmillan, 2014.

Perfect!

Of course, using Names for the columns makes this more transparent:

=author&". "&main_title&": "&subtitle&". "&place&":
"&publisher&", "&pub_year&"."

An easy way to think of the ampersands (OK, *concatenation operators*) is that they are used to separate content that comes from other cells (author, title, etc.) from content supplied by the formula itself (punctuation and spaces) and to mark the transitions from one to the other.

Dates

Nothing in the spreadsheets is going to cause you as much trouble as the date functions. In theory, working with dates is the sort of thing they should do really well, and when they work properly the spreadsheet date functions really are effective. However, when they don't they can be a real problem and a significant time waster. In other words, when they are good they are very very good, but when they are bad they are horrid! In fairness, differing date protocols and formats don't make the task any easier, but it's hard to avoid the impression that this is one area where Excel, in particular, doesn't perform to its best.

That said, there are some useful things librarians can do with dates in spreadsheets, as this is one area in which the neat regularity of base-10 mathematics collides with the messy reality of a year consisting of 365 days (more or less) and 12 months of varying length. To see what I mean, just try working out the number of days until your next birthday—unless it's tomorrow (or at least some day this month) you are going to struggle! Our spreadsheets make the task easier by giving each day a number so that we can carry out this calculation simply by subtracting the number for today from the number for our next birthday. Here it is in Sheets:

=B2-A2		
A	B	C
Today	**Next birthday**	**Days to wait**
02/17/2019	03/25/2019	36

I have entered today's date in cell A2 and the date of my next birthday in cell B2 and then in C2 the formula *=B2-A2*, which tells me how many days I will have to maintain my patience for.

A more professionally useful implementation of this function can be seen in the example below of Dulminster borrowing transactions:

=DateReturned-DateDue

Barcode Number	Lending Branch	Borrower Number	Date Borrowed	Date Due	Date Returned	Days Overdue
2095009571	East	4368	05/12/2018	06/12/2018	06/06/2018	-6
5261383263	South	3751	05/12/2018	06/12/2018	07/06/2018	24
5255919712	Central	4368	05/13/2018	06/13/2018	06/19/2018	6
2186837314	North	4368	05/14/2018	06/14/2018	06/27/2018	13
9381762514	North	1856	05/16/2018	06/16/2018	06/13/2018	-3
3684189788	East	6184	05/17/2018	06/17/2018	05/30/2018	-18
6961924774	Central	1856	05/17/2018	06/17/2018	06/22/2018	5
3983532110	West	6184	05/17/2018	06/17/2018	06/16/2018	-1
5455991514	Central	4368	05/17/2018	06/17/2018	06/11/2018	-6
745156686	North	1856	05/18/2018	06/18/2018	11/06/2018	141

Column E records the dates due and column F the dates on which books were returned, so because we have Named our ranges the calculation in column G is simply

$$=DateReturned-DateDue$$

Negative values occur when books have been returned before the due date.

EXERCISE

Download the spreadsheet for this exercise here:

http://bit.ly/30SSHP8

Have a look at the Named ranges.
Enter the formula =Date_Returned-Date_Due into cell G2, and copy it down the cells below. The results will be the same as those shown above.
In column H construct a formula that will show the total number of days between the date on which a book was borrowed and the date on which it was returned.

Spreadsheet date calculations are based on giving each date a serial number, starting with January 1, 1900, as 1. You can find out the number for today's date by entering the simple formula

$$=TODAY()$$

The cell that you enter this formula into needs to be formatted as a number in order for you to see this. If you were born on August 19, 1986, you could find out the number for your birthday by entering the formula

$$=DATE(1986,8,16)$$

Again you will need to format the cell as a number in order to see the answer (31640). All date formulas use these numbers, but often they are not visible—it's a good idea to know about them because when they suddenly appear they can be quite baffling!

Copying and Pasting Formula Results

When you use a spreadsheet formula to produce a result, it's this result that you see on your screen, but what is really "in" the spreadsheet cells is the formula. This is only as it should be of course because some of the formula inputs will change—if you receive an increase in your hourly rate pay, you want the spreadsheet to show how much you will be getting next week! However, there will be times when you want to copy and paste the results as they are now, showing the numbers or text as if you had typed them in. This is known as "pasting values."

Let's take a simple example. Say I wanted column A just to contain the numbers 1 to 100. In the cell A2 I type the number *1* and then in cell A3 I type the formula *=A2+1,* which I then copy down to cell A101 to create a sequential list of numbers. (There is another way of doing this, but I can't always remember what it is so this simple trick works well enough.) Because I no longer need the formulas, just the numbers, it's a good idea to get rid of the formulas at this point. I do this by highlighting column A and then pressing *Ctrl-C* to copy the content and then, rather than pressing *Ctrl-V,* which would paste the formulas, I choose *Edit/Paste special/Paste values only* so that only the numbers appear in the cells (as if I had spent five minutes typing them). Sheets has a useful *Ctrl-Shift-V* function that allows you to paste values automatically.

There are occasions when you will always have to copy and paste values. If you want to share the results of your spreadsheet as it is now with no risk of "accidental changes," then it's a good idea to do this rather than going to the trouble of locking down large portions of the spreadsheet with security measures. It's surprising how easy it is for another person to make a mess of your careful work when all they had asked to see was last month's circulation numbers! In a more specific example, if you've used a random number generator for sampling purposes, you need to permanently capture these exact numbers before the formula changes them when you next open the spreadsheet.

This is done by copying the numbers and using Paste values to save them permanently.

Formula Correction

Because we are human, and because entering formulas can be tricky, we will make the occasional mistake. Our spreadsheet software can be really useful in preventing us from doing this and explaining what it is we did wrong. Here's a simple example from Excel:

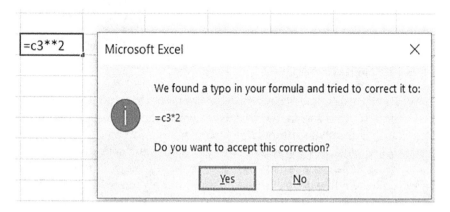

I had accidentally entered the multiplication operator twice; the software had spotted it and suggested a correction that I simply have to accept in order to get the correct result. In fact, it wouldn't allow me to continue until the formula made sense. These error corrections can be very useful, especially as some formulas can get quite complex with lots of parentheses and "nesting," but you should always check that the correction suggested is what you actually want. The spreadsheet is very good at determining what is, and what is not, a valid formula, but it has no ability to read your mind.

Sometimes It Just Goes Wrong: Learning From Your Errors

There will be times when you get it wrong, and your spreadsheet will come back with an error message. This can be annoying, but your spreadsheet should be able to help you work out what you did wrong.

#VALUE!

The most common form of error comes from trying to do something that is simply impossible, such as trying to multiply a book title by a number. If cell A2 contains the title of the book, and you enter the formula =A2*2 into cell B2, the output will be *#VALUE!* This is the standard form of an error message starting with a hashtag to notify you of the error and ending with an exclamation mark telling you to fix it! Now! This is a *Value* error because we are asking for a logical impossibility—only numbers can be multiplied with other numbers because multiplication is an arithmetic thing and arithmetic is a number thing not a word thing. We might have thought we were asking for two copies of the book, or asking for the title to be entered twice, but that's *not* what the formula means.

In Sheets, a mouseover of cell B2 gives us a very clear indication of what we did wrong:

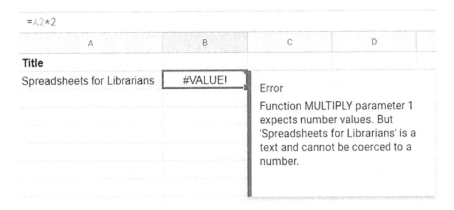

In simple terms this is saying, "if you want to multiply whatever is in cell A1, make sure it's a number." (It's not actually smart enough to know that *Spreadsheets for Librarians* is a book; it's just using the word *text* to mean that it's a bit of text not a number.) Excel also provides a lot of help in deciphering and fixing errors on the *Formulas* tab under *Error checking* and for a complex formula it will even walk you through each step.

#NAME?

If your spreadsheet really doesn't know what you mean, you will most likely get a *#NAME?* error, which is really a polite way of saying "you what?" The most common reason for this will be if you misspell the name of one of the many spreadsheet functions, which we will look at in the following chapters. For now, a simple example will show you what is meant. Sometimes a string of characters will contain invisible spaces at the beginning or end; because we can't see them we have no way of knowing that they are there, but they can cause problems. The TRIM function is a handy way of removing them, so if we want to create a version in cell B2 of the text in cell A2 without these leading or trailing spaces, we use the formula *=TRIM(A2)*. However, if we mistype this as *=TRIP(A2)*, then cell A3 will display *#NAME?*.

#REF!

The *#REF!* error occurs if a formula references a cell address that no longer exists or that is logically impossible. This is most likely to happen if you delete a range or a worksheet, in which case any formula that was linked to it will show the error. It's an important way of avoiding the introduction of accidental logical errors. Take, for example, a worksheet in which column A contained hours and column B contained minutes, and these were referenced from a formula in column E, which calculated the total time in minutes. If we deleted column A, then column B would become the new column A, but the formula now in column D (which used to be column E!) would show a *#REF!* error because its logic was based on a data element that no longer existed. What is really helpful is that the formula itself will now point out that it was trying to reference data that no longer exists—for example, a formula that tried to convert hours to minutes would now read =#REF!*60.

#DIV/0!

Division by zero errors can be really scary. Dividing zero by another number is simple—the answer is always zero! How many fives are there in ten—two. How many fives are there in zero—zero. But how many zeros are there in five—uh, that doesn't really make sense, so our spreadsheet gives us the *#DIV/0!* error instead. Now you might think, "but why would I ever want to divide something by zero?" Actually, it's easier than you might think.

Week starting	Books acquired	Total cost	Average cost	
7/29/2019	10	$852.90	$85.29	
8/5/2019	4	$364.50	$91.13	
8/12/2019	0	$0.00	#DIV/0!	Error
8/19/2019	15	$682.35	$45.49	Function DIVIDE parameter 2
8/26/2019	35	$1,415.00	$40.43	cannot be zero.

In this example column B records the number of books brought into stock each week and has the range Name *number_of_books_acquired*, while column C records the total cost (*total_cost*) while the formula in column D calculates the average cost:

=total_cost/number_of_books_acquired

Sometimes books will be donated, in which case they will not have a cost, and if in a given week the only books acquired are donated the total cost will be zero and the average cost will also be zero. The formula is able to manage this because the result of zero defined by a number is always zero. However, there will be weeks in which *no* books are acquired, and in this case not only will *total_cost* be zero but *number_of_books_acquired* will be zero as well. Now, your common sense might suggest that the average cost would also be zero, but according to the rules of mathematics division of any number by zero is an impossibility so instead your spreadsheet will give you a *#DIV/0!* error message.

Sometimes when you have a column with a division-based formula that has been set up to take data that will be input over a period of time, then these "waiting" cells will show *#DIV/0!*.

#N/A

This error occurs with lookup functions, which we will come to in Chapter 6. It stands for *Not Available,* which means that we went looking for an answer that we couldn't find. More on that later.

Error messages in spreadsheets aren't the end of the world, and you shouldn't be put off doing something just because of the risk of returning an error. There are ways of working around them, and just because we can't calculate the percentage increase or decrease in complaints after a week in which there weren't any doesn't mean we should be put off calculating it for all the other weeks of the year.

Think for Yourself!

As already mentioned, a spreadsheet doesn't really know what is in your mind or what you are intending to do. We think of them as being "smart," but that is something of an illusion—what they really are is just very very efficient, which is a different thing. Let's say we have a range called *Years* and another range with a formula that multiplies this by 365 to show the number of days. If you accidentally enter a number representing months or weeks into *Years*, the formula will dutifully multiply this number by 365 to produce a result that doesn't actually mean anything. However, there will be no error message because there is no error. This is because the spreadsheet has no idea what it was that you actually meant, and it will "assume" that any number in that column is valid—the error was one of execution and not of spreadsheet logic.

This might seem rather obvious, but because spreadsheets are so efficient, it's easy to fall into the trap of believing that they are doing your thinking for you, and strictly speaking words like "assume" should be avoided because they refer to human ideas and not to the operation of a computer. The results that they produce, however, depend entirely on the underlying logic, which is *your* responsibility. If at all possible have some means of carrying out a reality check—take one of the calculations and carry it out manually. Did it produce the same result as your spreadsheet? If it didn't, check back to see where you have gone wrong, to see if one of your formulas contains a logical error; you might have multiplied the number of years by 52 to calculate the number of months, for example, rather than by 12. If you think your calculations are too complex to be carried out manually, then you may be in very dangerous territory indeed! It might be possible to devise a wonderfully complex formula to allocate your book budget between different user groups, but if you can't explain it in simple terms to your committee, then your spreadsheet may simply be a high-tech form of smoke and mirrors.

The Sort Function in Sheets

In Chapter 2 we looked at sorting ranges using menu options in both Excel and Sheets. Sheets has a second method of sorting that uses a function and creates a new sorted version of a range in another location.

The following list is held in the range A2:D7.

	A	B	C	D
1	Title	Publication Date	Publisher	USD
2	A dictionary of animal behaviour	2014	Oxford University Press	$18
3	Adam's nose, and the making of humankind	2015	Imperial College Press	$38
4	An introduction to animal behavior	2012	Cambridge University Press	$145
5	Animal behavior	2018	Storytellers, Inc	$80
6	Animal behavior : an evolutionary approach.	2011	Apple Academic Press	$26
7	Animal nature and human nature.	2018	Taylor and Francis	$103

It is currently sorted by price in column D, but I want to create a copy sorted by the title in column A. To do this I simply go to any cell outside this range and enter

$$=SORT(A2:D7)$$

Because I didn't specify a column to sort by, it defaulted to the leftmost column and the new list is sorted by title. However, if I wanted to sort by date, this can be done by specifying the second column in the range followed by the word *TRUE*:

$$=SORT(A2:D7,2,TRUE)$$

This formula is entered in one cell only, at the top left corner of the new range. The word *TRUE* is needed to get it to sort in ascending order, and if you enter *FALSE* it will sort the other way round! You have to make sure that there is room on the worksheet for the whole range you are copying, or an error message will result. It's a fairly smart feature of Sheets, and if I inserted a row into the original list, this would be incorporated into the sorted list in its proper place, and the formula would automatically change to

$$=SORT(A2:D8,2,TRUE)$$

However, if I add a row to the end of the list, I need to alter the formula manually.

There is only one obvious shortcoming to the SORT function, and that is that it cannot be used with Named ranges with Header Rows as it will insert the Header Row into the sorted list at the appropriate place. If you've been paying attention, you will have noticed that Named ranges and Header Rows are among my favorite things, at least spreadsheet-wise. There are two possible workarounds. The first is to use literal addresses such as *A2:D8* as I have done here, while the second is to begin the definition of the Named range from the second row so that the range *vendor_data* would be defined as *A2:D*. This is somewhat clumsy but it works!

EXERCISE (SHEETS ONLY)

Using the spreadsheet that you opened for the previous exercise:

http://bit.ly/30SSHP8

Open a new worksheet by clicking the + symbol at the bottom left-hand corner. Copy the headings from the *Transactions* worksheet into the top row of the new worksheet; then in cell A2 enter the formula

$$=SORT(Transactions!A:F)$$

Observe what went wrong and fix it!
Now sort the data by Borrower Number. Then reverse the order.

Removing Duplicates

Before we proceed to look at data analysis in the following chapters, this might be a good time to consider the difficulties that can be caused by duplicate entries in a worksheet and also to look at other valid reasons for wanting to create lists of data without duplicates. If we look at a column, there might be good reason why the same entry appears numerous times—for example, the same person may have taken out several books, or if we are looking at a column containing the names of library branches, they may issue thousands of books a day, each transaction occupying a row of data. However, if the exact same transaction is recorded more than once, again this will distort any analysis of the data by treating each recorded instance as if it were a separate transaction. A single publication may have multiple authors from the same university or college—if each of them submits its details to the research management system, its details could appear on several rows of a spreadsheet output by the system. In this case it could be preferable to have two separate worksheets, one showing every instance and the other with no duplication.

Here are some brief records of journal articles taken from a research management system:

DOI	Title	Journal
10.1007/978-981-10-3394-0_15	Social and Emotional Learning and Indigenous Ideologies in Aotearoa New Zealand: A Biaxial Blend	Social and Emotional Learning in Australia and the Asia-Pacific
10.1016/j.scitotenv.2017.06.077	Separation and identification of hormone-active compounds using a combination of chromatographic separation and yeast-based reporter assay	Science of The Total Environment
10.1007/s00253-017-8199-3	Environmental and metabolic parameters affecting the uric acid production of Arxula adeninivorans	Applied Microbiology and Biotechnology
10.1007/978-981-10-3394-0_15	Social and emotional learning and indigenous ideologies in Aotearoa New Zealand: A biaxial blend	Social and Emotional Learning in Australia and the Asia-Pacific
10.1016/j.scitotenv.2017.06.077	Separation and identification of hormone-active compounds using a combination of chromatographic separation and yeast-based reporter assay	Science of the Total Environment
10.1002/bit.26249	Simultaneous detection of three sex steroid hormone classes using a novel yeast-based biosensor	Biotechnology and Bioengineering

If you look carefully, you will notice that two of the entries have been duplicated and, although they are not totally identical, they clearly refer to the same publications. Because it has proven difficult over the years to make absolutely uniform descriptions of journal articles, Digital Object Identifiers (DOIs) are widely used to uniquely identify them. As long as each DOI appears only once in the DOI column, we can be confident that there is no duplication of articles.

In Excel the *Remove Duplicates* feature can be found on the *Data* tab:

When you click on the *Remove Duplicates* icon, all columns containing data are automatically selected, a dialog box appears and you are given a choice, taken from the Header Row, of the ranges which will be used to base the duplicate removal decision on.

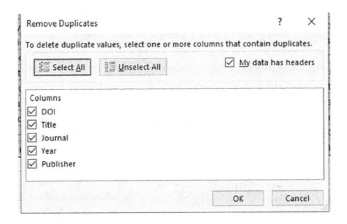

If you want to remove only those rows that are absolutely identical in all respects, leave all of the options ticked. (The only difference that will be ignored is case, so that a title in sentence case will be treated as identical to one with significant words capitalized, but otherwise even a missing comma could lead to two titles not being identified as identical.)

In this case, however, because the DOI is a unique identifier, we will choose to remove duplicates on that basis only:

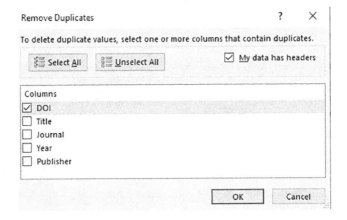

When we click *OK*, a message is received telling us the number of duplicates that have been taken out of the worksheet:

It's a good idea to check this carefully, and if you are unsure you can always use the *Undo* icon to restore the previous situation. In fact, before undertaking any major operation on a worksheet, it's good practice to take a copy of the worksheet by right-clicking on the tab at the bottom of the screen and choosing the *Create a Copy* option. You can always delete this backup sheet later on.

The process is more or less identical in Sheets through *Data/Remove duplicates*, but remember to click the *Data has header row* option in the dialog box:

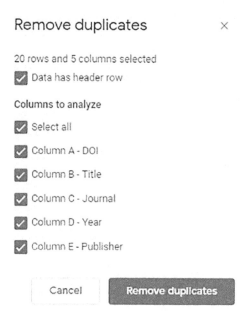

Conclusion

We have spent this chapter coming to grips with the fundamentals that underpin all spreadsheet functions. Even if you stopped reading now (please don't!), you would have learned enough to carry out some important tasks involving the manipulation of numbers and text and to put these into practice over thousands of lines of data. However, we have barely scratched the surface yet, and in the Chapter 4 we will proceed to look at spreadsheet functions that would turn these basic operations into powerful analytical tools. It's important though to understand that all of this functionality derives from simple arithmetic and a few word tools—the results produced by spreadsheets can appear magical, but they must always be grounded in sound logic and, as the human mind in control of the process, it is your job to create and control this logic. Unless it all adds up in your mind, there is a good chance that what you're looking at on your screen doesn't really add up either!

CHAPTER FOUR

Moving Forward With Formulas

Simple Sums and Average Arithmetic

So far we have used our spreadsheets mainly as fancy calculating machines, able to perform lots of additions or multiplications very quickly and to do some clever things with text. Now we are moving on to look at spreadsheet *functions*, which are commands that carry out specific mathematical or textual operations that would be much more difficult to perform using only the tools we have already learned.

Let's start with simple addition. If cells A2 to A6 contain numbers, we could work out a total just by adding them together with a + sign:

$$=A2+A3+A4+A5+A6$$

However, this would become very tedious, especially if it was a long range with hundreds of numbers to be added up, so instead we use the SUM function to do this work for us:

$$=SUM(A2:A6)$$

And of course, this becomes really transparent when we have used Named ranges:

$$=SUM(daily\_visitors)$$

Now, let's say we want to know the average of the numbers in the cells A2 to A6. There are five of them, so we could get the average by dividing the total by five:

=SUM(A2:A6)/5

This is clumsy, especially if it is a long range, so the spreadsheet has another function designed to give us the average:

=AVERAGE(A2:A6) or *=AVERAGE(daily_visitors)*

This is all pretty straightforward, and there is really only one mistake we can make, which is to overlook the fact that zero is a number. If we were averaging the number of daily complaints, there might be some days on which there were no complaints, for example. We might be tempted simply to leave the cell that records complaints on those days blank. However, if we do this the average number of complaints per day calculated by the spreadsheet will be higher than the true number. To understand this, we need to dig a little deeper into what an average is and how the spreadsheet calculates it. Here's a description of what we're trying to do:

average_number_of_complaints=total_number_of_complaints
÷number_of_days

To work out the number of days, we use the COUNT function, which counts the number of cells in a range containing a number. The formula

=COUNT(A2: A6)

will return the result 5 if there are numbers in all the cells, but if one of the cells is blank, or if it contains text or a space, it will return the result 4. Looking again at our AVERAGE function, it could also be written like this:

=SUM(A2:A6)/COUNT(A2:A6)

This makes it clear why we need to enter zeros rather than simply leaving days on which there were no complaints as blank cells. If there were 20 complaints over five days, but if on one of those days there were no complaints, the average number of complaints per day would be 4—the result of 20 divided by 5. Now, if for the day on which there were no complaints this is recorded as zero, then this is the result we get—zero is a number and the total number of days is 5—but if we leave the cell blank, then the total number of days becomes 4 and the average number of complaints per day rises to 5. This is not good and, more to the point, it is not correct.

This may seem like a minor point, but it demonstrates the importance of understanding what your spreadsheet is doing. It would be simple to do a reality check on the average of cells A2 to A6, but if this was a range with hundreds of entries you would have no intuitive sense of what the correct average would be!

While the COUNT function counts cells with numbers on them, the COUNTA function counts all nonblank cells. A worksheet may have a column (the Named range *Comments*) to record comments, but this will be used only occasionally. To find out quickly how many entries there are in the *Comments* range, we can use the formula = *COUNTA(Comments)*. The only potential difficulty with this could be the presence of spaces without any other text (known as "whitespaces"), which are invisible but which stop the cell from being nonblank and contribute to the COUNTA total. This might seem an unlikely thing to happen, but it's easy to fall into the habit of clicking on a cell and pressing the spacebar to remove its contents, rather than pressing the delete key. DON'T DO THIS! The cell will no longer be blank, but it will be indistinguishable from the blank cells unless you use some other smart move like counting the number of characters in the cell. Keep reading.

COUNTA is a pretty useful function. Let's say you have a spreadsheet consisting of separate worksheets for each month's transactions, called *January, February*, and so on. Column A in each worksheet will contain the date and time, and an entry in this column will indicate that there is a transaction, so that the total of nonblank cells will equal the total number of transactions. As well as the monthly worksheets there is a final sheet to summarize transactions for the year. The formula

$$=COUNTA(January!A:A)$$

will show the total number of transactions for the month of January.

Let's get back to averages. An average, also known as a mean, is a useful figure because it takes a total and divides it by the number of things counted—average salary, average house price, average book price, and so on. However, it doesn't always give a totally accurate picture of reality due to the presence of outliers in the data, or an uneven distribution of values sometimes known as "skew." Say you are sitting with a group of five colleagues, the youngest of whom is 19 years old and the oldest 35 years old. Altogether, your average age is 27. The town's senior resident, who is 102 years old, joins you, and the average age of the group rises to 40. Now, you didn't all age by 13 years, and anyone looking at the group would say that it's still a group of twentysomethings except maybe for that one person who seems a bit older. A better way of characterizing the group like this would be to look at the *median* age—line them up from youngest to oldest and pick the one in the middle. When we do this, we find that the arrival of the centenarian has only aged the group by two years, from 25 to 27. The formula we would use to calculate this if the ages were listed in a Named range would be

$$=MEDIAN(age)$$

So what has this got to do with libraries and spreadsheets? A simple example comes from OCLC's *Worldshare Collection Evaluation,* which uses both median and average to describe and evaluate publication dates of books in library collections. In some subjects, such as health sciences or engineering, the two methods will produce very similar results, but in the humanities it is common for the median date to be considerably more recent than the average date of publication. This is because of the fact that many humanities disciplines tend to "cumulate" knowledge over time, so that older works are still studied and considered relevant, while in the applied sciences older knowledge is characteristically replaced by more recent findings. The statistical result of this is that in the humanities the "long tail" stretches back further and the average publication date is driven down, while the median is the date that we would get if we put all the books in date order and then found the middle. This is a truer reflection of the age of our collection. Neither the median or the average is "right," but they are measuring different things, and it's important to understand which is the correct one to use in each circumstance.

EXERCISE

Open this list of orders:

http://bit.ly/2PjgSDe

Open a new worksheet to contain your formulas. There are a number of places of publication missing from column A of worksheet *OrderList,* but all books have prices. Use the COUNT and COUNTA functions to find out how many of these there are. Verify this by using a filter on the places to select only the blanks.
What is the median publication date of these books?
What is their average list price?
(Try using the Named ranges already contained in the spreadsheet.)

Array Formulas and Sumproduct

Sometimes we might want to undertake a complex calculation based on values from more than one column. Here's a spreadsheet containing simple prices and numbers of copies ordered:

	A	B	C	D
1	Title	USD	Quantity	Total
2	A dictionary of animal behaviour	$18	1	$18
3	Adam's nose, and the making of humankind	$38	3	$114
4	An introduction to animal behavior	$145		$0
5	Animal behavior	$80	2	$160
6	Animal behavior : an evolutionary approach.	$26	4	$104
7	Animal nature and human nature.	$103	2	$206
8	Animal vocal communication : assessment and management roles.	$94	3	$282
9				
10				$884

The costs listed in column D (*Total*) are the result of the simple multiplication:

$$=price*copies$$

or

$$=B2*C2$$

The total at the bottom of column D is the result of the formula

$$=SUM(D2:D8)$$

Now column D is certainly useful because it lets us know the amount being spent on each book as well as the total, but we could find the total without having to create column D through the use of an *array formula* that creates a sort of virtual column. The correct formula for this calculation is

$$\{=SUM(B2:B9*C2:C9)\}$$

or

$$\{=SUM(price*copies)\}$$

What you will notice about these formulas in Excel is that they are placed within curly brackets to indicate that they are array formulas. These are not entered through the keyboard but as a result of pressing *Ctrl+Shift+Enter* after the formula has been completed. If you do not do this, the result will be a *#VALUE* error. If you receive this error on entering the formula, simply place your cursor in the Formula bar and press *Ctrl+Shift+Enter*.

While Sheets uses the same formula, it works somewhat differently and contains a hidden trap. If you simply enter the formula

$$=SUM(B2:B9*C2:C9)$$

sheets will return an (incorrect!) answer rather than an error. When you press *Ctrl+Shift+Enter,* the formula will look like this:

$$=ArrayFormula(sum(B2:B9*C2:C9))$$

and will return the correct result.

Array formulas can be very complex, but as we have seen on this simple example, they can also result in saving time and avoiding the creation of extra columns. If you are using a spreadsheet created by someone else, you should be on the lookout for array formulas and always handle them with care.

Another way of arriving at the same result would have been through the function SUMPRODUCT which, as its name suggests, incorporates multiplication and addition. It looks a little strange because it uses two minus signs together in the following format:

$$=SUMPRODUCT(--B2:B9,C2:C9)$$

or

$$=SUMPRODUCT(--price,quantity)$$

Its advantage is that it doesn't require the unusual method of entry and looks the same in both Excel and Sheets. When we come to look at conditional formulas, SUMPRODUCT is particularly useful.

Simple Logic

Closely aligned to mathematics is *logic,* a system for evaluating whether statements are true or false. So far we have used the equals sign (=) as an indicator of the beginning of a formula, but used within a formula it is a logical operator, meaning that whatever is to the left of the equals sign is the same as whatever is on the right. The statement *three times two equals six* really means that those are two different ways of saying the same thing or expressing the same value, that the first thing (three times two) *is* the second thing (six). Now, an *is* statement is capable of being either *true* or *false;* either today is Monday or it is not, so the statement *today is Monday* will be true on Monday and false on every other day. So in spreadsheets we can use the equals sign within a formula as an operator to evaluate whether a statement is true. If we type the following into the formula box for cell A2

$$=3*2=6$$

the cell will show the value TRUE, but if we change it to

$$=3*2=5$$

the result will change to FALSE.

This equivalence logic also works for character strings (a fancy term for words and phrases) as well as numbers. The following formula is TRUE:

$$="elep"\&"hant"="elephant"$$

One thing to notice is that your spreadsheet will not take *case* into account when evaluating the equivalence of character strings, so that the following is also TRUE:

$$="elep"\&"hant"="ELEPHANT"$$

Of course, we don't really use a spreadsheet to work out simple little equations like this. Instead we are more likely to compare two cells to see whether they contain the same information, in the form of

$$=A2=B2$$

or

$$=home\_library=lending\_library$$

In the second example we could easily use filtering on the column containing this formula to count the number of transactions where the book was borrowed from the patron's home library (TRUE) and the number where it was borrowed from a different branch (FALSE).

As well as the equals sign, there are three other operators that use TRUE/FALSE logic, the *greater than* and *less than* signs and the *not equal to* sign. A left angle bracket signifies that the value to the left is *less than* the value to the right so that the following is TRUE:

$$=3<6$$

Similarly, a right angle bracket means that the right-hand value is greater, so the following is FALSE:

$$=3>6$$

If you want to increase your savings, the following needs to be TRUE:

$$= monthly\_income>monthly\_spending$$

Occasionally, you will want to say *greater than or equal to* or *less than or equal to* as in "books costing $20 or more" or "books costing $20 or less." In these cases the equals sign is combined with the angle brackets. If the value in cell A2 is 20, the following formulas both return the answer TRUE:

$$=A2>=20$$

$$=A2<=20$$

Finally, the logical operator for *not equal to* combines the other two symbols, so that the following is TRUE:

$$=3*2<>5$$

This can also be used on character strings so that the following is FALSE:

$$="elep"&"hant"<>"ELEPHANT"$$

Here's a funny thing! Because the notions *greater than* and *less than* are really numeric, we wouldn't expect them to work with words, but for some reason spreadsheets do evaluate character strings based on the position of the first letter in the alphabet, so that the following is TRUE:

$$="zebras">"aardvarks"$$

You can use this to prove conclusively that girls are greater than boys and dogs are greater than cats! Other than that, I'm not sure what the purpose of it really is, and it might make more sense for the spreadsheet to return an error message.

Slightly Less Simple Logic: AND, OR, XOR

So far, we have looked at logic as a means of comparing two values with one another, but there will often be circumstances when we want to determine the truth or falsity of a more complex set of circumstances. Think of the game *Guess Who* in which we ask questions like "is it a woman with long hair and glasses?" A more realistic example for us would be "houses in West Dulminster with more than three occupants." If we look at this phrase more closely, we can see that it breaks down into three elements:

Type of dwelling—house
Location—West Dulminster
Number of occupants—more than three

In turn these can be turned into three logical formulas:

type_of_dwelling="house"
location="West Dulminster"
number_of_occupants>3

Many librarians will already be familiar with, and recognize here, Boolean logic, which is used in database searching, and will have noticed that this is the form of a classic AND search in which a "hit" (in other words a TRUE result) is returned only if each of the subelements in a given row is true. We will find a match only if the dwelling is a house AND it is in West Dulminster AND it has more than three occupants. The spreadsheet formula for this uses the AND function and separates the different elements with commas:

=AND(type_of_dwelling="house",location="West
Dulminster",number_of_occupants>3)

If we were not using Named ranges, the formula in cell D3 could read

=AND(A3="house",B3="West Dulminster",C3>3)

Again, you'll notice that the values all occur in the same row and the different elements within the parentheses are separated by commas.

The resulting chart looks like this:

Dwelling	Location	Occupants	Match
House	East Dulminster	4	FALSE
House	West Dulminster	5	TRUE
Apartment	West Dulminster	5	FALSE
House	West Dulminster	3	FALSE

AND logic insists that *all* elements are true in order to return a TRUE result, but there will be cases in which we would be satisfied if any one of a number of options was true, and here we use the OR function. Let's say we changed the formula in column D to read

=OR(location="West Dulminster",location="East Dulminster")

In this case all the matches would be TRUE because we have matched on one element only, the location. However, we can combine these two functions to find houses with more than three occupants that are in either East or West Dulminster by using parentheses.

=AND(type_of_dwelling="House",OR(location="West Dulminster",
location="East Dulminster"),number_of_occupants>3)

Our chart now reads like this:

Dwelling	Location	Occupants	Match
House	East Dulminster	4	TRUE
House	West Dulminster	5	TRUE
Apartment	West Dulminster	5	FALSE
House	West Dulminster	3	FALSE

This logic can be flipped so we could find either houses or apartments with fewer than five occupants:

=OR(AND(type_of_dwelling="House",number_of_occupants<5),AND
(type_of_dwelling="Apartment",number_of_occupants<5))

Because this is our first substantial use of "nesting"—a formula within a formula—it is important to look closely at the use of parentheses. The overall formula is an OR statement, which begins and ends with a parenthesis. Within that statement are two AND statements, which also begin and end with parentheses, with the result that the formula ends with two parentheses, one for the second AND statement and the other for the overall OR statement. A handy rule of thumb is that the number of left parentheses should equal the number of right parentheses, and your spreadsheet will give you an error message if this is not the case, but your formula also has to "makes sense." Another interesting thing to notice here is that our PEMDAS (Parentheses, Exponents, Multiplication/Division, Addition/Subtraction) order of operations is not very helpful because we have parentheses within parentheses, but logically the inner sets, the two AND statements, are evaluated before the outer OR statement.

EXERCISE

Open the list of orders again:

http://bit.ly/2PjgSDe

In column G construct a formula that will return TRUE for all books published by Routledge in London before 2010. Alter it to include also books published by Routledge in New York.

Another point to note with Boolean AND and OR formulas is that they are combinations of logical formulas, so everything within them must be capable of returning TRUE or FALSE answers. If you try to mix or match other sorts of statements, you won't get an error message, but you will get a TRUE result that doesn't actually mean anything. For example:

$$=AND(5*3,4*6)$$

returns TRUE.

Because 5×3 and 4×6 are simple multiplications, they are not in themselves either true or false. This is another case where an error message would be useful!

The third major Boolean function is the NOT statement. If we wanted to include North Dulminster within the OR statement above, we could do this:

$$=OR(location="West Dulminster",location="East Dulminster",location="North Dulminster", location="Central Dulminster"))$$

However, you might have noticed that by this stage we have included every part of Dulminster except for South Dulminster, so a more elegant way of entering our formula would be

$$=NOT(location="South Dulminster")$$

The original formula would now read

$$=AND(type\_of\_dwelling="House",NOT(location="South Dulminster"),number\_of\_occupants>3)$$

As we have seen, there are logical operators for *greater than* (>) and *less than* (<), but there isn't one for *between*, as in the case of "between four and eight occupants." However, we can rephrase this to read "more than four and fewer than nine occupants," and the *and* in this phrase should give us the clue as to how we can express the idea of *between:*

=AND(number_of_occupants>3,number_of_occupants<9)

This can then be incorporated into a previous formula so that there are now two conditions relating to the number of occupants:

=AND(type_of_dwelling="House",NOT(location="South Dulminster"), number_of_occupants>3, number_of_occupants<9)

As *all* of the conditions have to be satisfied, a TRUE result will be produced only if there are more than three and fewer than nine occupants.

There is a final Boolean function which you are unlikely to use, but which I'm including for the sake of comprehensiveness. It's the XOR known as the Exclusive OR, and it means that you will have either one of two options but not both. It's not easy to think of examples for this, but let's say you have a branch library that will be open every Thursday and every last-day-of-the-month except when the last day of the month falls on a Thursday, in which case the formula to show when it should be open would be

=XOR(day="Thursday", last-day-of-the-month="yes")

Either of these conditions will trigger a TRUE result, but if they are both true it will be FALSE!

EXERCISE

Continuing with the order list we previously downloaded, enter the following formula into cell G2 and copy it down the column:

=AND(place="London",price>50)

This will return TRUE only for books published in London and costing more than $50. Filter column F to TRUE to verify that this is the case, but don't forget to turn the filter off before the next operation!

Now copy the formula into cell H2 and alter it so that it will return TRUE for books published in either London or Boston and costing between $50 and $80. Again copy it down the column and check it by using the filter.

Now copy that formula into I2 and reverse the logic so that it returns FALSE when it previously returned TRUE.

What Use is Logic?

We've spent quite some time looking at the various logic functions of spreadsheets—equivalence, greater than, less than, and Boolean logic (AND and OR). Each of these is a binary choice that produces one of two answers, TRUE or FALSE. In practical terms this might not appear tremendously significant or useful—after all, how often do we simply need to determine whether something is true or not? However, as we will see in coming chapters, this logic underlies many of the more powerful functions of spreadsheets. Within a spreadsheet of patron names, which included their home libraries, if we wanted to count the number of them who resided in East Dulminster, then we would use the COUNTIF function that incorporates equivalence logic:

=COUNTIF(location,"East Dulminster")

You will notice that this formula does not use the equals sign, but instead signifies the range (i.e., *location*) and the condition that has to be satisfied, and separates the two by a comma. To add a second condition, the number of items they borrowed last year, the COUNTIFS function uses AND logic:

=COUNTIFS(location,"East Dulminster",items_borrowed_last_year,">5")

Don't worry if this isn't absolutely clear yet as these functions will be more fully explained later on, but note that the second formula is the equivalent of counting the number of instances where the following formula is TRUE:

=AND(location="East Dulminster",items_borrowed_last_year>5)

Of course, it can be objected that reality does not consist of a set of binary true or false conditions. If I ask the question "is it raining?" the answer could be "yes" or "no," but it could equally well be "no, but it's about to" or "only just and nothing to worry about", or it could be "it's absolutely bucketing down!" Each one of these answers provides important information that could affect whether I go out for a walk that is not captured by the simple "yes" or "no" answer. The real problem here is that my question is based on too simple a model of reality, and I needed to ask about the prospects for rain in ten minutes time and to create a broader set of categories—no rain, insignificant rain, light rain, heavy rain, and so on. Then if there is no rain or insignificant rain I can go for my walk, if there is light rain I will take a coat, and if there is heavy rain I will stay at home and work on a spreadsheet! The takeaway here is that the categories we use in a spreadsheet must be as nuanced as we can practically make them in order to approximate to reality and produce useful recommendations for action.

CHAPTER FIVE

Working With Words

Just as we can use spreadsheet functions to carry out repeated calculations with numbers, we can use them to manipulate words as well. But although you might think that a *WORD* is a *Word* is a *word*, our language conventions contain a number of different formats that may or may not be appropriate in different circumstances. Book titles, for example, tend to show each significant word with an initial capital letter—*Studies in Pacific History: Economics, Politics, and Migration*—while library cataloguing or referencing protocols will often express this as a sentence—*Studies in Pacific history: Economics, politics, and migration*. We can look at these examples and easily enough turn them into a set of rules. In the first instance every word apart from "in" and "and" begins with a capital letter, while in the second the first word begins with a capital and the first word after the colon begins with a capital, but other words begin with a lowercase letter unless they are the name of a person or a place.

Changing Cases

Many word processing packages like Microsoft Word or Google Docs have formatting options to change selected text to Title Case or UPPERCASE (or vice versa), so it's not surprising that spreadsheets are able to do the same thing through the use of formulas. Let's say we have downloaded some book titles from an Integrated Library System into column A, which we will call *original_titles*. Coming from a library system they are in sentence case, meaning that only the first word and the names are capitalized. The formula to change them to uppercase is

=UPPER(original_title)

Our title now looks like this:

STUDIES IN PACIFIC HISTORY: ECONOMICS, POLITICS,
AND MIGRATION

The formula to change them to title case is not TITLE but PROPER:

=PROPER(original_title)

However, this doesn't produce a perfect result:

Studies In Pacific History: Economics, Politics, And Migration

I don't know about you, but I would have preferred *in* and *and* NOT to be capitalized.

Partly to avoid these sorts of problems, some library vendors prefer to capitalize book titles when providing data in spreadsheet format. It is possible to convert this into title case using the PROPER function, but unlike our word processors, spreadsheets do not have the function to convert text to sentence case. The nearest you get to it is through the LOWER function:

=LOWER(original_title)

but that produces rather a weird-looking result:

studies in pacific history: economics, politics, and migration

We will look at ways of fixing this later on.

There is another useful character string function that is designed to fix the problem of invisible spacing, known as "whitespaces." These can occur between words or at the end of a character string where they can be impossible to see. In the following example, cell C2 contains this formula:

=name1=name2

and produces this result:

Name 1	Name 2	Identical
East Dulminster	East Dulminster	TRUE

However, if I sneak in an extra space at the end of one of the names, the result changes even though I can't see the difference:

Name 1	Name 2	Identical
East Dulminster	East Dulminster	FALSE

Obviously, I don't want to have to go through each cell looking for whitespaces at the end, so I use the TRIM function to ask the formula to ignore them:

$$=TRIM(name1)=TRIM(name2)$$

No matter how many spaces I insert between the two words, this formula will return the TRUE result unless you change one of the meaningful characters. A more permanent solution is to use TRIM to remove all the whitespaces from a range of data, and we will look at how to do this at the end of this chapter. Unfortunately, there is no spreadsheet function to remove punctuation from a character string so that a book with a colon between the title and the subtitle will not be identical to the same one with a dash in the same place. We will look at solutions to this problem later as well.

Words Within Words: Find and Search

It can often be useful to find out if a particular word or phrase occurs within a longer character string. If we have a range named *locations* that includes not only North, South, East and West Dulminster, but many other place names as well such as North and South Funbury, not to mention Greater and Lesser Tedium, then we could add a column to show which cells in the range include the word "Dulminster." To do this we can use the FIND function, which takes the following form:

$$=FIND("Dulminster",location)$$

What this gives us is a number indicating the position within the larger string where the string we are searching for begins. If the location is East or West Dulminster, the answer is 6, but if it is North Dulminster, the answer is 7. Because the result of this formula has to be a number, it will give the error message *#VALUE!* if the word *Dulminster* is not present in the string:

7

#VALUE!

8

Error

In FIND evaluation, cannot find 'Dulminster' within 'North Funbury'.

This is wonderfully cryptic, but what it's telling us is that the formula expected a number and didn't get one.

If we placed our formula in a new range called *is_Dulminster,* it would return numbers for those rows where the word occurred, and error messages for the others, and we could use this to filter or sort the spreadsheet to eliminate the rows that contained *#VALUE!* This wouldn't be very elegant or meaningful, however, if the main purpose of the *is_Dulminster* range is to identify rows in which that word occurs in the specified location, so we can use another function which indicates whether or not the output of a formula is a number. It is helpfully called ISNUMBER, and now our formula looks like this:

=ISNUMBER(FIND("Dulminster",location))

ISNUMBER is an *information function,* and like a logical function it returns an answer of either TRUE or FALSE for the formula above:

Location	Is Dulminster?
East Dulminster	TRUE
West Funbury	FALSE
East Dulminster	TRUE
North Dulminster	TRUE
North Funbury	FALSE
Lesser Tedium	FALSE

By answering the question "does a FIND search for the word *Dulminster* return a number?" the formula also answers the question "does the word occur in the character string represented by the Name *location?*"

The FIND function is case sensitive. We have already seen that the logical equivalence operator ignores case so that

="elephant"="ELEPHANT"

will return the answer TRUE. However, the following will be FALSE:

=ISNUMBER(FIND("elephant","The Elephant's Birthday"))

To instruct the spreadsheet to ignore case, instead use the SEARCH function. The following will be TRUE:

=ISNUMBER(SEARCH("elephant","The Elephant's Birthday"))

In fact, given the widely varying use of cases within bibliographic data, it is probably prudent to use SEARCH unless there is a good reason to use FIND.

EXERCISE

Continuing with the list of orders, use the ISNUMBER(FIND technique to identify the titles with publishers that are university presses—in other words those publishers with "University Press" in their name. Copy the formula down the column, and use filtering to check that you got it right.

http://bit.ly/2PjgSDe

Cell Lengths

Sometimes we might want to know how many characters there are in a cell. The LEN function is used for this and it takes the form

$$=LEN(A2)$$

We will shortly see some very interesting uses of this function, but here is a simple enough example. We have imported some bibliographic data that includes both books and journals, and there is a column headed *IS* that contains both ISBNs and ISSNs. We will name this range *standard_number* and use the fact that an ISSN takes the form 0002-6980 and should always have nine characters, while an ISBN will have either 10 or 13 characters. The formula

$$=LEN(standard\_number)$$

will give us the length of the number, while the following will tell us whether or not it is an ISSN:

$$=LEN(standard\_number)=9$$

If the string is nine characters long, the answer will be TRUE; otherwise it will be FALSE.

This is a good time to remind ourselves that when a cell contains the *output* of a formula, any operation carried out on it relates to that output and not to the formula that created it. Here is a simple illustration of what that means; cell A2 contains the character string *Truth is stranger than fiction, but it is because fiction is obliged to stick to possibilities; truth isn't,* while cell B2 contains three characters only:

$$=A2$$

However, the formulas *=LEN(A2)* and *=LEN(B2)* both return the same result (*107*, if you're interested!).

LEFT, RIGHT, and MID

Chopping up character strings is a surprisingly useful pastime, and there are three tools that allow you to do this. The first is the LEFT function that returns the first (or leftmost) *x* characters in the string or cell. Let's say the book title *The Elephant's Birthday* is in cell A2; if we enter the following formula, we will get the word *The*:

$$=LEFT(A2,3)$$

The format is

$$=LEFT(character\text{-}string,\ number\text{-}of\text{-}characters)$$

As it happens in this case, and probably in most cases, the character string is a cell address.

The RIGHT function works in the same way, counting off *x* characters to the right of the string. So as there are eight characters in the word *Birthday*, I can use this formula to output that word:

$$=RIGHT(A2,8)$$

To extract the word *Elephant's,* we use the MID function, which specifies the position of the first character of the substring and the number of characters. As our substring starts at the fifth character and is 10 characters in length, we use the following formula:

$$=MID(A2,5,10)$$

returning the word *Elephant's.*

Slicing and Dicing with FIND, LEFT, RIGHT, and LEN

Once we have mastered these tools, we can begin to do some clever things with items of text data, such as book titles. Let's say the full title of our book is in fact *The Elephant's Birthday: Studies in Animal Awareness of Age,* so that it consists of a title and a subtitle. It's actually in a spreadsheet with numerous other titles, many of which follow the same format, and we want to create a formula that will split off the title from the subtitle to correspond to the MARC fields 245a and 245b. The titles are in column A, which is named *full_title,* and we can use the position of the colon within the string to split the title into its two components.

The first task then is to locate the position of the colon, and we can do this using the FIND function. This is how we begin constructing the formula in column B:

=FIND(":", full_title)

This returns the number 24, which can then be used along with the LEFT function to extract the text preceding the colon:

=LEFT(full_title, FIND(":", full_title))

You can see what has happened here—we have used the FIND subformula *FIND(":", full_title)* as input to the LEFT function, as if it were the number 24. It returns the following result:

The Elephant's Birthday:

As we are splitting the title into two parts, we don't really need the colon, so we can eliminate it by subtracting 1 from the result of the FIND operation. Our formula now reads

=LEFT(full_title, FIND(":", full_title) -1)

and returns the following result that will equate to the 245a field:

The Elephant's Birthday

If we had not been using Named ranges and the title had been in cell A2, the formula would read like this:

=LEFT(A2,FIND(":",A2)-1)

The formula in column C will extract the subtitle, and to do this we will use the RIGHT function, which uses the number of letters between the colon and the end of the string. Fortunately, we have two pieces of data that will allow us to determine this—the position of the colon and the length of the full title. Working in column C, we can begin the formula like this:

$$=LEN(full\_title)$$

The length of the full title is 59, and we can now subtract the position of the colon—$FIND(":", full\_title)$—to calculate the length of the portion to the right of the colon:

$$=LEN(full\_title)-FIND(":", full\_title)$$

The answer to this sum is 35, but as there is a blank space between the colon and the beginning of the subtitle, this needs to be removed by subtracting 1, which makes the formula

$$=LEN(full\_title)-FIND(":", full\_title)-1$$

which returns the number 34, which will now be the input to the RIGHT formula:

$$=RIGHT(full\_title, LEN(full\_title)-FIND(":", full\_title)-1)$$

which accurately returns the subtitle, *Studies in Animal Awareness of Age.*

If we had not been using Named ranges and the title had been in cell A2, the formula would read like this:

$$=RIGHT(A2,LEN(A2)-FIND(":",A2)-1)$$

EXERCISE

Open the worksheet for this exercise:

http://bit.ly/2HGriZb

Column A is the range *full_title,* and it contains a number of titles containing colons between the first and second parts of the title.
In cell B2 type the following formula to find the position of the colon:

$$=FIND(":", full\_title)$$

The answer is *17*, and in cell C2 use this fact to extract the first part of the title using the LEFT function:

=LEFT(full_title, 17)

Now cell C2 will contain the first part of the title including the colon, so remove the colon by altering the formula to

=LEFT(full_title, 16)

However, if you copy this formula down cells C3 to C10, you'll get some pretty wacky results as the colon occurs at different points in each title. So go back and replace the number 16 with the subformula that identified it, *FIND(":",full_title)-1*, changing the formula in C2 to read

=LEFT(full_title, FIND(":", full_title)-1)

This will give you the first part of the title. Copy it down the rows.

In cell D2 use the following formula to calculate the number of characters to the right of the colon:

=LEN(full_title)-FIND(":", full_title)

The answer is *30*. Now in cell E2 combine this with the RIGHT function to extract the subtitle:

=RIGHT(full_title, LEN(full_title)-FIND(":", full_title)-1)

Copy it down the other rows.

You can now delete columns B and D so that the first part of the title is now in column B and second part in column C. Name these ranges *title* and *subtitle*.

The only difficulty with these formulas is that they won't work if there is not a colon in the full title; as we have already seen that if FIND or SEARCH are looking for a specific character (in this case a colon) that is not present, they will return the error message *#VALUE*. We will look at how to deal with this in Chapter 6.

Using UPPER and LOWER, LEFT and MID

The full title of our book is

The Elephant's Birthday: Studies in Animal Awareness of Age

which is in title case with all "significant" words capitalized, but many bibliographic styles would want it to look like this with capitals only at the beginning of the title and the subtitle:

The elephant's birthday: Studies in animal awareness of age

As already noted, spreadsheet software is able to convert character strings to lowercase (LOWER—no capitals at all), title case (PROPER—every word capitalized), and uppercase (UPPER—every letter capitalized), but there is no function for sentence case. Fortunately, we have already split the first and second parts of the title between two different columns (Named ranges *title* and *subtitle*), so we are able to use the UPPER and LOWER functions to convert them to sentence case, and then we can join them together again and reinsert the colon. To do this we will use column D. The first step is to capitalize the first letter of the *title* string (i.e., *The Elephant's Birthday*), so in the case of the formula converting the title (i.e., the bit before the colon), it goes like this:

=UPPER(LEFT(title,1))

To this we add the rest of the title, beginning at the second character, in lowercase, and we can use the MID function to do this. This function requires two pieces of information, the starting point and the number of characters; we know that the starting point will be 2, and the number of characters will be the length of the cell minus one, so using the LEN function the formula for that will be

=MID(title,2,LEN(title)-1)

We now convert this to lowercase

=LOWER(MID(title,2,LEN(title)-1))

which gives us

he elephant's birthday

Now we can put the initial letter at the start of the formula (using the &) to give us the title in sentence case:

=UPPER(LEFT(title,1))&LOWER(MID(title,2,LEN(title)-1))

The elephant's birthday

Then we repeat the process with the subtitle and join both formulas together, inserting a colon and a space between them using ampersands:

=UPPER(LEFT(title,1))&LOWER(MID(title,2,LEN(title)-1))&":
"&UPPER(LEFT(subtitle,1))&LOWER(MID(subtitle,2,LEN(subtitle)-1))

The output now reads

The elephant's birthday: Studies in animal awareness of age

This might seem to be a long and complicated formula, but it has been simplified by the fact that we used columns B and C to split out the title and subtitle from the full title appearing in column A. If we had done all the work in column B, we would have had to use the subformula

LEFT(A2,FIND(":",A2)-1)

every time we referred to the *title* and the subformula

RIGHT(A2,LEN(A2)-FIND(":",A2)-1)

every time we referred to the *subtitle*. The resulting formula would have been twice as long and almost impossible to understand!

This approach won't be perfect as, when we convert the title to lowercase, this is applied to the names of places, people, and organizations as well as to "ordinary" words. For example, the title

Studies in Pacific History: Economics, Politics, and Migration

will be converted to

Studies in pacific history: Economics, politics, and migration

I would very much prefer the word *Pacific* to be capitalized, so there will be some further editing to do. Because you can't alter anything that is output by a formula (other than by altering the formula), it will be necessary to convert all the output from the range containing the final version to plain text, which we will look at shortly.

EXERCISE

Go back to the Title and Subtitle spreadsheet from the previous exercise, and enter the following formula into cell D2:

=UPPER(LEFT(title,1))&LOWER(MID(title,2,LEN(title)))&": "&UPPER(LEFT (subtitle,1))&LOWER(MID(subtitle,2,LEN(subtitle)))

Copy it down the other rows, and note the problem with the name of a country. Remember that you will need to have Named the ranges *title* and *subtitle* as in the earlier exercise.

What's in a Name?

Matters get even trickier with names of people, which can take a bewildering variety of forms. The name *Tracy Jane Simmons* can also be

> *Simmons, Tracy Jane*
> *Tracy J. Simmons*
> *Tracy J Simmons*
> *TJ Simmons*
> *T J Simmons*
> *T. J. Simmons*
> *Simmons, T. J.*
> *Simmons, Tracy Jane, 1982–*

and so on. Librarians will be familiar with all these permutations and more, and it is a favorite pastime of journal editors to think up new variations, but fortunately there is a suite of spreadsheeting functions and tools that allow us to convert one of these forms to another. Let's look at how we could convert

> *Simmons, Tracy Jane, 1982–*

to

> *TJ Simmons*

For the sake of simplicity we'll assume that the name is in cell A2 in a range named *fullname*. Our first task will be to extract the last name into column B, which we will name *lastname*. Extracting the last name should be pretty straightforward by now as we have the comma with which to split the full string. The fact that there are two commas in the string shouldn't worry us as both FIND and SEARCH will always find the first instance of the string they are searching for. So, our first formula typed into cell B2 will be

=LEFT(fullname, FIND(",", fullname)-1)

Simmons

We can now use this first comma in *fullname* to split off the right-hand part of the name into column C by entering

=RIGHT(fullname, LEN(fullname)-FIND(",", fullname)-1)

This still leaves the date of birth hanging at the end of the string, but as already noted this is of no significance:

Tracy Jane, 1982–

We now name range C *firstnames* and use a combination of LEFT, MID, and FIND to extract the initials into column D:

=LEFT(firstnames,1)&MID(firstnames,FIND(" ",firstnames)+1,1)

Note that we have found the second initial by locating the position of the space and adding 1 to it. What the formula says is "the leftmost character and the next character along from the space." The *+1,1* relates to the MID subformula and means "move along one character and then select one character." The output from this formula is *TJ* with no intervening space.

We are aiming for *TJ Simmons* as output, and you will remember that we left the last name (*Simmons*) parked in the *lastname* range in column B, so it's a simple job to add this to our formula for the initials with a space between the two elements. There is no need to move into another column at this point, so the full and final formula in column D reads

=LEFT(firstnames,1)&MID(firstnames, FIND(" ", firstnames)+1,1)& " "&lastname

Once again, with some spreadsheeting heroics, we could have squeezed all of this into one formula in cell B2 and saved the use of two extra columns, but it lacks transparency and is not easy to copy and paste:

=LEFT(RIGHT(A2,LEN(A2)-FIND(",",A2)-1),1)&MID(RIGHT(A2,LEN(A2)-FIND(",",A2)-1),FIND(" ",RIGHT(A2,LEN(A2)-FIND(",",A2)-1),1)+1,1)&" "&LEFT(A2,FIND(",",A2)-1)

Exercise

Download the spreadsheet:

http://bit.ly/2VWsWKr

It contains a list of names in the format of two first names followed by a last name, and the aim is to reformat it to the last name followed by a comma and then the two first names. Column A has the Name *name*.
In column B, split off the first name by using the formula

=LEFT(name,FIND(" ",name)-1)

Note that the space is the divide indicator throughout this exercise. Now in column C extract the last two names:

=RIGHT(name,LEN(name)-FIND(" ",name))

In column D split off the first of these:

=LEFT(C2,FIND(" ",C2)-1)

And in column E the second, which is the last name:

=RIGHT(C2,LEN(C2)-FIND(" ",C2))

Then in column E put it all together, including the comma:

=E2&", "&B2&" "&D2

Using Substitute to Clean Text

It can be very useful to compare two character strings with one another to see if they are identical. This process underlies the various lookup functions that we will come to in later chapters, to see, for example, if any of the items in our vendor's latest spreadsheet are already in our collection by matching between different ranges within our spreadsheet. However, there is a problem here in that identical really does mean *identical*, exactly the same. Well, that's not exactly true because we have seen that there is some latitude for case so that the formula

*="Studies in Pacific History: Economics, Politics, and Migration"="STUDIES IN
PACIFIC HISTORY: ECONOMICS, POLITICS, AND MIGRATION"*

will return the answer TRUE.
However, if we so much as remove a single comma from either side of this formula, the answer becomes FALSE! Now, although there are quite strict

rules governing punctuation, unfortunately there is more than one set of them, and in any case lots of people don't follow rules very consistently. I know that I much prefer *Economics, Politics and Migration* (without the second comma) to *Economics, Politics, and Migration,* but I couldn't really tell you why, and in any case I don't want to go through two ranges of titles fixing the punctuation just so that I can compare them with one another.

If *Studies in Pacific History: Economics, Politics, and Migration* is in cell A2 and *Studies in Pacific History: Economics, Politics and Migration* is in cell B2, is there a way we can make the formula

$$=A2=B2$$

return the answer TRUE? Without changing whatever is in the cells, which would be cheating. As it happens there is a function, SUBSTITUTE, which will allow us to solve the problem with commas. It takes the following format:

=SUBSTITUTE (string, existing_substring, substitute_substring)

This will take any character string—look for the specified existing substring and replace it with a substitute substring. In our case the specified substring will be a comma, and it will be substituted with nothing, in other words removed entirely. The "nothing" is indicated by two double quote marks with no space between them. So here is the formula in cell C2 to remove the commas in cell A2:

=SUBSTITUTE(A2,",", "")

And the result is that C2 now outputs

Studies in Pacific History: Economics Politics and Migration

We haven't actually changed anything in A2; nor do we want to. The aim of the exercise is not to eliminate commas and other punctuation from book titles, but simply to see if the book in A2 is the same as the one in B2.

Now we could use cell D2 to repeat the same process on B2 using the same formula

=SUBSTITUTE(B2,",", "")

and then use E2 to check whether these two cells were the same, but as all we're really looking for is a TRUE or FALSE, we can do all the work in C2 with the following formula:

= SUBSTITUTE(A2,",", "")=SUBSTITUTE(B2,",", "")

Again, without doing anything to the cells we are comparing, we have created two comma-free versions of them in the computer's memory and compared them with one another instead.

Of course, commas are only one form of punctuation, and there could be other differences between two character strings describing the same title. The use of a colon to separate title and subtitle is only a convention and the book

Studies in Pacific History: Economics, Politics, and Migration

could equally well be described as

Studies in Pacific History - Economics, Politics, and Migration

using a dash (-) to separate the two elements. We can now use SUBSTITUTE to alter our comma-free string to also become dash-free, and this is done by adding an outer shell to the previous formula so that it now reads

=SUBSTITUTE(SUBSTITUTE(A2,",", ""),"-", "")=SUBSTITUTE (SUBSTITUTE(B2,",", ""),"-", "")

This will still return FALSE, however, because there is still a colon in B2, so we need to remove that as well. Then because there are spaces on either side of the dash, we need to TRIM both sides of the equation to remove the additional whitespace:

=TRIM(SUBSTITUTE(SUBSTITUTE(SUBSTITUTE(A2,",", ""),"-", ""),":",""))

=TRIM(SUBSTITUTE(SUBSTITUTE(SUBSTITUTE(B2,",", ""),"-", ""),":",""))

This returns the result TRUE.

If you want to instruct your spreadsheet to ignore most types of punctuation (including parentheses), these formulas can get pretty long and complicated:

=TRIM(SUBSTITUTE(SUBSTITUTE(SUBSTITUTE(SUBSTITUTE (SUBSTITUTE(SUBSTITUTE(SUBSTITUTE(SUBSTITUTE(A2,
"(",""),
")",""),
"-","")
".",""),
",",""),
"!",""),
" ",""),
":",""))

Here the *Alt+Enter* key has been used in the formula bar to place each substitution on a separate line—this is a useful trick that lasts only as long as the next time you save the spreadsheet. Notice that each element (representing a separate character) ends with parenthesis-comma and that there are as many SUBSTITUTEs as there are elements. If you like to imagine things visually, think of cell A2 as the center of a Russian doll, with each additional shell working on the contents of those inside it to remove one piece of punctuation—by the time we get to the outer shell, any punctuation that existed in cell A2 has been stripped out.

EXERCISE

Open a new copy of the spreadsheet of titles with colons:

http://bit.ly/2HGriZb

In column B write a formula to replace the colons with dashes. Don't forget to leave a space before the dash.

Other Uses of Substitute: Dealing with Spelling Variations and Diacritics

One of the many delights of English is the variation in spelling between the American and British varieties of the language. (I am struggling with it through the writing of this book!) Probably the most common ones are favour/favor, colour/color, honour/honor, and favourite/favorite. Let's say we are wanting to compare two book titles in cells A2 and B2:

Your four favourite flavours

Your four favorite flavors

In cell C2 the simple formula A2=B2 will return FALSE because they are not the same, so we could try

=B2=SUBSTITUTE(A2, "our", "or")

Unfortunately, this will return the value FALSE because we have in fact altered the string in cell A2 to read

Yor for favorite flavors

This must seem a bit odd, but we must remember that we are not actually changing anything in cell B2; we are simply coming up with a notional version of it with all the *our* substrings changed to *or*. What we need to do then is to apply the substitution to both sides of the equation:

=SUBSTITUTE(A2, "our","or")=SUBSTITUTE(B2, "our","or")

What this is saying is

Yor for favorite flavors = Yor for favorite flavors

TRUE! They may both be nonsense, but at least they are the same nonsense.

EXERCISE

Open a copy of the spreadsheet:

http://bit.ly/2KbhfwX

Column A contains titles that use one spelling system for words like *organization;* column B contains the same titles using the alternative system. If you enter formula

=A2=B2

into cell C2, it returns FALSE. Change the formula so that it returns TRUE, and copy it down the rows below.

The SUBSTITUTE function is also very useful in dealing with *diacritics,* such as the e-acute in the word *café,* which a spreadsheet will read as a different word from *cafe;* this is sometimes known as an *accent* or an accented character. I have a personal close-to-home example in the spelling of vowels in the Māori language. The line above the letter *a* in the word *Māori* and in other words like *whānau, kō,* and *āta* is known as a macron, and it signifies that the vowel sound is to be lengthened. It really signifies a completely different letter from the short *a,* and its absence or presence can completely alter the meaning of the word. However, the macron has only been used for the last 25 years or so, and its use is by no means consistent—computer keyboard software needs to be installed for one thing, and it is a convention that is not much used outside of New Zealand, although references to Māori words are common in the international literature. We cannot go through our spreadsheet adding macrons to words that don't have them, but we wish to be able to treat words with and without the macron as if they were the same thing. Here is the formula for cell A2 to create a macron-free version of a string in cell B2:

=SUBSTITUTE(SUBSTITUTE(SUBSTITUTE(SUBSTITUTE(SUBSTITUTE
(SUBSTITUTE(SUBSTITUTE(SUBSTITUTE(SUBSTITUTE(SUBSTITUTE
(A2,"ā","a"),"ē","e"),"ī","i"),"ō","o"),"ū","u"),"Ā","A"),"Ē","E"),"Ī","I"),"Ō","O"),"Ū","U")

The SUBSTITUTE function is case sensitive, so it has been necessary to add pairs of capital letters in addition to lowercase letters.

Inconsistencies with diacritics can create real problems when trying to compare character strings or search for substrings within strings. For example, there is a type of postgraduate educational and research institute in France known as an *École Normale Supérieure*. In the affiliation data of one database that I checked, it appeared as *École Normale Supérieure, Ecole Normale Supérieure,* and *Ecole Normale Superieure*, none of which would give a match with any one of the others in a spreadsheet. The following formula will replace most diacritics with equivalent unaccented characters:

=SUBSTITUTE(SUBSTITUTE(SUBSTITUTE(SUBSTITUTE(SUBSTITUTE
(SUBSTITUTE(SUBSTITUTE(SUBSTITUTE(SUBSTITUTE(SUBSTITUTE
(SUBSTITUTE(SUBSTITUTE(SUBSTITUTE(SUBSTITUTE(SUBSTITUTE
(SUBSTITUTE(SUBSTITUTE(SUBSTITUTE(SUBSTITUTE(SUBSTITUTE
(SUBSTITUTE(SUBSTITUTE(SUBSTITUTE(SUBSTITUTE(SUBSTITUTE
(SUBSTITUTE(SUBSTITUTE(SUBSTITUTE(SUBSTITUTE(SUBSTITUTE
(SUBSTITUTE(SUBSTITUTE(SUBSTITUTE(SUBSTITUTE(SUBSTITUTE
(SUBSTITUTE(SUBSTITUTE(SUBSTITUTE(SUBSTITUTE(SUBSTITUTE
(SUBSTITUTE(SUBSTITUTE(SUBSTITUTE(SUBSTITUTE(SUBSTITUTE
(SUBSTITUTE(SUBSTITUTE(SUBSTITUTE(SUBSTITUTE(SUBSTITUTE
(SUBSTITUTE(SUBSTITUTE(SUBSTITUTE(SUBSTITUTE(SUBSTITUTE
(SUBSTITUTE(SUBSTITUTE(SUBSTITUTE(SUBSTITUTE(A2,"(","")),")"),""),"á",
"a"),"é","e"),"í","i"),"ó","o"),"ú","u"),"ã","a"),"ê","e"),"â","a"),"é","e"),"è","e"),"ī","i"),"ï","i"),
"ç","c"),"ä","a"),"ö","o"),"ü","u"),"ß","ss"),"ş","s"),"ı","i"),"ğ","g"),"ę","e"),"ń","n"),"ś","s"),
"ź","z"),"ā","a"),"â","a"),"à","a"),"ą","a"),"đ","d"),"ě","e"),"ı̄","i"),"í","i"),"ô̝","o"),"ô","o"),
"ư","u"),"ả","a"),"ế","e"),"ī","i"),"ơ","o"),"ŏ","o"),"ạ","a"),"ú","u"),"ý","y"),"ạ","a"),"é","e"),
"ỳ","y"),"ệ","e"),"ề","e"),"ệ","e"),"ủ","u"),"ë","e"),".",""),"Ġ","g"),"ø","o"),"ñ","n"),"‹","),
"ĥ","h"),"ķ","k"),"ļ","l"),"ł","l"),"ŗ","r"),"ů","u")

This formula contains 64 nested layers, which is the limit of what a spreadsheet can handle, and it covers lowercase letters only! Fortunately, we can make use of the fact that the output of one cell can be the input of another, so if this formula appears in cell B2, there can be an identical one in cell C2 to deal with capitals. Between them the two will transform *École Normale Supérieure* into *Ecole Normale Superieure*.

Actually, there is an easier way to do this that allows unlimited substitutions. Take a look at this portion of a larger worksheet:

	A	B	C	D
1		á	à	â
2		a	a	a
3	Casa de Velázquez	Casa de Velazquez	Casa de Velazquez	Casa de Velazquez
4	Thomas à Becket	Thomas à Becket	Thomas a Becket	Thomas a Becket
5	Les châteaux de la Loire	Les châteaux de la Loire	Les châteaux de la Loire	Les chateaux de la Loire

In cell A3 is the name of a French educational institution—*Casa de Velázquez*, which contains the lowercase letter *a* with an *acute* accent—*á*. The same letter occurs in cell B1, and below it in cell B2 is the letter *without* the accent. This pattern is followed along rows 1 and 2, with the accented letter in row 1 and its unaccented counterpart in row 2. The following formula is placed in cell B3:

=SUBSTITUTE(A3,B$1,B$2)

Look carefully at what the formula does. For the content in cell A3, the title with all of its diacritics in place, it replaces the cell B1 value (*á*) with the cell B2 value (*a*). As a result *Casa de Velázquez* is transformed into *Casa de Velazquez*. You will notice that in the formula the $ symbols occur before the *row* numbers but not before the *column*, so if we copy it into cell C3 it now reads

=SUBSTITUTE(B3,C$1,C$2)

There are two things to notice here. First, because of relative referencing the cell in C3 is now working on the content of B3 so that if there is a *grave* à (the letter in C1) in the phrase (as it happens there isn't), this would also be replaced by its unaccented equivalent in C2. The second thing is that the $ symbols mean that whichever cell it occurs in the formula will always be referencing the top two rows of the column. If it is copied to cell G10, it will read

=SUBSTITUTE(F10,C$1,C$2)

How the system works then is that the top two rows of the worksheet make up a table of accented and unaccented characters, and as the formula is copied along the row it works on the original content of column A, changing it one letter at a time until the final column on the right shows the finished product. In this example diacritics have been used, but a similar system could be used to remove punctuation, or punctuation symbols could be included in row 1 and the cells in row 2 left empty so that they are replaced with nothing.

EXERCISE

Open a copy of the spreadsheet:

http://bit.ly/2W9MWhz

Examine the range Names to understand the relationship between the two worksheets and why column B of *Inputs & outputs* is able to deliver a version of the content of column with the diacritics removed.

Change the contents of row 1 of *Conversion* to punctuation symbols, leaving the cells below in row 2 empty, and practice removing punctuation from phrases.

The reason why the SUBSTITUTE function is so important is that it allows us to compare the contents of two cells that may have minor differences by creating idealized or "clean" versions of both cells, which can then be tested to see whether or not they are identical. Put like that, all this comparing might seem like a relatively trivial occupation, but in fact it forms the basis of much (or indeed all) information searching and analysis. When we search for a book by title in the library catalog, what we are really saying is "find me a book whose title is identical to the string that I typed into the search box." That is a fairly structured information search, but we use the same formulation when asking "what is the population of Dulminster?" This really means "find the town whose name is (identical to) Dulminster and tell me its population." By reducing the potential differences between cells and ranges by eliminating punctuation, or replacing accented letters with their plain vanilla equivalents by using SUBSTITUTE, we greatly increase the chances that our comparisons will produce true results. It could be argued that one way of doing this would simply be to eliminate punctuation and diacritics (accents) from our spreadsheets altogether, but this would often be undesirable. Punctuation plays an important role in meaning, and although diacritics are not a major feature of the English language, they are critically important in many languages, and the meanings of words can be changed if they are altered or removed. By using the SUBSTITUTE function, we are able to maintain these features while still recognizing that the *École Normale Supérieure, Ecole Normale Supérieure*, and *Ecole Normale Superieure* are all one and the same thing!

Dependencies

This is a good time to point out that in the example above the contents of B3 and C3 *depend* on cell A3 and any changes made to that cell will be reflected in the other two. We already knew this, but what we haven't considered yet is what happens if cell A3, or the range or column which it appears, is deleted. Here is an input range for the system described above and the corresponding output:

	A		B
1	**Phrase**		**Without punctuation or diacritics**
2			
3	Casa de Velázquez		Casa de Velazquez
4	Thomas á Becket		Thomas a Becket
5	Les châteaux de la Loire		Les chateaux de la Loire
6	École française de Rome		Ecole francaise de Rome
7	Institut Français d'Archéologie Orientale		Institut Francais d'Archeologie Orientale

Now, there is a small, but not entirely nonexistent, risk that I will get up too early one morning, look at my input range and think "I've removed the diacritics from this so I no longer need the input column." So I delete the entire column. Big mistake.

	A
1	**Without punctuation or diacritics**
2	
3	#REF!
4	#REF!
5	#REF!
6	#REF!
7	#REF!

The #REF! error indicates that the formula is trying to reference something that does not exist. Fortunately, in this case I was able to use the *Undo* icon to restore the missing data, but you should be aware that once you have deleted a worksheet in Excel, it is not possible to restore it. Sheets is more forgiving and will undo a worksheet deletion.

Excel, however, has a *Formula Auditing* function that is lacking from Sheets. If you are planning to delete a range or a worksheet, click on one of the cells and then on the Formula tab click on *Trace Dependents*. If the cell and the dependent cell are on the same page, an arrow will link them:

	A	B
1		á
2		a
3	Casa de Velázquez	Casa de Velazquez

In this case cell B3 is dependent on A3. If the dependent cell is on another worksheet, this will be indicated also:

	A	B	C
1	Phrase	Without punctuation or diacritics	
2			
3	Casa de Velázquez	Casa de Velazquez	
4	Thomas à Becket	Thomas à Becket	

Before you delete anything, it's a really good idea to check on its dependents, and if you are trying to understand a formula, there is also a Trace Precedents tool that will take you back to the source of the input data.

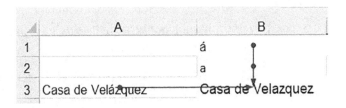

This tells us graphically something we should already have known, that cell B3 references A3, B1, and B2.

Sheets is not able to show links to different worksheets in formulas, but if you click on the formula box, it does a nice job of highlighting input cells in different colors.

Converting Formula Outputs to Plain Text

Once you have extracted a substring from a cell or range into a new cell or range, it's often a good idea to save the output in plain text format, that is, as if you have typed it into the cells. Only do this if you are sure that the data in the original cells is not going to change, or if you do not wish these changes to be reflected in the new locations. This is done by copying the range containing the formula output and then carrying out the paste-values operation that we saw in Chapter 2.

Here's a simple example of how we could use a formula to tidy up some text and then use paste-value to replace the original. Imagine that column A contains a list of names that have been manually input, some of which contain trailing whitespaces at the end. These could alter string lengths and potentially interfere with the operation of formulas, so we want to get rid of them rather than having to add a TRIM function to every formula that references this range. To do this we can insert a column to the right of column B, and in cell B1 we will enter the formula

$$=TRIM(A1)$$

and copy it down as far as we need to. We then copy column B, place the cursor in cell A1, and use the *paste-value* operation to overwrite the contents of column A. When we are sure that this has worked properly, we can delete column B. Fortunately, users of Sheets don't need to do this as on the Data tab there is a *Trim whitespace* utility that can be applied to a selected range.

Putting it all Together

Practical Example 1

Using AND, OR, ISNUMBER, and SEARCH to identify a set of books by words in title and year of publication

Follow the example by opening or downloading a copy of the spreadsheet:

http://bit.ly/2Xdn7cN

Here are three columns from the beginning of a worksheet containing data sourced from a Library Management System—titles (field 245|a), subtitles (245|b), and publication years:

	A	B	C
1	245|a	245|b	Year
2	Animals		1990
3	History of animals		1932
4	Psychic animals	an investigation of their secret powers	1987
5	A guide to the zoological literature	the animal kingdom	1994
6	CRC handbook of animal diversity		1986
7	Zoology		1991
8	Animal diversity		1981
9	Animal biology		1969
10	Man and wildlife		1975
11	Nightmares of nature		1995

Our task is to identify the books published before 1981 that mention *color* in their titles. The first thing to note is that our word has two different spellings, *color* and *colour*, and numerous different endings referencing the same idea—*colored*, *coloration*, and so on. There is another related word that we would also be interested in—*camouflage*—so at some point we are going to have to introduce the OR function, but let's just start with the simple word *color*.

We don't need to worry about "wildcards" at this point (more about these in Chapter 6), as we are simply going to use ISNUMBER and SEARCH to verify that our character string occurs within the target strings that are in the *title* range, using the following formula in column D, which will produce either TRUE or FALSE:

=ISNUMBER(SEARCH("color", title))

You will notice that I have used SEARCH rather than FIND because sometimes the word will occur at the beginning of a title with an initial capital, and sometimes it will be in another position. SEARCH is not case sensitive, whereas if I had used FIND it would not match titles beginning with *Color* or *Coloration*. Now filter column D to TRUE to see your results, but don't forget to remove the filter before you proceed.

Because I have a second word, *colour*, to look for I now use the OR function to include this word as well in the examination of the range *title*. Enter this formula into column E, and keep using new columns as you move through this worked example so you can compare results at each stage in the process:

=OR(ISNUMBER(SEARCH("color",title)),ISNUMBER
(SEARCH("colour",title)))

Filter column E to TRUE—how many extra titles have you found?

It might occur to me at this point that a simple way to avoid having to use OR would be just to trim one letter off our search word, cutting it back to *colo*. There is a problem with this though, which is that our ISNUMBER and SEARCH technique will identify any string containing that snippet, which would include words like *ecology* and *colony*. So we are stuck with having to use both word stems, and then we have to throw in the word *camouflage* as well:

=OR(ISNUMBER(SEARCH("color",title)),ISNUMBER(SEARCH("colour",title)),
ISNUMBER(SEARCH("camouflage",title)))

And then, I have to include the same for the range *subtitle*:

=OR(ISNUMBER(SEARCH("color",title)),ISNUMBER(SEARCH("colour",title)),
ISNUMBER(SEARCH("camouflage",title)),ISNUMBER(SEARCH("color",subtitle)),
ISNUMBER(SEARCH("colour",subtitle)),ISNUMBER(SEARCH
("camouflage",subtitle)))

However, this is unnecessarily cumbersome. Although there is no range combining title and subtitle, there is nothing to stop us from combining the two ranges within our formula, using an &, like this:

=OR(ISNUMBER(SEARCH("color",title&subtitle)),ISNUMBER(SEARCH ("colour",title&subtitle)),ISNUMBER(SEARCH("camouflage",title&subtitle)))

If you are sharp-eyed, you will have noticed that the subformula

title&subtitle

does not contain a space between the two elements and so creates something of a nonsense. Applied to the third row of our data, it would result in this:

Psychic animalsan investigation of their secret powers

However, there is no problem with this as we are constructing a merely notional string within which to locate the starting points of our two terms.

The next step is to add in the year restriction, so that only books published in the year 1980 or earlier return the response TRUE. This is done by using AND, which is wrapped around the existing formula, meaning that the restriction applies to everything within its outer parentheses. We use the symbol for *less than or equal to,* but we could equally well have simply specified anything less than 1981. Our full formula now reads like this:

=AND(OR(ISNUMBER(SEARCH("color",title&subtitle)),ISNUMBER(SEARCH ("colour",title&subtitle)),ISNUMBER(SEARCH("camouflage",title&subtitle))), Year<=1980)

When we filter the final column to TRUE, we find the following:

	A	B	C
1	245|a	245|b	Year
174	Chromatophores and color change	the comparative physiology of animal pigmentation	1973
256	Colour for survival		1979
486	Adaptive coloration in animals		1940
488	Animals and their colours	camouflage, warning colouration, courtship and territorial display, mimicry	1974
489	The nature of animal colours		1960
490	Life's color code		1973
491	Animal camouflage		1959

Practical Example 2

Using LEN and SUBSTITUTE to count the numbers of authors of journal articles

You can copy the spreadsheet for this example here:

http://bit.ly/2YZZa9p

Situation. The Research Support Team at Dulminster University Library has been asked to provide data on the research publications and bibliometric impact of the university's faculty. Although it is possible to use locally available data to count the number of journal articles authored by university staff, an objection has been made that a raw count of articles does not take into account the fact that research articles usually have multiple authors (up to 3,000!), only some of whom will be from Dulminster University. The team have been asked to look at a substantial sample of Dulminster-authored articles and work out

1. the total number of authors for each article, and
2. the number of those authors from Dulminster University

From those numbers it will be possible to find averages.

As being the first author of a paper carries special status, the team also wishes to identify those articles where the first author is affiliated to Dulminster University.

The first step is to find a source of journal article records that include well-structured "affiliation data"—that is, author addresses for each article. The Scopus database contains the information that the team wants in a format that lends itself to further examination by a spreadsheet. The team searches the database for Dulminster University affiliations and downloads a number of .csv files, which it combines into a spreadsheet of 6,200 lines covering journal publications over the last five years. The spreadsheet has a column headed *Affiliations*, which are then given that name as a range. Here is what a typical entry in this range looks like:

Department of Natural Resource Management, Dulminster University, Dulminster, WD, United States; Ecdysis Foundation, Estelline, SD 57234, United States; West Dakota Game and Fish Department, Dulminster, WD, United States; Department of Life Science and Environmental Biochemistry, Pusan National University, Miryang, 50463, South Korea; Department of Natural Resource Management, Dulminster University, Dulminster, WD, United States; Department of Cellular Biology & Anatomy, Louisiana State University Health Sciences Center-Shreveport, Shreveport, LA, United States

Solution. One of the team notices some patterns. There are six addresses that are separated by semicolons. Two of the addresses are identical, which means that each time an address has occurred it has been included—each author is given their own address even when more than one comes from the same institution. Therefore, counting the semicolons will give an accurate count of the total number of authors, but although there are six addresses there are only five semicolons because there is no semicolon after the last address. From this there arises the possibility of finding three separate pieces of information:

1. they can count the number of authors by counting the number of semicolons in the cell and adding one
2. they can count the number of Dulminster authors by counting the number of times the string *Dulminster University* occurs in the cell
3. they can determine whether the *first* author is from Dulminster University by determining whether that name occurs before the first semicolon

The first two tasks would be really easy if there was a spreadsheet function that counted the number of times a character or string occurred within another string. (As we have already seen, there is a COUNT function, but it does something rather different.) Fortunately, there is a method for counting string occurrences, which would work like this for semicolons:

1. find out the length of the cell
2. remove the semicolons
3. find out the length of the cell without the semicolons
4. subtract the second number from the first

Of course, we don't need to actually remove semicolons—this just happens notionally as a SUBSTITUTE within the formula:

=LEN(Affiliations)-LEN(SUBSTITUTE(Affiliations, ";",""))+1

The important thing to notice here is that there is no space between the final two double quotes—the semicolon has been replaced by *nothing*, which is a method of deleting it. Each semicolon adds 1 to the length of the string, so when they are removed in the second part of the formula the difference between the two lengths gives us the number of semicolons. And, of course, we have added 1 to the total to account for the last address, which is not followed by a semicolon.

If this seems slightly hard to understand, try the following. In cell A2 there are two authors A and B, separated by a semicolon and a space like this:

A; B

This gives A2 a total length of *four*. If we remove the semicolon, it looks like this:

A B

with a total length of *three*. Therefore, if we subtract the length of the cell *without* the semicolon from its length *with* the semicolon the answer is one. We add the extra *1* to this to give us the total number of authors, which is 2. This operation is expressed by the following formula:

=LEN(A2)-LEN(SUBSTITUTE(A2, ";",""")+1

The next step is to count the number of times the string *Dulminster University* occurs in the statement of affiliations, and the team can use the same technique to do this by using SUBSTITUTE to remove it and then using the consequent difference in cell lengths to calculate the number of instances of the phrase. If you go back and look at the full list of addresses, you will see that the phrase "Dulminster University" occurs twice; the team will know that their formula is correct if it returns the answer 2. They try this formula:

=LEN(Affiliations)-LEN(SUBSTITUTE(Affiliations,
"Dulminster University",""))

It returns the answer 42. This is a little puzzling at first, until someone points out that there are 21 letters in *Dulminster University*, so that each time that string is deleted the length of Affiliations decreases by that amount. To find out the number of authors, they need to calculate the difference between the two lengths and then divide the result by that number. This formula would work:

=(LEN(Affiliations)-LEN(SUBSTITUTE(Affiliations,
"Dulminster University","")))/21

but it's not very transparent, so instead they opt for this:

=(LEN(Affiliations)-LEN(SUBSTITUTE(Affiliations,
"Dulminster University","")))/LEN("Dulminster University")

The answer, of course, is 2.

Finally, the team need to determine whether or not the first author address contains the phrase *Dulminster University*. By now this is pretty easy. They know that the first author address ends at the location of the first semicolon, which they can calculate by using FIND or SEARCH. The answer will of course be a number. They can also use SEARCH to identify the location of the first occurrence of *Dulminster University*, another number. By subtracting this second number from the first one, they will get a result that is either positive or negative, which will indicate whether *Dulminster University* occurs to the left (positive) or the right (negative) of the semicolon. A positive result will mean that the first author is from Dulminster University. The formula reads like this:

=SEARCH(";",Affiliations)-SEARCH("Dulminster University", Affiliations)

In this example the answer is 52, so they do have a Dulminster first author. If you copy it down the rows below in the worked example, it will return a #VALUE! error for all the rows without a Dulminster author because the subformula

SEARCH("Dulminster University",Affiliations)

does not return a valid number. This looks messy but won't cause you any actual harm, and you will learn how to fix it in Chapter 6.

As a final step, rather than relying on whether the number is positive or negative, you can turn the result into TRUE or FALSE with the following:

=SEARCH(";",Affiliations)-SEARCH("Dulminster University", Affiliations)>0

EXERCISE

Make your own spreadsheet.

In cell A2 you have the title *Farmers, farms and farming life*. Write a formula in cell B2 that will find the starting location for the words *farm* or *farms*, but not for the words *farmers* or *farming*. Make sure that it would work for any title containing either of the target words.

Hint—you can use the presence of a space to indicate that a word has finished, but bear in mind that words can be followed immediately by a comma or a period. You should also consider the possibility that the target word could be the last word in the title.

Experiment with your formula over a range of titles to see that it works in all cases.

Looking Ahead

It might seem that this chapter has covered rather a miscellaneous range of topics. In Chapters 6 through 8 we will be looking at the use of spreadsheets in the organization and analysis of information, so it has been important to deal with some of the more basic functions first. We've seen spreadsheets as giant adding machines, allowing you to add up all the visitor numbers for a year and then divide them by the number of days, but they are hugely more than this. As already suggested, the ability to compare items of information to see whether they are identical or not lies at the heart of information searching and analysis. Counting the number of visitors over a year might be interesting, and might allow you to compare last year with the year before, but what would be really interesting would be to know whether there were more or fewer visitors on rainy days than on dry days, or if East Dulminster residents borrowed more books from the Central library on weekends than on weekdays. To do this we need to be able to compare multiple pieces of information at the same time.

Here are two of the most important words in our language—*is* and *if*. The first of them deals with reality, the second with possibility and conditionality. Imagine yourself as a child hearing these two sentences:

"The present on the table *is* for you."
"The present on the table is for you *if* you are good."

Clearly these do not mean the same thing because the second sentence hides within itself an alarming possibility:

"The present on the table is *not* for you." Oh dear!

Fortunately, we will not be dealing with such alarming possibilities, but rather more prosaic questions such as:

"Count the number of transactions but only if they happened at South Dulminster."
"Count the number of visitors but only if the weather was rainy."

The ability to make conditional calculations like this can make what would otherwise just be plain old number crunching into explanation and even prediction. Maybe the number of books borrowed in October was way down on the previous year because the weather was unusually dry. If rain is forecast for Thursday and schools are on holiday, we can expect the children's library to be extra busy.

One of the big breakthroughs of the social sciences was the discovery that, although as individuals we may appear to act somewhat randomly (I know I do), in the mass we behave in quite uniform and predictable ways. For example, if the price of the product goes down sales go up, unless it's a luxury item, in which case sales go up when the price increases. (Nobody said this had to make sense, just that it happened according to certain well-established patterns.) In fact, the word "predictable" tells us a lot about how we view the world, that our expectation of what will happen in the future is firmly based on our knowledge of what has happened in the past. The better and more fine-grained our understanding of past performance and behavior, the better our ability to predict the future will be. Of course, the fact that things do not always turn out as we expected is what keeps us buying newspapers and exclaiming over extraordinary events, but what makes them extraordinary and interesting is the fact that most of the time things *do* happen within our range of expectations. It is our job as librarians, and particularly as library managers, to know what is "normal and expected" and to recognize when something unusual is on the horizon. The following chapters will allow you to begin making these judgments.

Conditional Functions

In Chapter 5 we spent considerable time looking at functions that produced the binary outputs TRUE or FALSE. These functions were either logical (*equal to, greater than*) or informational (*this is a number*). You might have wondered what the purpose of all that effort was—while we could use filtering to identify which rows of our worksheet return to the answer TRUE and which returned FALSE, and we could have counted those rows, but this seems like a clumsy way of extracting information from our worksheet. Added to this is the fact that we could extract only one piece of information at a time—for example, we could find out if a number was less than 50 or greater than or equal to 50, but we couldn't look at a range of numbers and show which were less than 50, which were between 50 and 100 ,which were between 100 and 200, and so on. We couldn't simultaneously count the number of books our library had purchased that cost less than $50, and the number that cost more than $200. We couldn't count the number of books we had purchased from publisher A and compare their average cost with that of books from publisher B. If we were into bibliometrics, we couldn't look at the average number of citations to articles published in the *Journal of Industrial Deregulation* in 2016 and compare them with citations to articles in the *Journal of Green Technology*.

All of these things, and many more, are possible, and in this chapter we will look at *conditional functions*, those that rely on one of the shortest and most important words in the English language—*IF*. It is this word that allows us to imagine different possibilities and to create future scenarios—*if* it is raining today, I will stay at home, *otherwise* I will go to the beach. Already though, I have fallen into the trap of being excessively binary and of using a very incomplete decision-making model—what I should have said was "if it is sunny I will go to the beach, if it is cloudy I will go for a walk (and if it is windy as well I will go somewhere sheltered), and otherwise I will stay at home." We can immediately see the possibilities that this sort of scenario creates for libraries—if this book is by a popular author and costs less than $50, then buy two copies for each branch, if it costs more than $50, buy two copies for the large branches and one for the others, and so on. And if we run out of money, flag it for the waiting list!

The IF Function

Going back to Chapter 5 we can see that an IF statement was already embedded in the logical and informational functions. When we used the simple formula

$$= A2="East\ Dulminster"$$

we were really saying "if the value of cell A2 is *East Dulminster,* then return the answer TRUE, otherwise return the answer FALSE." Combined with nesting, which we have seen already, simple if-then-else logic forms the basis of all the conditional functions of spreadsheets.

Here is how it works. When we use an IF statement on a logical proposition that could return either TRUE or FALSE, rather than using these answers we get to specify what the outcome will be in either case. It takes the form

$$=IF(logical\_proposition,\ outcome\_if\_true,\ outcome\_if\_false)$$

So rather than answering TRUE or FALSE, we could change our formula in cell B2 to output *Yes* or *No:*

$$=IF(A2="East\ Dulminster",\ "Yes","No")$$

There are two possible outcomes:

Location	East Dulminster?
East Dulminster	Yes

or

Location	East Dulminster?
North Dulminster	No

So far, so binary, but what if we changed the *outcome_if_false* option to another formula, this time testing for the presence of a North Dulminster location? Because this question is no longer binary, a simple *yes* or *no* will no longer suffice, and for the second subformula I need another option. At the same time, rather than simply saying *yes* or *no*, the output for the formula will indicate the day of the week on which the mobile library visits each district:

=IF(A2="East Dulminster", "Monday", IF(A2="North Dulminster", "Tuesday", "Not in Schedule"))

The double parentheses at the end indicate that the second part of the equation is nested within the first part. If cell A2 contains *East Dulminster,* the first part of the formula outputs *Monday,* and there is no need for further processing. If it doesn't, we move on to the second subformula where we test for North Dulminster. At this point the possible outputs are either *Tuesday* or *Not in Schedule.* (If I hadn't wanted to be this pedantic, I could have left final option as simply two pairs of double quotes, but there would have to be some option in that space.) Here are some outputs:

Location	Mobile Library Visit
North Dulminster	Tuesday

Location	Mobile Library Visit
South Dulminster	Not in Schedule

We can now proceed to cover all the Dulminster possibilities with each new subformula appearing as the *outcome_if_false* of the preceding one:

=IF(A2="East Dulminster"," Monday", IF(A2="North Dulminster", "Tuesday", IF(A2="West Dulminster", "Wednesday", IF(A2="South Dulminster", "Thursday", IF(A2="Central Dulminster", "Friday", "Not in Schedule")))))

Location	Mobile Library Visit
South Dulminster	Thursday

Location	Mobile Library Visit
East Hicksville	Not in Schedule

You'll notice that there are now five parentheses at the end of the formula, equating to the five IF functions nested within. Logically the *Not in Schedule* option comes at the end because we only know that it is true after we have tested all the other possibilities.

The next step is to change the entries in column A, which we will now name as the range *address*, to the full addresses:

94 Chesterfield Street, South Dulminster 11521

Of course, our formula will no longer work, but as we saw in Chapter 5 we could test for the presence of the character string *South Dulminster* by using the following formula, which will produce a TRUE or FALSE outcome:

=ISUMBER(SEARCH("South Dulminster", address))

We can use this to write a formula that will extract the location information we need from these full addresses:

=IF(ISNUMBER(SEARCH("East Dulminster", address)),"Monday",
IF(ISNUMBER(SEARCH("North Dulminster", address)),"Tuesday",
IF(ISNUMBER(SEARCH("West Dulminster", address)),"Wednesday",
IF(ISNUMBER(SEARCH("South Dulminster", address)),"Thursday",
IF(ISNUMBER(SEARCH("Central Dulminster", address)),"Friday",
"Not in Schedule")))))

Address	Mobile Library Visit
94 Chesterfield Street, South Dulminster 11521	Thursday
156D Anderson Avenue, East Dulminster 11517	Monday
14 Monroe Grove, North Dulminster 11514	Tuesday
1088 East Dulchester Drive, West Dulminster 11525	Wednesday
19 Paradise Parade, East Hicksville 11543	Not in Schedule

Notice that it is necessary to be careful with the use of parentheses within these long nested formulas. Because the formula

=ISUMBER(SEARCH("South Dulminster", address))

ends with two parentheses, it's necessary for these two parentheses to be used when it's a subformula. However, the subformulas are only separated by commas, as each one of them is actually part of the preceding formula—it's the *outcome_if_false*.

This is a different type of nesting from the "Russian dolls" nesting that we saw with the SUBSTITUTE function where each new substitution wrapped around the outside of the previous one and the cell address sat nestled in the middle. Think of *if-then* nesting as a series of doors at each of which we ask a yes/no question—let's call it the Emperor's New Clothes game. You are faced with two doors and you ask the question "are the Emperor's new clothes blue?" If the answer is "yes," you go through the door to the left and call out "the Emperor's new clothes are blue!" If the answer is "no," you go through the door to the right and find two more doors. Again you ask the question, this time enquiring if the clothes are green. This process continues until you get the answer "yes" and exit the game through one of the left-hand doors, triumphantly calling out the answer. If you come to the final door and the answer is still "no," you pass through that door and call out "the Emperor has no clothes!"

If-then nested formulas really only work if the different options are mutually exclusive—an address can only refer to one district, so at each point in the process the question is still binary, *yes* or *no*. Someone can live in East Dulminster or West Dulminster, but not in both. It is possible, though, to imagine a situation in which the formula could produce a false answer. Let's say that the first mayor of South Dulminster had originally come from North Dulminster and named one of its main streets North Dulminster Drive; if that was the case, our formula would identify the string "North Dulminster" within the address and would produce a false result for each resident in that street. We could get around that by placing the South Dulminster question before the North Dulminster question in our formula, so that addresses from South Dulminster Drive would already have exited the formula before the North Dulminster question was asked. This might sound slightly far-fetched, but it is always a good idea to watch out for "false positives." In general, the order of questions in an if-then nested formula doesn't matter, but there may be cases where you need to ask one specific question before another.

A further thing to note is that we could have based our question on postcodes and still returned the answer as a set of days of the week:

$$=IF(ISNUMBER(SEARCH("11517", Address)),"Monday",$$
$$IF(ISNUMBER(SEARCH("11514", Address)),"Tuesday",$$
$$IF(ISNUMBER(SEARCH("11524", Address)), "Wednesday",$$
$$IF(ISNUMBER(SEARCH("11521", Address)), "Thursday",$$
$$IF(ISNUMBER(SEARCH("11511", Address)), "Friday", "Not in Schedule")))))$$

However, because there is more than one postcode per district, we would need to include a set of OR statements to avoid unnecessary repetition:

$$=IF(OR(ISNUMBER(SEARCH("11517", Address)),ISNUMBER(SEARCH("11518", Address))),"Monday", IF(OR(ISNUMBER(SEARCH("11514", Address)),ISNUMBER(SEARCH("11515", Address))),"Tuesday", IF(OR(ISNUMBER(SEARCH("11524",$$

Address))),ISNUMBER(SEARCH("11525", Address))),"Wednesday",
IF(OR(ISNUMBER(SEARCH("11521", Address)),ISNUMBER(SEARCH
("11520", Address))),"Thursday", IF(OR(ISNUMBER(SEARCH("11511",
Address)),ISNUMBER(SEARCH("11512", Address))),"Friday",
"Not in Schedule")))))

One advantage of using the postcodes is that it avoids the ambiguity caused by the presence of North Dulminster Drive in South Dulminster! Unique identifiers of this kind, such as ISSNs standing in for journal titles and DOIs pointing to the location of unique document versions on the web, are often used by librarians to avoid the ambiguities that arise from the use of words. For example, a search for the *Journal of Educational Psychology* may also capture results from the *International Journal of Educational Psychology*, and although it would be possible to construct a spreadsheet formula that distinguished one from the other, it might be easier to use the ISSNs—*0022-0663* and *2014-3591*—that have been uniquely assigned to each title.

Working from the Inside Out

The best way to construct a formula like this is to begin from the inside and work outward. Enter the address into cell A2, and then write a SEARCH formula in cell B2 to make sure that it returns a number when the required string is present and something else (an error message) when it is not. Then wrap the ISNUMBER function around this to turn that determination into a binary answer. Around this you then wrap the OR function to test for more than one possible search string, checking that it still returns either TRUE or FALSE. Only when this is all working properly do you turn it into a series of nested if-then statements. By then you will have placed a variety of different addresses in column A to make sure that your formula is producing the correct result under all possible circumstances.

This is how the sequence would go in cell B2 if *94 Chesterfield Street, South Dulminster 11521* was in A2 and column A had been given the Name *Address:*

=SEARCH("11521",Address) Step 1—column B

The answer is 42, which is the position of the character string *11521* in the full Address. Now, we are not interested in this number, only in confirming that *11521* occurs in the full Address. If it does not occur, then we will get an error message—*#VALUE!*—and we can use this fact by adding the informational function ISNUMBER as the next shell:

=ISNUMBER(SEARCH("11521",Address)) Step 2—column C

This returns TRUE in this case, but FALSE if one of the other postcodes appears in the *Address* range. Our next step then is to expand the number of postcodes that will return TRUE by using OR:

=OR(ISNUMBER(SEARCH("11521",Address)),ISNUMBER(SEARCH
("11520",Address))) Step 3—column D

The presence of either of these postcodes in the Address will now return TRUE, and as these two postcodes relate to South Dulminster, we can use this fact combined with an IF function to return this piece of information:

=IF(OR(ISNUMBER(SEARCH("11521", Address)),ISNUMBER(SEARCH
("11520",Address))),"South Dulminster", "Not South Dulminster")
Step 4—column E

This is still a binary choice though, so we continue to add IF statements so that the formula progresses through all the possibilities, including *Not Dulminster* as the final option:

=IF(OR(ISNUMBER(SEARCH("11521",Address)),ISNUMBER(SEARCH
("11520",Address))),"South Dulminster",IF(OR(ISNUMBER(SEARCH("11517",
Address)),ISNUMBER(SEARCH("11518",Address))),"East Dulminster",
IF(OR(ISNUMBER(SEARCH("11514",Address)),ISNUMBER(SEARCH
("11515",Address))),"North Dulminster",IF(OR(ISNUMBER(SEARCH
("11524",Address)),ISNUMBER(SEARCH("11525",Address))),"West Dulminster",
IF(OR(ISNUMBER(SEARCH("11511",Address)),ISNUMBER(SEARCH
("11512",Address))),"Central Dulminster","Not Dulminster")))))
Step 5—column F

So far we have used the place names rather than days of the week because it gives us an easy visual check on the accuracy of our formula, but the final step is to substitute days for districts to indicate when the mobile library will visit. Here again is the final formula:

=IF(OR(ISNUMBER(SEARCH("11517",Address)),ISNUMBER(SEARCH
("11518",Address))),"Monday",IF(OR(ISNUMBER(SEARCH("11514",Address)),
ISNUMBER(SEARCH("11515",Address))),"Tuesday",IF(OR(ISNUMBER
(SEARCH("11524",Address)),ISNUMBER(SEARCH("11525",Address))),"
Wednesday",IF(OR(ISNUMBER(SEARCH("11521",Address)),ISNUMBER
(SEARCH("11520",Address))),"Thursday",IF(OR(ISNUMBER(SEARCH
("11511",Address)),ISNUMBER(SEARCH("11512",Address))),"Friday","
Not in Schedule"))))) Step 6—column G

EXERCISE

Open a copy of the spreadsheet:

http://bit.ly/2WcUHhD

This is a helpful guide if you don't like making clothing choices first thing in the morning and don't mind wearing the same colors on the same days of the week. You will notice that column A has the range Name *day*, and column B has the formula

=IF(day="Monday","Green","Hey, that's not a real day!")

Because the formula is incomplete, it is giving the *outcome_if_false* answer to all the valid days of the week. Change the formula to

=IF(day="Monday","Green", IF(day="Tuesday","Blue","Hey, that's not a real day!"))

and copy down the rows, and you'll see that the value for Tuesday is now correct.

Complete the formula so that each day is showing a color of your choice and anything other than a valid day of the week gets the appropriate message. You will need to keep the parentheses on the right balanced with the number on the left.

Because you quite like the color blue, you want to wear it on at least three days of the week. Copy the formula into column C, and use the OR function to achieve this outcome.

You will have to delete some parentheses from the right!

Dealing with Errors

You might recall that in Chapter 3 we looked at the following formula to calculate the average cost of books acquired by a library in a given week:

=total_cost/number_of_books_acquired

http://bit.ly/2GxRNzn

This works only if there were in fact any books acquired that would provide a number to use as a divisor; otherwise you are trying to divide by zero, and you will get a #DIV/0! error. Now, it is perfectly reasonable to assume that there will be weeks in which no books come into stock, but as this results in a division by zero we want to be able to tell the formula to ignore the error. To do this we wrap the whole formula within the IFERROR function like this:

$$=IFERROR(total\_cost/number\_of\_books\_acquired,"")$$

The double quotes at the end tell the formula what to do in case of an error resulting from the application of the formula to a zero value in *number_of _books_acquired*, in this case leave the cell blank—although it could have been any character string or number or even another formula. If the *number _of_books_acquired* value had been a valid number other than zero, then the result from the main part of the formula would have been returned.

The IFERROR function can seem slightly like cheating, but it's actually a really useful tool, as we've seen in the division by zero case, because it allows us to carry out a reasonable and information-generating procedure while ignoring cases where it doesn't work. A lot of blank cells in the *Average cost* column looks normal while the same number of #DIV/0! messages looks as if something went badly wrong. When we come to the LOOKUP and INDEX/ MATCH functions, we will discover that a #N/A! error simply means that we didn't find anything to match what we were looking for. This isn't really an error at all, and the message is not particularly helpful, so it becomes routine to wrap these formulas in IFERROR.

There is also an ISERROR function that is somewhat less useful as it only returns a true/false result. For example, =A3/B3 will return an error if the value B3 is zero, so you could wrap it in the formula

$$=ISERROR(A3/B3)$$

to test if it is a valid operation, but you will only get back either TRUE or FALSE. You will occasionally see this done:

$$=IF(ISERROR(A3/B3),"",A3/B3)$$

which says that if the result of this formula is an error return a blank; otherwise do this (repeated) formula. Using IFERROR is much simpler:

$$=IFERROR(A3/B3,"")$$

This is because we are usually testing whether the output of a subformula is an error because we wish the output of the subformula to be the output of the whole formula, and there is no point in repeating the subformula if its output is valid. Occasionally, however, we might want the output of the whole formula to be something different. We have already done something similar with ISNUMBER. This formula

$$=ISNUMBER(SEARCH("11521",Address))$$

returns TRUE if the postcode is found in the address and FALSE if it is not, but it could equally well be expressed as

$$=ISERROR(SEARCH("11521",Address))$$

The difference is that it would return the opposite result to the ISNUMBER formula, so that the ISERROR would say FALSE when ISNUMBER said TRUE. Here's a cut-down version of our earlier formula that linked postcodes to days of the week using ISNUMBER:

$$=IF(ISNUMBER(SEARCH("11521",Address)),"Thursday","")$$

In this case *Thursday* is returned if the postcode is found in the address; otherwise the result is a blank. When we use ISERROR, this order is reversed:

$$=IF(ISERROR(SEARCH("11521",Address)),"","Thursday")$$

Here, when the postcode is *not* found, an error message is returned and the output is a blank; otherwise the output is *Thursday*.

As already said, IFERROR will generally suffice, but there will be occasions, particularly with lookup functions, which we will come to in Chapter 7, when a valid subformula will lead to one operation and an error will lead to another.

It's All Conditional: COUNTIF

So far, we have used our IF function to perform operations on a single cell, but what if we wanted information about the contents of a range? Here are three columns from a worksheet of transactions:

Barcode Number	Lending Branch	Borrower Number
2095009571	East	4368
3617777997	Central	3751
6496938991	East	1856
1829733880	West	6184
5410260319	Central	4368
5261383263	South	3751
9590633665	East	4368
1089515500	East	3397
5926421139	North	2258
5255919712	Central	4368
4889092566	North	1856
5814673452	East	6184

The middle column is named *Lending_Branch,* and if we wanted to know the total number of transactions from East branch, we could filter this column to East and count the number of rows. However, this is cumbersome, and we would still have to record the total somewhere, so instead we will use the COUNTIF function to do this:

=COUNTIF(Lending_Branch,"East")

Note that the format is

=COUNTIF(range, characterstring)

What is being counted is not the number of rows *containing* the word *East* but the number of rows that are *identical* to that word, so that if a cell in the range contains the string *East Dulminster,* it would not be included in the count. Fortunately, in this case, the range follows a set of rules that specify that only a single word is used to describe each branch.

COUNTIF also works with logical operators such as *greater than* or *less than* so that for our vendor-supplied list of titles and prices we could count those that cost more than $50 using the following formula:

=COUNTIF(usd_cost,">50")

This is slightly unexpected and can be difficult to remember. We've seen logical operators before in formulas like this:

=G8<50

which will return either TRUE or FALSE depending on the value in cell A8. However, when used in a COUNTIF function, the logical operator is enclosed in quotes (*usd_cost,">50"*). Unfortunately, if you leave the quotes out, the formula will not return an error message but will instead give you the value zero (0). If you had missed out the quotes around the logical operator (*usd_cost,>50*) from the COUNTIF formula above, you could be led to mistakenly think there were no books in the list that cost more than $50. Be warned and remember that it is always good to do a reality check on the results of your formulas!

Actually, these two uses of the COUNTIF function are really variations of the same thing because when we asked to count the lines containing "East" we were really asking for a logical equivalence. You might recall that when used within a formula the equals sign (=) is a logical operator determining whether whatever is to its left is identical to whatever is to its right. It returns either TRUE or FALSE. So when in our formula

=COUNTIF(Lending_Branch,"East")

we were insisting that whatever was in the *Lending_Branch* range needed to be the character string *East* in order to be counted. We could have written the formula like this:

=COUNTIF(Lending_Branch,"=East")

And, believe it or not, if you do that it will work just fine!

EXERCISE

Open a copy of the spreadsheet:

http://bit.ly/30SSHP8

Open a new worksheet and list the five libraries in column A—you could copy column B from the *Transactions* worksheet and remove the duplicates in order to do this. Then write a formula in column B of the new worksheet, counting the number of transactions for each branch.

Wildcards

Finding equivalence between strings is easy enough when the information in the range is relatively simple as in the example above, but won't work when we have anything less standardized, such as the addresses of library users in the format *94 Chesterfield Street, South Dulminster 11521*. If we had a large range of these, we might want to count the number of entries for *South Dulminster* or *11521* or even for *Chesterfield Street* but, as all of these items of information are combined into the one string, COUNTIF as described above cannot be used. Somehow or other we have to convert the long address and the short search term (e.g., *11521*) into entities that can compared with one another, and this is done through the use of wildcards; many librarians will already be familiar with wildcards from their use in databases and search engines. The wildcard is an asterisk (*) and can be used at the beginning and the end of a string, so that the following

11521

really means

fromthebeginning11521totheend

In other words, any character string containing the bit between the asterisks will meet the equivalence test. We can now count the number of occurrences of *11521* in our list of addresses:

=COUNTIF(Address,"*11521*")

This can also be used for districts:

=COUNTIF(Address,"*East Dulminster*")

and even streets:

=COUNTIF(Address,"*Monroe Grove*")

This works really well, except that we would have to keep changing our formula every time we wanted to count the occurrences of a postcode, a district, or a street. The answer is to place the search terms in a range of their own and then build this into the formula. The range of districts is simplest to show because there are only five of them, and we can place them in a range like this with the Name *District:*

District
North Dulminster
South Dulminster
East Dulminster
West Dulminster
Central Dulminster

We then use the & combined with the * to build this range into the formula, which reads like this:

=COUNTIF(Address,"*"&District&"*")

This produces the result:

District	Count
North Dulminster	602
South Dulminster	415
East Dulminster	758
West Dulminster	260
Central Dulminster	117

In the first line the subformula

"*"&District&"*"

is the equivalent of

$$"*North\ Dulminster*"$$

EXERCISE

Go back to the Addresses spreadsheet that we opened earlier:

http://bit.ly/2IgJ6JF

You will notice that column A of the *Addresses* worksheet has the range Name *Address*.

Open a new worksheet, list the five districts of Dulminster in column A, and give this column a range Name. In column B write a formula that counts the number of occurrences of each district in the range *Address*.

But we just saved ourselves a lot of typing and unnecessary repetition.

Conditional Sums and Averages

There are two other conditional mathematical formulas, SUMIF and AVERAGEIF. Just as the SUM function added numbers together rather than counting them, SUMIF does this for a specific condition. As adding can only be done with numbers, this must be a condition relating to numbers, in other words *greater than, less than,* or *equal to.* If we wish to determine the proportion of our spending that went toward books costing more than $200, we could use the following formula:

$$=SUMIF(usd\_cost,">200")$$

We then use SUM to calculate the total amount spent (without the condition), and the final formula will give us our answer:

$$=SUMIF(usd\_cost,">200")/SUM(usd\_cost)$$

This result can then be formatted as a percentage.

The same principle can be applied to finding conditional averages, so if we wish to know the average price of books costing less than $100, we could use the following:

$$=AVERAGEIF(usd\_price,"<100")$$

Functions with Multiple Conditions: COUNTIFS

You will by now have some idea of the power of conditional functions, but the questions we have been asking are relatively simple ones, such as "how many residents of West Dulminster are registered with the library?" Or "how many of these books are published by Wiley?" Here's the beginning of a list of book titles with date, publisher, and price details. You can see the full list here:

http://bit.ly/2XtfOxJ

	A	B	C	D
1	Title	Publication Date	Publisher	USD
2	A dictionary of animal behaviour	2014	Oxford University Press	$18
3	Adam's nose, and the making of humankind	2015	Imperial College Press	$38
4	An introduction to animal behavior	2012	Cambridge University Press	$145
5	Animal behavior	2018	Storytellers, Inc	$80
6	Animal behavior : an evolutionary approach.	2011	Apple Academic Press	$26
7	Animal nature and human nature.	2018	Taylor and Francis	$103
8	Animal vocal communication : assessment and management roles.	2017	Cambridge University Press	$94
9	Domestic animal behavior for veterinarians and animal scientists	2018	Wiley	$59
10	Exotic pet behavior : birds, reptiles, and small mammals.	2006	Saunders Elsevier	$95
11	Fossil behavior compendium.	2010	Taylor & Francis	$126
12	Handbook of bird biology	2016	Wiley-Blackwell	$96
13	How animals think and feel : an introduction to non-human psychology.	2016	Greenwood	$58
14	In the company of animals: a study of human-animal relationships	1996	Cambridge University Press	$25
15	Mixed-species groups of animals : behavior, community structure, and conservation.	2017	Academic Press, an imprint of Elsevier	$56
16	Perspectives on animal behavior	2009	Wiley	$163

If you are working along, note the Named ranges and open a new worksheet. To find out the number of titles published by Wiley, we could use the formula

$$=COUNTIF(publisher, "Wiley")$$

which returns the answer 2. We have asked for an exact match, but if we had used wildcards

$$=COUNTIF(publisher, "*Wiley*")$$

then the answer would be 3 because the formula would also have captured the Wiley-Blackwell title. Our next step is to extend the question to ask "how many books that were published by Wiley cost more than $100?" This question has more than one condition, publisher, *and* price, so we need to proceed to a new function, COUNTIFS. It takes this form:

=COUNTIFS(range_1,condition_1,range_2,condition_2,range_3,condition_3)

Our question about Wiley books costing more than $100 is expressed as

=COUNTIFS(publisher, "*Wiley*",usd, ">100")

The answer is now *1*.

You might have noticed that what we are using here is a logical AND—*publisher=Wiley AND price > $100*—but that it is expressed rather differently. The S in COUNTIFS signals that an AND statement is to follow. We can now proceed to three conditions by asking how many Cambridge books costing less than $100 and published before 2010 are in the list:

=COUNTIFS(publisher,"*Cambridge*",usd,"<100",pub_date,"<2010")

In Chapter 5 we saw that it was possible to determine whether a value fell *between* two other values by doing an AND search:

=AND(pub_date>2014,pub_date<2017)

If this formula is placed in a column on the same worksheet as the Named range *pub_date*, it will return TRUE for rows in which the date is 2015 or 2016 and FALSE for any other date. We can apply this logic then to COUNTIFS:

=COUNTIFS(publisher,"*Cambridge*",usd,"<100",pub_date,"<2010",
pub_date, ">1990")

So far we have been looking for specific publishers, but the next step is to list all the publishers in our spreadsheet and find the numbers of titles for each one, plus any other data on prices or dates that we wish to extract. We will do this on a separate worksheet.

Making a List: SUMIFS and AVERAGEIFS

The first step is to create a single list of all the publishers and sort this by date. As some publishers appear more than once, and in real life may appear many times in a worksheet of this kind, we need to copy the list of publishers and remove all duplicates so that each publisher appears only once. To do this, simply go to the *publisher* range and copy it and paste it into the new worksheet. Go to the *Data* tab and remove the duplicates; then sort the list of publishers alphabetically.

Once we have a sorted list, the formula goes in the adjacent column and simply references the entries in this list, so that if the list is in column A, then the formula in cell B2 to count the entries for the first publisher in the list will read

$$=COUNTIF(publisher,A2)$$

Remember here that the Name range *publisher* contains all the entries in the worksheet *Animal behavior,* while the A2 references the range *A:A* in the new worksheet. It might be a better idea to Name range this range *pub_list*, meaning the sorted list of publisher names with duplicates removed. The formula now reads

$$=COUNTIF(publisher, pub\_list)$$

Our list now looks like this:

	A	B	C	D
1	Publisher	Titles	Total value	Average price
2	Academic Press, an imprint of Elsevier	1	56	56.00
3	Apple Academic Press	1	26	26.00
4	Cambridge University Press	4	369	92.25
5	Fordham University Press	1	29	29.00
6	Greenwood	1	58	58.00
7	Imperial College Press	1	38	38.00
8	Oxford University Press	1	18	18.00
9	Routledge	2	145	72.50
10	Saunders Elsevier	1	95	95.00
11	Storytellers, Inc	1	80	80.00
12	Taylor & Francis	1	126	126.00
13	Taylor and Francis	1	103	103.00
14	W. W. Norton & Company	1	92	92.00
15	Wiley	2	222	111.00
16	Wiley-Blackwell	1	96	96.00

Once this has been done, we can add two more columns and two more formulas to capture the sum total of prices for each publisher. The first uses SUMIFS, which gives us the total amount spent for each publisher:

$$=SUMIFS(usd,publisher,pub\_list)$$

The range that is being summed goes first and doesn't have any additional criteria, and then the other ranges setting the conditions follow on. The format goes like this:

=*SUMIFS(range_to_be_summed, condition_range, condition)*

In our example the *range_to_be_summed* is *usd*, the *condition_range* is *publisher* and the *condition* is *pub_list*. This last one might seem a bit confusing until we consider that what *pub_list* really means is "the cell in this row that is also in the range *pub_list* (i.e., column A)." We could go on to add a second condition, for example, if we wanted to know the sum total of prices for a publisher for a given year:

=*SUMIFS(usd, publisher,pub_list, pub_date, "2017")*

And, of course, we can do exactly the same thing with averages to find the average price of a book from each publisher over all the years:

=*AVERAGEIFS(usd,publisher,pub_list)*

If a specific year is included, the AVERAGEIFS function has to be wrapped in an IFERROR to avoid the Division by zero error:

=*IFERROR(AVERAGEIFS(usd,publisher,pub_list,pub_date,"2017"),"")*

Here's what our chart would look like for the all-years option:

	A
1	**Publisher**
2	Academic Press
3	Apple Academic Press
4	Cambridge University Press
5	Elsevier
6	Fordham University Press
7	Greenwood
8	Imperial College Press
9	Oxford University Press
10	Routledge
11	Storytellers
12	Taylor and Francis
13	W. W. Norton
14	Wiley

Before we proceed to the next section, it's important to reiterate that all of these calculations are done on the basis of exact equivalence, so that the item on the *publisher* range has to be identical to the item in the *pub_list* range for a match to be made. The only exception to this is case, so that *Academic Press* and *Academic press* will be regarded as the same thing for the purposes of these calculations, but a stray comma or semicolon or even an extra space on one of the publisher names will result in no equivalence being found. In a later chapter we will see that we could have performed all the operations just described by using pivot tables, but as they also work on exact equivalence it's really useful to know how to use functions and formulas to deal with the sorts of complexities that we will now consider.

Using Wildcards to Tidy the List

If you look closely at the list of publishers, you might see some anomalies. *Academic Press*, for example, is described as *Academic Press, an imprint of Elsevier,* but this is based on the description appearing in the book and is not really the name of the publisher, which is simply *Academic Press*. If we had a long list of titles, then we could be almost certain that both these names will appear and that, using the duplication removal methods described above, they would both produce different and incomplete results. *Wiley* and *Wiley-Blackwell* are another example where we are simply interested in books published by Wiley regardless of the exact imprint. Going back to Academic Press, we might also be interested in titles published by Elsevier even under a slightly different imprint. A further complication arises with *Taylor and Francis* and *Taylor & Francis*.

Sometimes there is no simple way to fully remove these anomalies, so we are now going to copy the list into a new column and manually edit it to reflect the groupings of publishers as we see them. So here's what it looks like now:

	A
1	**Publisher**
2	Academic Press
3	Apple Academic Press
4	Cambridge University Press
5	Elsevier
6	Fordham University Press
7	Greenwood
8	Imperial College Press
9	Oxford University Press
10	Routledge
11	Storytellers
12	Taylor and Francis
13	W. W. Norton
14	Wiley

As well as the change to Academic Press, you will notice that a separate row has been added for Elsevier, Taylor and Francis has been reduced to a single entry, as has Wiley, and the corporate add-ons from Storytellers, Inc. and W. W. Norton & Company have been lopped off. We will name this range *pub_list2*. The formulas we have already used for *pub_list* will no longer work on many of the entries in this new list because they were based on exact equivalence, so instead we have to use the wildcards we saw in the Chapter 5. We use these at the beginning and end of *pub_list2* so that any character string in the range *publisher* that contains the string from *pub_list2* will give a match:

$$=COUNTIF(publisher,"*"\&pub\_list2\&"*")$$

This has mixed results:

	A	B
1	**Publisher**	**Titles**
2	Academic Press	2
3	Apple Academic Press	1
4	Cambridge University Press	4
5	Elsevier	2
6	Fordham University Press	1
7	Greenwood	1
8	Imperial College Press	1
9	Oxford University Press	1
10	Routledge	2
11	Storytellers	1
12	Taylor and Francis	1
13	W. W. Norton	1
14	Wiley	3

It has correctly identified that there are three Wiley titles and that there are two titles with the word *Elsevier* in their publisher lines. However, it has given the result of two titles for Academic Press because it has added in the Apple Academic Press title. We could have avoided this by missing out the left-hand wildcard so that the formula read

$$=COUNTIF(publisher,pub\_list2\&"*")$$

but this would be at the cost of not capturing the two Elsevier titles. There is probably not a lot we can do about this apart from recognizing it as a problem, and this is a case where some later manual tidying of the data may be necessary.

There is good news, however, and that is that the Taylor and Francis/Taylor & Francis problem can be solved by smart use of the SUBSTITUTE function. While it would be possible to go to the *publisher* range and use find/replace on the *Edit* tab to replace all the *&*s with *ands*, this is a messy procedure and would need to be carried out every time new data was added at the bottom of the worksheet. So here is a better way.

If the *publisher* range contains Taylor and Francis 10 times and Taylor & Francis 4 times, we can get the correct result by adding the two numbers together. In theory then we could count the total number using the following formula:

=COUNTIF(publisher,"Taylor and Francis")+COUNTIF(publisher,"
Taylor & Francis")

This is obviously not very practical as it only works for the one publisher, but by using the SUBSTITUTE function we can generalize it like this:

=COUNTIF(publisher,pub_list2)+COUNTIF(publisher,SUBSTITUTE
(pub_list2,"and","&"))

What this does in relation to Taylor and Francis (and, of course, any publisher with the possibility of an ampersand in their name) is to count both versions and add the results together. Unfortunately, however, the formula does the same thing for *every* publisher's name—if there is no *and* in the name, then there are still two versions, and they just happen to be identical—so the result is that we get the correct result for Taylor and Francis/Taylor & Francis but double the correct result for Cambridge University Press and everything else! The answer to this is to get the SUBSTITUTE function to work only for those publishers with "and" in their name, and this is done by the use of our old friend IF(ISNUMBER(FIND:

=IF(ISNUMBER(FIND("and",pub_list2)),COUNTIF(publisher,pub_list2)
+COUNTIF(publisher,SUBSTITUTE(pub_list2,"and","&")),COUNTIF
(publisher,pub_list2))

What we're doing here is first of all identifying whether or not the publisher name contains the character string *and*. If it does then we add together the entries for that publisher containing the ampersand and those containing the word *and*. This does not need to be done for publishers without *and* in their names—*COUNTIF(publisher,pub_list2)*.

The final step is to add the wildcards to the publisher names so that we can capture *Wiley-Blackwell* simply by having the name *Wiley* in *pub_list2*. This formula will do it:

=IF(ISNUMBER(FIND("and",""&pub_list2&"*")),COUNTIF(publisher,"*"
&pub_list2&"*")+COUNTIF(publisher,SUBSTITUTE("*"&pub_list2&"*","and",
"&")),COUNTIF(publisher,"*"&pub_list2&"*"))*

However, as we have seen, this formulation means that "Apple Academic Press" gets counted in with "Academic Press," so we could compromise by leaving off the truncation to the left, which would give us

=IF(ISNUMBER(FIND("and",pub_list2)),COUNTIF(publisher,pub_list2&"")
+COUNTIF(publisher,SUBSTITUTE(pub_list2&"*","and","&")),COUNTIF
(publisher,pub_list2&"*"))*

This means that we can't pluck *Elsevier* out of *Sanders Elsevier* or *Academic Press, an imprint of Elsevier*, but this is a case where we have to make a choice—there is no perfect outcome.

The Conditional Power of IF

Conditional functions, particularly those where we set multiple conditions, are a fundamental feature of spreadsheeting and a source of a great deal of its power. By setting conditions we are able to drill down into large sets of data to find exactly what we want and also to create scenarios that help us make decisions. Here are the first few lines and some selected columns of a very large data set on the Open Access status of a set of journal articles:

http://bit.ly/2QRSXJQ

	A	B	C	D	E
1	OA Status	Journal	Year	Publisher	Crossref citations
2	diamond	Journal of High Energy Physics	2016	Springer Nature	24
3	green	Journal of the American Academy of Audiology	2016	American Academy of Audiology	2
4	diamond	Journal of High Energy Physics	2017	Springer Nature	27
5	gold	Foods	2017	MDPI AG	1
6	closed	High Altitude Medicine & Biology	2017	Mary Ann Liebert Inc	4
7	hybrid	Philosophical Transactions of the Royal Society B: Biological Sciences	2017	The Royal Society	7
8	diamond	Journal of High Energy Physics	2017	Springer Nature	10
9	diamond	Journal of High Energy Physics	2016	Springer Nature	3
10	closed	Meat Science	2017	Elsevier BV	1
11	gold	eLife	2017	eLife Sciences Organisation, Ltd.	22

Column A shows the Access status of each article according to the following brief definitions:

Closed: There is no open access to these articles, which are behind a paywall, meaning that members of the general public have to pay to download and read them.
Gold: These articles are published in fully Open Access journals, and a publication charge has been paid.
Diamond: These articles are published in fully Open Access journals, but no publication charge has been paid.
Hybrid: These articles are published in journals that are not fully Open Access, and a charge has been paid to make them accessible.
Green: These articles are accessible to everyone through repositories run by institutions and organizations.

Column A has the range Name *oa_status*. Column B has the range Name *journal*, column C as the range Name *year*, and column D as the range Name *publisher*. Column E contains data from Crossref (the bibliographic cooperative that issues Digital Object Identifiers), showing how many times each of the articles has been cited and it has the range Name *citations*. (You should note that I have left out the article titles, but each row of data refers to a specific article.)

What I'm trying to find out is the total number of articles and the average citation rate for each publisher and each Open Access status. This will tell me, for example, whether closed articles are cited on average more or less than green or hybrid articles and whether there is any difference by publisher. The first step is to create a unique list of publishers, which I can do by removing the duplicates as already described. I will place my list of publishers on a separate worksheet, and after sorting it looks like this:

	A	
1	**Publisher**	
2	AACE Corp (American Association of Clinical Endocrinologists)	
3	Addleton Academic Publishers	
4	American Academy of Audiology	
5	American Association for the Advancement of Science (AAAS)	
6	American Astronomical Society	
7	American Chemical Society (ACS)	
8	American Dairy Science Association	
9	American Medical Association (AMA)	
10	American Meteorological Society	
11	American Physical Society (APS)	
12	American Psychological Association (APA)	

I'm going to name the range *publisher_list,* and it sits in column A of the new worksheet—there are 91 separate publishers in the list. Column B will be headed *Total* and column C *Gold.* To see the total number of articles for each publisher published in 2017, I can use the formula in column B:

$$=COUNTIFS(publisher,publisher\_list,year,"2017")$$

and then in column C I can count the number of papers for status Gold:

$$=COUNTIFS(publisher,publisher\_list,year,"2017",oa\_status,"gold")$$

Then it's a simple change to calculate the average numbers of citations in column D:

$$=AVERAGEIFS(citations,publisher,publisher\_list,year,"2017",oa\_status,"gold")$$

Unfortunately, we ran into a problem at this point:

$$\#DIV/0!$$

This is because we are asking for the total number of citations divided by the gold publications for each publisher in 2017, and if there were none, we are asking for the citations to be divided by zero, which is a mathematical non-sense! To avoid this I need to wrap the formula in an IFERROR function:

$$=IFERROR(AVERAGEIFS(citations,publisher,publis$$
$$her\_list,year,"2017",oa\_status,"gold"),"")$$

You will notice that I have chosen to use a blank space rather than the number zero because this would imply that there were gold articles for that publisher in that year and that they had not been cited. Filtered to publishers with at least one gold article, my table now looks like this:

	A	B 2017 articles	C Gold articles in 2017	D Average citations
1	Publisher			
5	American Association for the Advancement of Science (AAAS)	2	1	37.00
29	Cogitatio	1	1	0.00
33	Dove Medical Press Ltd.	1	1	3.00
35	eLife Sciences Organisation, Ltd.	2	2	14.50
36	Elsevier BV	102	1	9.00
38	F1000 Research, Ltd.	1	1	0.00
39	Frontiers Media SA	10	10	4.50

EXERCISE

Open a copy of the spreadsheet:

http://bit.ly/2QRSXJQ

Open a new worksheet and, as described above, make a list of publishers with duplicates removed in column A, and give it the range Name *publisher_list*. In row 1 label columns B to F "closed," "gold," "diamond," "hybrid," and "green." Now create formulas showing the numbers in each category for each publisher for the year 2016; then in columns G to K create formulas showing the average citation rates for each publisher in each category. Don't forget to allow for zero counts.

Bonus point—can you rewrite these formulas to use the column labels in row 1 so that they are essentially all the same formula, taking advantage of relative referencing to make it easier to copy them over a number of columns?

Conditional SUMPRODUCT

In Chapter 4 we looked at the SUMPRODUCT function, which allows us to take a result from a "virtual" range—if we have a range called *price* and one called *quantity*, then we don't need to create a further range to multiply one by the other when all we want is the overall cost. The formula used is

$$=SUMPRODUCT(--price,quantity)$$

This is not strictly speaking an array formula but it produces the same effect. It really comes into its own if we wish to specify a condition. Here is a list of book titles with prices and the quantity ordered:

http://bit.ly/2Vyfhuv

The Named ranges are *place, publisher, price,* and *quantity.* There is no column to show the product of multiplying price by quantity, but instead we could calculate the total by using the formula above. However, if we wished to take this one step further and find out the total cost of orders for the publisher Sage, this can be added into the formula as a condition, like this:

=*SUMPRODUCT(--(publisher="Sage"),price,quantity)*

However, as we have seen, a publisher like Wiley has a variety of forms of its name. Fortunately, the condition can be modified to include all versions of the name by using ISNUMBER:

=*SUMPRODUCT(--ISNUMBER(FIND("Wiley",publisher)),price,quantity)*

And then, of course, a cell address can be used in place of the name:

=*SUMPRODUCT(--ISNUMBER(FIND($A2,publisher)),price,quantity)*

Any number of conditions can be added in this way, so if we wanted to calculate the total spent with each publisher on titles costing more than $50, the formula looks like this:

=*SUMPRODUCT(--ISNUMBER(FIND($A2,publisher)),(price>50),*
price,quantity)

To calculate the subset of these published in New York, the formula is

=*SUMPRODUCT(--ISNUMBER(FIND($A2,publisher)),*
(place="New York"),price,quantity)

Each set of conditions is closed in parentheses, while the two ranges to be multiplied appear at the end of the formula separated by a comma.

EXERCISE

http://bit.ly/2Vyfhuv

On the worksheet SUMPRODUCT, column B contains the formula to calculate the total spent for the publishers in column A. In cell C2 write a formula that calculates the total for the city in cell C1 and copy this to all the other cells.

What was the total spent for Pearson titles published in Boston?

Summary

Conditional functions are a major tool, perhaps *the* major tool, in the task of transforming data into information and facts into knowledge. Counting things tells how many things there are, but counting different groups of things and comparing them with one another tells us whether thing A is more common than thing B, which begins to look like useful information. If we then discover that we could buy 10 of thing A for the cost of one of thing B, then we might be on the way to discovering, or at least illustrating, a fundamental rule of economics. It is always important, of course, to compare apples with apples, but a conditional formula might be able to tell us that the price of apples is higher on a Friday than on a Tuesday, while the price of bananas remains the same. And that's information!

We can begin to see the usefulness of this sort of data analysis in the operation of our libraries. It might be obvious that the Central Dulminster Library is busier on a Saturday afternoon than at any other time of the week, although we know that most of the people who use this library reside in South Dulminster and travel into the city center Monday to Friday for work. To find out who is borrowing books on a Saturday afternoon, the transaction row on our spreadsheet needs to include not only the borrower number and the branch that the book was borrowed from, but also information about where the borrower resides. Of course, when somebody takes a book out, this last piece of information is not asked for during the course of the transaction. It might be argued that the information is somehow "included" in the borrower number, but this isn't really the case, unless the library has different prefixes for different "home branches," which would cause problems every time someone moved between districts. The information about the borrower's "home district" will certainly be available in the borrower record, but this does not mean that it forms part of the transaction and will be available in the transaction record that makes up a row of a spreadsheet. What is needed is a mechanism to include it within that row by going off and retrieving it from somewhere else, and this is what we are going to look at in Chapter 7.

CHAPTER SEVEN

Lookups and Matches

Looking up is what librarians do. Before computers, if you wanted to know the population of Dulminster, you looked it up in a gazetteer or in the printed census. If you wanted to know whether or not the library had a copy of a specific book, you looked it up in the card catalog. If you wanted to know about a specific subject, you looked it up in the catalog or in an abstract/ index journal like *Biological Abstracts*, *Historical Abstracts,* or *Library and Information Science Abstracts*. To find the meaning of a word, you looked it up in a dictionary. With electronic libraries and databases we look up books or subjects or meanings by typing words into search boxes, and everybody with access to a computer looks things up by searching Google or some other similar search engine. We even look things up by asking our phones.

When we look something up, we begin with a value *that we know* and obtain a *new* piece of information relating to that value—the meaning of a word or the population of Dulminster. The dictionary or the gazetteer works by bringing those two things together, but it also places them in order by the first value so that we are able to find the new information. Let's take the example of a printed staff list. To find someone's room number, you find their name, and next to it (in the adjacent column) is the number. The name is the value we wanted information about, and the room number is the information itself. This is simple and works well, but it makes two important assumptions—that each person has a single number and that the list of names is ordered alphabetically. The underlying logic behind this is the alphabet itself, both our knowledge of it and the alphabetical arrangement of the list. If we now imagine the staff list as a worksheet, with the names in column A and the numbers in column B, we have what is known as a *lookup table,* which uses the name in column A to locate the row in which the entry occurs and then returns the number from column B. Here's the beginning of a typical staff list stored as a table in a Word document:

Name	Room	Telephone number
Aberdein, D	5.54	311
Adams, B	1.22	293
Adlington, B	3.98	143
Akhter, R	1.82	302
Aldrich, D	3.59	134
Anderson, K	2.99	188
Back, D	3.14	335
Baltzer, A	5.12	452

Now, if this is a printed list and we wanted to find the room number for *Tracy Simmons,* we would simply turn to the page where the letter *S* began and scan down the left-hand column to *Simmons* and then find the number in the right-hand column. If the list was a document on a computer, we could simply scroll down to the name. In both cases we rely on the list being sorted alphabetically.

Exact Matches Using VLOOKUP

Looking more closely at our room list, it is obvious that it takes the form of a spreadsheet, with column A containing the names, column B the room numbers, and column C the telephone numbers. If we place the entire list into a spreadsheet, we can then use a *lookup function* to find the name we want in column A and return the room number from column B. Because the list is vertical with the names running from top to bottom, a vertical lookup is used, and this function is known as VLOOKUP. To find the room number for *Baltzer, A,* we use this formula

=VLOOKUP("Baltzer, A",A:C,2,FALSE)

and it returns the result *5.58.*

Let's unpack the formula to see how it works. The first element is the *lookup value,* the thing we wanted information about (*Baltzer, A*); the second is the range that represents the lookup table A:C. The left-hand column of this range is known as the *lookup column,* and this is where the lookup value will be found, and this always has the value 1, meaning that it is the *first* column in the range. The third element (the number 2) is the column number within the lookup table from which the "answer" is to be taken (in this case the *second* column), and the fourth element (FALSE) indicates that we want an exact match. (If this last element seems a bit confusing, that's because it is!) The formula finds the lookup value in the left-hand column of the table (the lookup column) and returns the answer from the column to the right of that indicated by the column number. Note again that the lookup column has the number 1, so the column immediately to its right is column 2, and so on. As the lookup table has a third column, the formula to find telephone numbers reads

$$=VLOOKUP("Baltzer, A",A:C,3,FALSE)$$

And, of course, we could use a cell address as the lookup value rather than entering the actual name by using the following formula in cell E2 to look up the room number for any name entered into D2:

$$=VLOOKUP(D2,A:C,2,FALSE)$$

And this one will return the telephone number:

$$=VLOOKUP(D2,A:C,3,FALSE)$$

However, this will only work if cell D2 contains the name in the exact format used in the spreadsheet—*first_name, initial*—so if we simply wanted to enter the name *Baltzer*, we would need to add on a wildcard:

$$=VLOOKUP(D2\&"*",A:C,3,FALSE)$$

Be warned that there is a trap with this! If the lookup column (column A) contains more than one person with the same last name, the formula will return a result from the *first one found*. Lookups really only work on unique information elements, and as librarianship is a very word-based discipline, there is a risk of returning "false positives" on book titles and author names. For this reason the use of unique identifiers such as ISBNs, Digital Object Identifiers (DOIs), and ORCID IDs is often necessary to minimize ambiguity.

EXERCISE

http://bit.ly/2mcvliN

Enter formulas into cells E2 and F2 to return the room number and telephone number of any last name entered into cell D2.

What would happen if you tried to find the information for Simon Gordon? You could solve the problem by including the comma and initial, but you would need to know that there was a duplication. Is there any way you could build in a warning that there is more than one entry in the list for this last name? (Hint—think IF and COUNTIF with wildcards.)

Using VLOOKUP Within a Formula

So here's an example of how a lookup table and the VLOOKUP function allow us to perform operations that would be extremely cumbersome, or impossible, to carry out using the tools we have learned so far. Librarians buy books, journals, and services from all over the world, and these are charged for in a variety of currencies. For the purposes of estimating costs, it is essential to convert them to a single currency using the various exchange rates as a multiplier. Here's a simple formula that would convert British pounds into U.S. dollars:

$$=price* 1.25937$$

Because the exchange rate fluctuates, we might want to place it in a cell with the Name GBP so that the formula would read

$$=price*GBP$$

For the sake of simplicity we place the Named cell GBP on a separate worksheet called *Exchange_rates*. If there were several different currencies, we would need a column next to the price column indicating which currency related to each price plus a Named cell for each currency. In this example cell B2 has the Name AUD to indicate that it holds the exchange rate for the Australian dollar, B3 is Named CAD, and so on:

	A	B
1	Symbol	USD
2	AUD	0.68705
3	CAD	0.74556
4	EUR	1.12095
5	GBP	1.25937
6	USD	1

Because the table shows the value of these currencies *against* the U.S. dollar, the value USD will always be 1.

Here then is our list of books on its own worksheet (*Price_list*), with the currency symbols in column C and prices, in those currencies, in column D.

	A	B	C	D	E
1	Year	Title	Currency	List Price	USD
2	2019	Writing guidelines for business students	AUD	125	
3	2007	Practical media relations	GBP	265	
4	2012	Public relations writing and media techniques	USD	65	
5	2016	Reframing organizational culture	GBP	344	

We could then use the IF function to determine the price in U.S. dollars of each item. Here is the formula in cell E2:

$$=IF(C2="AUD",D2*AUD, IF(C2="GBP",D2*GBP, IF(C2="EUR",D2*EUR, IF(C2="USD",D2*USD))))$$

You will recall that the multiplier for *USD* is *1* because it is the "target currency," but it has still been necessary to include it in the formula. With only three currencies, potentially out of hundreds, this formula is already becoming complex, and each time a currency was added we would have to change the formula. What is worse, if we hadn't used Named cells for each of the exchange rates, the formula would read like this:

$$=IF(C2="AUD",D2* 0.68705, IF(C2="GBP",D2* 1.25937, IF(C2="EUR",D2* 1.12095, IF(C2="USD",D2))))$$

Good luck with changing that every Wednesday morning!

Fortunately, as already noted, our list of exchange rates is held on the *Exchange_rates* worksheet with the currency symbols in column A and the current exchange rates in column B. This becomes our lookup table, and using the VLOOKUP function we can access this table directly without having to use a sequence of nested IF statements. If the table is in columns A (symbol) and B (exchange rate) of the worksheet *Exchange_rates*, this formula will retrieve the exchange rate values for the symbol in cell C2 of *Price_list:*

$$=VLOOKUP(C2,Exchange\_rates!A:B,2,FALSE)$$

As each exchange rate has a currency symbol to act as a unique identifier, there is no concern about duplication.

Once again we note that VLOOKUP consists of four elements:

* the value to be searched for (the *lookup value*), in this case the currency symbol in cell C2 of the *Price_list* worksheet.
* the range that is to be searched consisting of one or more columns generally on a different worksheet—this is the *lookup table*. The lookup value is searched

for in the left-hand column, and it is a vertical search that will cease when a match is found.

- the number of the column from which the answer is to be returned. The left-hand column is always numbered 1, so in this example column number 2 is column B of the worksheet *Exchange_rates*. If the currency in cell C2 of *Price_list* is GBP, VLOOKUP looks down column A of *Exchange_rates* until it finds a match and then returns the value from column B.
- a final statement known as the *range_lookup*, which indicates whether an exact match is to be found or not. Rather confusingly, the value here is FALSE because an exact match is required—if it were TRUE an incorrect answer could be returned. (I don't get it either.)

The VLOOKUP value can now be used as the multiplier in a formula that converts prices in different currencies to U.S. dollars. As the currency symbol in our list of books is in column C and the price is in column D, then this is the formula in cell E2 of *Price_list*:

=D2* VLOOKUP(C2,Exchange_rates!A:B,2,FALSE)

Not only is this much simpler than the formula above, but it now allows for almost unlimited expansion in the possible values held in the lookup table. It works perfectly in the case of exchange rates because each currency has a unique symbol and a currency has only one exchange rate at a time. Of course, it would be possible to have multiple values against the same currency symbol, say last week's exchange rate in column B of the lookup table and this week's exchange rate in column C, and we could use different formulas to compare fluctuations in prices:

=D2* VLOOKUP(C2,Exchange_rates!A:B,2,FALSE) (last week)

=D2* VLOOKUP(C2,Exchange_rates!A:C,3,FALSE) (this week)

The important point is that there would be only one entry for the currency symbol and all columns in the same row would relate to that entry.

EXERCISE

Open a copy of the spreadsheet:

http://bit.ly/31tlXwi

On the worksheet *Price_list*, the currencies appear in column C and the prices appear in column D. Look carefully at the layout of worksheet

Exchange_rates, and then create a formula in column E of *Price_list* to express each price in U.S. dollars.

Continue this until all the currencies in the header row can be calculated.

The currency of Hungary is the forint, and its symbol is HUF. At the time of writing its exchange rate to the U.S. dollar is 0.0033. Add it to the list of exchange rates, and alter one of the currency symbols in the price list to HUF to check that it's working. If you are feeling really smart, you can calculate the exchange rate of the forint for the other currencies in the Header Row; otherwise you will get error messages or zeros for those columns. If you are feeling lazy, wrap the formulas in the IFERROR function to replace the error messages with blanks.

As already noted, lookup functions are really designed for situations in which there is only one possible set of answers. If more than one country used the USD or GBP symbols, then the VLOOKUP would not work and the world financial system would also become unworkable. No, seriously. However, reality does not always conform to unique and mutually exclusive spreadsheet-ready units of data. The very words we use to describe reality are themselves a notorious example of ambiguity—almost every common word seems to have a variety of meanings or means different things in different contexts, while every meaning has a number of words that could be used to reference it. A spreadsheet could be used to create a dictionary, with the word in column A and its meaning in column B, and this is occasionally done to create bilingual dictionaries to power flash-card apps for language learners, but in practice it's not a very satisfactory method of creating a dictionary.

To summarize the features of the VLOOKUP function using exact matches:

- the lookup value must occur in the left-hand column of the lookup range
- the formula must be set to FALSE to ensure that only exact matches are found
- it is not necessary for the data in the lookup range to be sorted, but a match will be returned on the first row found
- for this reason it is essential that the values in the left-hand column are unique

Approximate Matches Using VLOOKUP

The question arises of why we wouldn't want an exact match and why we would ever set the VLOOKUP function to TRUE to find an approximate match, which returns the highest value that is *less* than the value being searched for. This is how an approximate match works:

- the data *must* be sorted by the value in the left-hand column
- the VLOOKUP function goes down the left-hand column, and unless there is an exact match it goes to the row *beyond* the value of the lookup value and then selects the row immediately *above* that as the match, in other words the highest value that is *less* than the lookup value

The classic example for this is turning test scores into grades. Let's say we have a grading system where a score of 50 to 64 was a C, 65 to 74 was a B, and anything over 75 was an A. Here is the grading schedule set out as a worksheet Named *Schedule*:

Cutoff	Grade
50	C
65	B
75	A

And this formula will turn a score into a grade:

=VLOOKUP(A2,Schedule!A:B,2,TRUE)

If the score is 65, then there is an exact match and grade B is returned. If the score is greater than 65 but less than 75, the formula "looks" at the first value in column A beyond 65, sees that it is greater than the score, so drops back to the row above and returns a B.

EXERCISE

Open the copy of the spreadsheet:

http://bit.ly/2XSpylm

On the worksheet *Grades* you will notice that if you enter a score of less than 50, an error message is returned. Expand the schedule to accommodate all possible scores.

Alter the formula to give a warning if a score of more than 100 or less than zero is entered.

Now, this may seem a bit remote from libraries where we are not generally giving scores and grades to our customers. However, you might recall that in Chapter 6 we used this formula to assign branch library names to postcodes:

=IF(OR(ISNUMBER(SEARCH("11517",address)),ISNUMBER(SEARCH("11518", address))),"East Dulminster",IF(OR(ISNUMBER(SEARCH("11514",address)), ISNUMBER(SEARCH("11515",address))),"North Dulminster",IF(OR (ISNUMBER(SEARCH("11524",address)),ISNUMBER(SEARCH("11525", address))),"West Dulminster",IF(OR(ISNUMBER(SEARCH("11521",address)), ISNUMBER(SEARCH("11520",address))),"South Dulminster", "Not Dulminster"))))

Knowing what we now know, this is an obvious candidate for a VLOOKUP formula, and we could create a lookup table to convert numbers to words:

Postcode	Branch
11511	Central
11512	Central
11513	Central
11514	North
11515	North
11516	North
11517	East
11518	East
11519	East
11520	South
11521	South
11522	South
11523	West
11524	West
11525	West

This is all very well, but it would become cumbersome if there were a large number of postcodes. Looking carefully at the codes, we notice that they are grouped so that the numbers from 11511 to 11513 relate to Central Dulminster, those from 11514 to 11516 to North Dulminster, and so on. We could use this sequential clustering to create a simple VLOOKUP formula based on a cut-down version of the table:

Postcode	Branch
11511	Central
11514	North
11517	East
11520	South
11523	West

You will notice that the value is always assigned to the lower limit of the range, so that 11516 defaults back to the value assigned to 11514. The formula to assign branch names using this table would be

$$=VLOOKUP(A2,Postcodes2!A:B,2,TRUE)$$

EXERCISE

Open a copy of the *Visits* spreadsheet:

http://bit.ly/30Zh9yv

Look at the *How_busy* worksheet to see the three descriptors that have been used to characterize each month's number of visitors.
Why is zero set as the limit for Quiet?
In columns E and F of the *Visits* worksheet write formulas to apply the descriptors to each month.
Which month went from Quiet to Busy?
Add a Super-Busy category for months that had more than 5,000 visitors.

Strictly speaking it is not necessary to use the TRUE element to specify an approximate search, as TRUE is the default setting if this final argument is left out. However, it is good practice to keep a clear distinction between exact (FALSE) and approximate (TRUE) uses of the VLOOKUP function.

To summarize the features of the VLOOKUP function using approximate matches:

- the lookup value must be in the left-hand column of the lookup range
- the rows must be sorted by the left-hand range
- the value in the left-hand cell of a row represents the lower boundary of a range, and the value in the cell below represents the beginning of the next range

- the formula should be set to TRUE
- you may need to be careful to specify what happens if the value entered is less than or greater than the allowable ranges—for example, the number of visitors cannot be less than zero, although the VLOOKUP function will cheerfully tell you that this was a quiet day unless you add an IF function to deal with this contingency

HLOOKUP

Unsurprisingly, the HLOOKUP function is identical to VLOOKUP but works horizontally rather than vertically. It looks *along* the top row of a worksheet to find a match on the lookup value and then moves *down* a specified number of rows to find the result. Because spreadsheet data tends to be arranged by row, it is used less often than VLOOKUP, but it can be useful in certain circumstances. For example, a lookup table for exchange rates could be placed in the first two rows of a worksheet listing book titles, currencies, and prices rather than taking up a whole worksheet on its own. Let's say the first two rows of the worksheet *Book_list* look like this:

AUD	GBP	GBP	CAD	CNY	EUR	JPY	NZD	USD
0.68705	0.68705	1.25937	0.75	0.14438	1.12095	0.00921	0.6492	1

A formula in row 4 to find the exchange rate if the symbol GBP occurred in cell C4 would look like this:

=HLOOKUP(C4,1:2,2,FALSE)

Note that the column letters we are used to seeing (e.g., A:B) have been replaced by row numbers (1:2). In theory a horizontal lookup table like this could run down for as many rows as you chose, so a horizontally arranged list of historical exchange rates (one for every month over 10 years, for example) could produce a formula like this to extract the exchange rate from the 95th row of the worksheet *Historical_XR*:

=HLOOKUP(C4,Historical_XR!A1:I120,95,FALSE)

Lookup Functions with Wildcards

As we saw with the room list, lookup functions can be used with wildcards. This is different from approximate matches that find values within upper and lower boundaries, and is more like the wildcard operations we used with COUNTIF and AVERAGEIF. We have already seen the variety of forms that publisher names can take—Wiley, Wiley Blackwell, Wiley Inc., John Wiley & Sons, and so on. Let's say there is a very long list of these in column A of a worksheet called *Publisher,* and each publisher has a unique identifying number in column B. Over time every version of the name has been added to the list, but care has been taken to ensure that the same identifying number has been used for each publisher. If I get tired of looking down the list and having to remember that Blackwell appears as Wiley Blackwell, I can create a new worksheet called *Lookup* and enter the name I am looking for into cell A2. I then use this formula in cell B2 to return the customer number:

=VLOOKUP("*"&A2&"*",Publisher!A:B,2,FALSE)

So all I have to do is to type Wiley or Blackwell into cell A2 to capture the publisher number. Because this is a slightly risky process—VLOOKUP will return a result on the first match that it finds—I can add an extra formula to confirm the version of the name that the match was made on:

=VLOOKUP("*"&A2&"*",Publisher!A:B,1,FALSE)

Because the column value is *1,* the match is returned from column A.

In practice, wildcards are not commonly used in lookup functions because you are generally trying to find an exact match for your lookup value. This is why we have tended to use numbers rather than words to reduce ambiguity and improve accuracy. One possible use is when you suspect that the data in the left-hand column of the lookup table may contain trailing whitespaces that have not been removed—the data may have been imported from another source, for example, and removing whitespaces would have added an additional manual process. In this case adding a truncation symbol would be a useful way of dealing with this:

=VLOOKUP(A2&"*",Importer_data!A:B,2,FALSE)

The Joys of Index Match

The functions VLOOKUP and HLOOKUP work only if the lookup value is to be found in the left-hand column of the lookup table and the result comes from another column somewhere to the right. It also depends on counting columns, so if the match is found in column C and the result is to be taken from column AD, then it is necessary to count the difference between those two columns and enter this number into the formula. As you begin to capture data in the form of CSV files from other systems, you will soon find that they do not always conform to this neat left-to-right layout. A DOI (Digital Object Identifier) is a superb example of a unique alphanumeric lookup value that unambiguously identifies a publication, but I regularly use imported data with a DOI that appears in column AD while the title of the publication appears in column F. While it is possible to rearrange the data to fit the VLOOKUP format, by inserting a new column A to the left of the existing one and copying column AD into this new column, in practice this is a cumbersome process requiring careful instructions if anyone else is to use your spreadsheet—or in fact if you yourself come back to it after a six-month break! For this reason we use INDEX/ MATCH, which allows us to choose *any* column to be the one containing the lookup value and *any other* column as the one from which the result is to be taken. I hesitated for some time before using this function as it appears slightly more complex than VLOOKUP and HLOOKUP, but once you get used to it you will probably come to use INDEX/MATCH in preference to those functions. However, you haven't wasted time by coming to grips with them first because they are a good set of "trainer wheels" for INDEX/MATCH and can be easier to use (and faster) when there are only a few columns to process.

Like VLOOKUP, INDEX/MATCH has four elements—(1) a value that is to be searched for (the *lookup value*), (2) a column in which this value is to be found (the *lookup column*), (3) a column from which the result is returned (the INDEX), and (4) a TRUE or FALSE statement indicating whether or not the search is to be exact or approximate. The differences are that, as already noted, the *Index* column does not have to be to the right of the *Match* column, and these two columns are explicitly named rather than being identified by the number of columns separating them. When using INDEX/MATCH range Names really come into their own.

Let's begin with a simple example to see how this works. Here is a spreadsheet containing a few details about some libraries in Maine (http://bit.ly /2o2PAoQ):

	A	B	C
1	Library	City	Zipcode
2	GOODALL MEMORIAL LIBRARY	SANFORD	04073
3	SPRINGVALE PUBLIC LIBRARY	SPRINGVALE	04083
4	SANGERVILLE PUBLIC LIBRARY	SANGERVILLE	04479
5	SCARBOROUGH PUBLIC LIBRARY	SCARBOROUGH	04074
6	CARVER MEMORIAL LIBRARY	SEARSPORT	04974
7	SPAULDING MEMORIAL LIBRARY	SEBAGO	04029
8	SHAPLEIGH COMMUNITY LIBRARY	SHAPLEIGH	04076

The data is held in columns A to C, and the row 1 headers have been used as column Names. The lookup value is a *zipcode* entered into cell E3. If we want to find the name of the library with the zipcode 04029, we can first use the MATCH function to find it in column C, which is Named Zipcode. This will find the row number within the lookup column where the lookup value is found. Because the MATCH function operates only on the lookup column, there is no need for a column number, but otherwise it looks very much like the other lookup functions:

=MATCH(E2,Zipcode,FALSE)

This formula returns the row number in the range *Zipcode* in which the number 04029 is found, in this case 7—our spreadsheet recognizes that the Header Row is not part of the range. We can now use this number in the INDEX function to find the name of the library from the range Named *Library*, which happens to be column A:

=INDEX(Library,7)

The INDEX function locates the line number within the Named range (*Library*) and returns the appropriate value from cell A7, in this case SPAULDING MEMORIAL LIBRARY. Now we can incorporate the MATCH subformula within the INDEX function to produce the desired result in one step:

=INDEX(Library, MATCH(E2,Zipcode,FALSE))

Using range addresses rather than names, the formula would read:

=INDEX(A:A,MATCH(E2,C:C,FALSE))

INDEX/MATCH can take a little while to get your head around, but it is definitely worth persisting with. Here are the two important points to note:

- INDEX is the column from which your answer will come
- MATCH is the lookup column in which your lookup value will be found

When you are used to using VLOOKUP, where the lookup column comes first, this is slightly counterintuitive, but the great thing about INDEX/ MATCH is that the columns can be in any order—the "answer" doesn't have to be to the right of the "question"—so that numerous questions can be asked about the same set of data.

INDEX/MATCH with Big Data

Here is a larger portion of the same spreadsheet downloaded from the U.S. Institute of Museums and Libraries' *Public Libraries Survey*. It's still been cut down considerably and contains data only from cities beginning with *S*:

	A	B	C	D	E	F	G
1	STABR	LIBNAME	ADDRES_M	CITY_M	ZIP_M	PHONE	City_State
2	AK	ST. PAUL ISLAND SCHOOL/COMMUNITY LIBRARY	P.O. BOX 207	ST. PAUL	99660	9075463334	ST. PAULAK
3	AK	SELDOVIA PUBLIC LIBRARY	P.O. BOX DRAWER H	SELDOVIA	99663	9072347662	SELDOVIAAK
4	AK	SEWARD COMMUNITY LIBRARY AND MUSEUM	P.O. BOX 2389	SEWARD	99664	9072244082	SEWARDAK
5	AK	SITKA PUBLIC LIBRARY	320 HARBOR DRIVE	SITKA	99835	9077478708	SITKAAK
6	AK	SKAGWAY PUBLIC LIBRARY	P.O. BOX 394	SKAGWAY	99840	9079832665	SKAGWAYAK

The worksheet *Pub_libs* contains details of over 800 public libraries:

http://bit.ly/2RqDKQj

The names in the Header Row remain unchanged from those used in the survey, and this is good practice—it is then easy and transparent to make them the names of the ranges we will use in our formulas, which will also accommodate future downloads from the same data source. The exception is column G (*City_State*), which has been added to the original data as a "helper" that we will use in Excel. It is generated by the formula

$$=CITY\_M\&STABR$$

This column has been given the range Name of CITY_STATE and the header names have been used as the Names of the other ranges as well.

On a second worksheet Named *Index_Match* we will create a lookup that allows us to enter the name of a city in cell A2, and the state abbreviation in cell B2, to find the name and other details of any library in the worksheet *Pub_libs*.

The first thing to notice is that our range that we want to match to our lookup value, in this case the name of the city, is not in the left-hand column, and some of the details we want to find (library name and address, telephone number) are to the left of it, so a VLOOKUP will simply not work. The first piece of information we look for is the name of the library corresponding to the city name that has been entered. This will be taken from column B of the worksheet *Pub_libs,* which has been given the range Name LIBNAME—this is the INDEX column. We will be matching the city name with column D of *Pub_libs,* which has the range Name CITY_M—this is the MATCH column. So our formula will look like this:

$$=INDEX(LIBNAME,MATCH(A2,CITY\_M,FALSE))$$

The specification FALSE means that an exact match is required. If we enter *Sunfield* into cell A2, this result appears in cell A3:

SUNFIELD DISTRICT LIBRARY

Expressed without range Names it looks like this:

$$=INDEX(Pub\_libs!B:B,MATCH(A2,Pub\_libs!D:D,FALSE))$$

EXERCISE

Open a copy of the *Public Libraries* spreadsheet:

http://bit.ly/2RqDKQj

Click on Data/Named ranges to see the names that have been assigned. Note the formula in column G, which is used to make this a helper column for Excel.

On the *Index_Match* worksheet, *San Marino* is entered in cell A2 and the state abbreviation in cell B2. In cell C2 enter the formula that will give you the full name of the San Marino library.

Use columns D to F to retrieve the postal address, the ZIP Code, and the telephone number.

Change the value in cell A2 to *Santa Monica*.

INDEX/MATCH Using Multiple Criteria

This system appears to work well but, like VLOOKUP, INDEX/MATCH looks for the *first* match for the lookup value in the Match column and returns the appropriate result from that row. This will work perfectly well for borrower numbers and exchange rates, which are *unique*, but runs into a problem when we try to look up information for the city of Springfield because that name appears no fewer than 14 times in the worksheet *Pub_libs* in states ranging from Colorado to Vermont. Because the worksheet is arranged by state, the formula we have used will return the result for Colorado. We need a mechanism to create a unique match, and this is provided by the city/state combination in column G, our helper column, which runs together the name of the city with the state initials, so that the Springfield in Nebraska is identified as "SPRINGFIELDNE" while the Springfield in Oregon is "SPRINGFIELDOR." The formula in column G that creates this unique string is

=CITY_M&STABR

The lookup value also has to change, to concatenate both city and state, so that rather being simply *A2* it is now *A2&B2*.

Because INDEX/MATCH can work from right to left, it is a relatively simple operation to make the match in column G and return the name of the library from column C:

=INDEX(Pub_libs!B:B,MATCH(A2&B2,Pub_libs!G:G,FALSE))

With Springfield entered in cell A2 and OH in cell B2 of the worksheet *Index_Match*, we get this result from the formula in cell C2:

CLARK COUNTY PUBLIC LIBRARY

Using range Names the formula reads like this:

=INDEX(LIBNAME,MATCH(A2&B2,CITY_STATE,FALSE))

EXERCISE

Change the formulas you created for the previous exercise to return the correct values if *Springfield* is entered in cell A2 and *OH* in cell B2. Test them by changing the value in B2 to OR.

To deal with cases where no match is found—maybe there is no library in that city or locality—wrap the formulas in the IFERROR function and include an error message. Test this by changing the value in cell B2 to *CA*.

A helper column can be used to set multiple criteria for an INDEX/MATCH formula, as long as the different elements appear in the same order in both the helper column and the lookup value.

At the time of writing this chapter, Google Sheets has a significant advantage over Excel, in that there is no need for a helper column. Instead, the concatenation of the matching columns can be carried out within the formula itself. You will recall that the column with the range Name *CITY_STATE* was created using this formula:

=CITY_M&STABR

This can be used to substitute for the range *CITY_STATE* so that this formula

$$=INDEX(LIBNAME,MATCH(A2\&B2,CITY\_STATE,FALSE))$$

is replaced by this one

$$=INDEX(LIBNAME,MATCH(\$A2\&\$B2,CITY\_M\&STABR,FALSE))$$

As we saw in Chapter 3, it is possible to use concatenation through the & symbol to create a *notional range*, in this case one that we search in for a match for our two conditions, which have also been concatenated—$A2&$B2. In Excel it has been necessary to create an actual range while in Google Sheets the notional range will suffice. However, by the time you are reading this Excel may have introduced this feature as well, so it is worth trying it out to see if it works. There are other methods of using INDEX/MATCH with multiple criteria using array formulas, but the concatenation method is relatively straightforward and transparent.

Putting It All Together

http://bit.ly/2ZnxzPw

Here's a system-generated list of library transactions that uses barcode numbers and borrower numbers to stand in for the names of books and people:

	A	B	C	D	E	F
1	Barcode Number	Lending Branch	Borrower Number	Date Borrowed	Date Due	Date Returned
2	5814673452	North	1856	05/12/2018	06/12/2018	05/22/2018
3	4286222619	East	4431	05/12/2018	06/12/2018	06/03/2018
4	5455991514	North	3397	05/13/2018	06/13/2018	05/27/2018
5	2186837314	North	3871	05/13/2018	06/13/2018	05/19/2018

The list appears on the *Transactions* worksheet—it is sorted by the date on which the book was borrowed, and the same book may appear in the list several times as it is returned and taken out again. When a book is still out on loan the *Date Returned* column is empty:

1	Barcode Number	Lending Branch	Borrower Number	Date Borrowed	Date Due	Date Returned	BarcodeReturned
24	9381762514	East	3397	05/20/2018	06/20/2018	06/03/2018	9381762514r
25	6961924774	North	4368	05/21/2018	06/21/2018		6961924774x
26	1003004258	North	6184	05/21/2018	06/21/2018	06/01/2018	1003004258r

You will notice that to the right of the Date Returned column there is a helper column (column G) with the range Name *BarcodeReturned*, which consists of the barcode with a single letter indicator of whether there is a *Date Returned* entry for this transaction. If the book has been returned this indicator is set to *r*, and if it is still on loan it is set to *x*. This formula has been used to combine the barcode with the indicator:

$$=A2\&IF(LEN(F2)>0,"r","x")$$

The formula creates a unique marker of each transaction and also allows us to distinguish between completed transactions for which there is a return date and uncompleted transactions where the book is still out on loan. This will become very useful in a moment.

The *Books* worksheet links the barcode numbers to book titles:

	A	B
1	Barcode Number	Book
2	2186837314	The elephant's birthday
3	1089515500	Animal behaviour : a very short introduction
4	9381762514	A life with wildlife
5	2095009571	Animal
6	5261383263	Animal life in Australia

Note that the barcode numbers are unique while titles may be duplicated.

The *Borrowers* worksheet contains information about the people:

	A	B	C	D	E
1	Borrower Number	Postcode	Branch	Name	Telephone number
2	1856	11514	North	Craig Russell Lee	07-754-3010
3	3751	11522	South	Tracy Jane Simmons	07-754-3011
4	4368	11517	East	Eric Johnson	07-754-3012

Our task is to use the *Current_status* worksheet to deliver the following information in columns B and C about the barcode numbers that are listed in column A:

- The title
- The date due if it is out on loan or a blank if it is not

Then for those books that are on loan columns C, D, and E will show:

- The borrower number
- The borrower name
- The telephone number

We have given columns A and B of the worksheet *Books* the range Name *Titles*, and as the barcode number is to the left of the title the task of retrieving the title can be done by a simple VLOOKUP in column B:

$$=VLOOKUP(A2,Titles,2,false)$$

Our next task is to use the barcode number to find out whether the book is out on loan or not and to find the borrower number for items that are currently on loan. You will recall that we have created a helper column named *BarcodeReturned* and that uncompleted transactions (i.e., books still out on loan) were marked by the letter *x* appended to the barcode. We can now use this to find borrower numbers or assign a *Not on loan* status (for entries lacking an *x*) by using INDEX/MATCH inside an IFERROR statement:

$$=IFERROR(INDEX(Borrower\_number,MATCH(A2\&"x",BarcodeReturned, \\ false)),"Not on loan")$$

To understand this formula, you need to know that the range *Borrower_ number* is column C of the *Transactions* worksheet.

Because the Borrower number is in the left-hand column of the worksheet *Borrowers*, we can use VLOOKUP rather than INDEX/MATCH to extract the borrower name from column D of that worksheet. This formula in cell D2 would work:

$$=IFERROR(VLOOKUP(C2,Borrowers!A:D,4,false),"")$$

However, lookup operations take a lot of processing and, as we now know which barcode numbers relate to books that are not currently out on loan, it is a waste of this computer effort looking for them again in this way. Instead we can stipulate that these numbers are not looked up a second time:

$$=IF(C2="Not on loan","",VLOOKUP(C2,Borrowers!A:D,4,false))$$

If *Not on loan* appears in cell C2, then cell D2 is left blank; otherwise the borrower's name is retrieved from column D of the worksheet *Borrowers*.

EXERCISE

http://bit.ly/2ZnxzPw

In column A of the worksheet *Current_status* is a list of barcode numbers. Use the formulas shown above to fill in the other columns. You will need to create your own formulas for the telephone number and Date due information. Have a look at the Named ranges, which may help you create the formulas.

Clean Your Data Before Matching

We've noted the importance of unambiguous and unique data in making lookup matches. This is why unique identifiers, such as barcode numbers, borrower numbers, or digital object identifiers, are really useful. It is true that we have been able to use the names of cities and localities to find the names and details of libraries, but this is because names of towns and cities generally consist of only one or two words and do not include punctuation. However, we won't always have the luxury of substituting numbers and similar identifiers for strings of words. It might be argued that as each book has an ISBN, this number could simply be used to stand in for the title in the same way that borrower numbers can substitute for people's names, but in practice each edition of a book may have a different ISBN, so that the same title could be represented by a dozen different numbers or more. If we wish to make full use of the data-matching potential of lookup functions in library contexts, then there will be many occasions on which we wish to compare two book titles with one another to determine whether or not they are the same.

Back in Chapter 3 we looked at the use of the SUBSTITUTE function as a method of removing punctuation and diacritics from character strings and of replacing the *&* symbol with the word *and*. The value of this technique will now become apparent as we use it to regularize the character strings that we will be comparing. Punctuation is an incredibly useful feature of language because it allows us to parse a sentence and to tell the difference between

"She likes cooking her family and her dog"

and

"She likes cooking, her family and her dog."

However, not all cases are this clear, nor are the rules for the use of punctuation always consistent. Take, for example, the preference for, or dislike of, the "Oxford comma." Some writers swear by

"France, Italy, and Spain"

while others prefer

"France, Italy and Spain."

This might all seem a bit academic until we get hold of the book

"The Budget Traveller's Guide to France, Italy, and Spain".

Or should that be

"The Budget Traveller's Guide to France, Italy and Spain"?

Or, horror of horrors

"The Budget Traveller's Guide to France, Italy & Spain"?

By now we have learned enough about spreadsheets to know that these three titles are not the same and that if we try to match them it's not going to work. So, in the absence of a spreadsheet function called PUNCTUATETHIS-THEWAYILIKEIT, the best we can do is to eliminate the punctuation entirely and replace the & with *and* by using SUBSTITUTE. If we do this identically for both the lookup value and the lookup range, then we should be able to compare accurately the two sets of data.

Here is a spreadsheet containing data on books from two different library vendors:

http://bit.ly/S4LVendList

VendorList_1 is longer than *VendorList_2* but lacks prices. Titles in both lists contain colons, commas, and ampersands (&), but they have not been used consistently. *VendorList_2* tends to place a space before the colon as well as after it, while *VendorList_1* does not place spaces before colons, but without checking we are not sure whether this has been done consistently in both cases. Ampersands seem to have been used rather randomly, and everything in *VendorList_2* is in upper case

Here are the first few lines of *VendorList_1*:

	A	B	C
1	**Title**	**Publisher**	**Year**
2	Writing guidelines for business students	Cengage Learning	2019
3	Practical media relations	Gower	2007
4	Public relations writing & media techniques	Longman	2012
5	Reframing organizational culture	Sage	2008

And of *VendorList_2*:

	A	B	C	D
1	**PUBLISHER**	**Year**	**TITLE**	**LIST PRICE**
2	GUILFORD PRESS	2012	THE PSYCHODYNAMICS OF WORK AND ORGANIZATIONS : THEORY & APPLICATION	$413.00
3	CORWIN PRESS INC.	2011	RELATIONSHIP-DRIVEN CLASSROOM MANAGEMENT : STRATEGIES THAT PROMOTE STUDENT MOTIVATION	$462.00
4	THOMSON/WADSWORTH	2006	PRINCIPLES OF INSTRUCTIONAL DESIGN	$336.00

Our aim is to add prices to the titles in column A of *VendorList_1* whenever matches can be found in *VendorList_2*. Our first step will be to create a helper range in column E of *VendorList_2*, and we will use the SUBSTITUTE function to strip out the punctuation and replace the ampersands with *AND*. Here is the formula that will do this:

$$=TRIM(SUBSTITUTE(SUBSTITUTE(SUBSTITUTE$$
$$(C2,":",""),",",""),"&","AND"))$$

In the case of the colon and the comma, the double quotes without a space between means that these punctuation symbols have been replaced by nothing. The whole thing is enclosed in a TRIM function to deal with the double spaces that result from deleting colons with spaces before and after them. (Using TRIM is a good idea in any case as there may have been double spacing within the original data.) The result looks like this:

	A	B	C	D	E
1	**PUBLISHER**	**Year**	**TITLE**	**LIST PRICE**	**Cleaned**
2	GUILFORD PRESS	2012	THE PSYCHODYNAMICS OF WORK AND ORGANIZATIONS : THEORY & APPLICATION	$413.00	THE PSYCHODYNAMICS OF WORK AND ORGANIZATIONS THEORY AND APPLICATION
3	CORWIN PRESS INC.	2011	RELATIONSHIP-DRIVEN CLASSROOM MANAGEMENT : STRATEGIES THAT PROMOTE STUDENT MOTIVATION	$462.00	RELATIONSHIP-DRIVEN CLASSROOM MANAGEMENT STRATEGIES THAT PROMOTE STUDENT MOTIVATION
4	THOMSON/WADSWORTH	2006	PRINCIPLES OF INSTRUCTIONAL DESIGN	$336.00	PRINCIPLES OF INSTRUCTIONAL DESIGN

You might point out that we could have achieved the same result by sim-ply doing a *Find/Replace* in column C and cleaning it up that way. There are, however, good reasons for using a formula and a helper row to achieve the same result:

- It is transparent—we know exactly what we have done, and we have not had to interfere with the original data
- It can easily be added to or amended
- It is a good idea to avoid manual processes wherever possible, because these would need to be separately documented, whereas a formula is more or less self-documenting
- A formula makes it easy to add new data to the spreadsheet or to reuse it with other data

This helper range can now be used in a formula in the worksheet *Vendor List_1* to create a match between the titles in column A of that worksheet and column E of *VendorList_2*. But first we need to "clean" those titles of punctua-tion and ampersands, and the best way to do this is to create a helper range in column D using the identical formula (but in this case referencing column A rather than column C):

$$=TRIM(SUBSTITUTE(SUBSTITUTE(SUBSTITUTE$$
$$(A2,".","""),",","""),"&","and"))$$

The formula to retrieve the prices from *VendorList_2* is now relatively simple:

$$=IFERROR(INDEX(VendorList_2!D:D,MATCH$$
$$(D2,VendorList_2!E:E,FALSE)),"")$$

And here is the result:

	A	B	C	D	E
1	Title	Publisher	Year	Clean	List Price
2	Writing guidelines for business students	Cengage Learning	2019	Writing guidelines for business students	
3	Practical media relations	Gower	2007	Practical media relations	
4	Public relations writing & media techniques	Longman	2012	Public relations writing and media techniques	65

We could have used some spreadsheet heroics and built the SUBSTITUTE statements into this formula, but the result would have been needlessly com-plex, and it would not have been as straightforward as comparing the two helper ranges. For example, if we came across another piece of punctuation that needed to be removed, then applying the same process to each helper range would be really simple.

A Few Words About Data Matching

Data matching has rather a bad name at the moment, and it's true that it forms the basis of much of the so-called "surveillance economy"! It's also true that as librarians we need to exercise caution on these grounds—storing information on which books people have been reading or who has been reading particular books is not only unethical but also potentially illegal. However, most of the uses of the lookup functions we have been considering are innocuous and also highly useful. For example, the data on public libraries includes really useful information like the numbers of books, ebooks, and videos held by each library, the number of loans, the number of visits to the library, and the number of reference inquiries. A new spreadsheet comes out every year, so if we wanted to track trends over time we could bring several of them together, then use our lookup functions to pull the information we wanted onto a single worksheet with a column for each year. Because there won't be one data source containing everything you ever wanted to know, the use of multiple sources will be quite normal.

The key to good data matching is having a good lookup value, the common element between two worksheets that allows us to rely on the fact that all of the data that we are combining relates to the same entity. Numbers and unique identifiers are particularly useful, which is why ISBNs, ISSNs, and DOIs have become such a valued feature of the library world, but we have already seen that in the case of ISBNs that they are not in fact unique in relation to titles, so we have had fall back on the use of words as identifiers. While this is generally fine, it is not without risk, and we need to bear in mind the importance of always having a reality check. This is particularly the case for books with short titles—*Persuasion* may be a book by Jane Austen, but there could also be a dozen marketing books of the same name!

In Chapter 8 we are going to look at advanced techniques of data analysis, which will be based on the existence of rich and complex data, and in Chapter 9 we will look in more detail at the process of gathering data from various sources, so what you have learned in this chapter will be highly relevant. If you have struggled with INDEX/MATCH, it will be well worth the effort of going back over the examples and the exercises in this chapter to make sure that you have thoroughly mastered it, because a simple reliance on VLOOKUP will deprive you of access to much of the really valuable information that could make a big difference to your library and to you.

CHAPTER EIGHT

The Power of Pivot Tables

A Closer Look at Filters

We have spent a lot of time looking at things we can do with data, counting it, averaging it, matching it with other data, and so on, and generally our data has sat in separate worksheets that we have operated on from outside, that is, from another worksheet. One of the things we will have noticed, however, is that our raw data will not be perfect, that it will contain variations, inconsistencies, and misspellings that will affect the operation of some of our formulas. Given that much of our data is textual and that it will have come from a variety of sources, probably entered by a number of individuals, some degree of variability is probably inevitable. We may also come to realize that what our formulas do is present generalizations about data, such as that 10% of books account for 80% of the loans from our library, but that this doesn't tell us what those books are. It's useful, therefore, to be able to drill into our data find variations, and to uncover patterns and filtering is a good way of doing this. Once we have mastered the use of filters, we will move on to look at pivot tables, which combine the functions of formulas that we have already seen with an ability to apply these to slices of data based on filters.

Here are some lines of data from our vendor's list of book titles, publishers, and prices:

http://bit.ly/2LqnD4U (Sheets)
https://bit.ly/2W2k489 (Excel—download and save)

	A	B	C	D	E
1	**Place**	**Publisher**	**Year**	**Title**	**List Price**
2	New York	Longman	1998	An Introduction to Human Factors Engineering	$24.45
3	Crans-Pre	RotoVision	2007	Still Life and Special Effects Photography: A Guide to Professional Lighting Techniques	$50.11
4	Milton Qld.	John Wiley & Sons Australia, Ltd	2002	Managing Organisational Change	$127.66
5	Hoboken N.J.	Wiley	2010	Becoming a Master Manager: A Competing Values Approach	$93.43

As we saw in Chapter 2, it is possible to make selections from within this data by using filters. Let's say we want to identify all rows relating to the Blackwell publishing house, which could be described in various ways— Blackwell, Basil Blackwell, Wiley Blackwell, and so on. Because of these different iterations of the name simply sorting the spreadsheet on the *Publisher* column will not be effective, so we need to look *inside* the publisher names instead. This is done by limiting the display of the worksheet only to rows in which the *Publisher* column contains the word *Blackwell*. In Sheets we click on the *Filter* icon and then on the drop-down arrow for the *Publisher* header:

Filter by values is selected by default and, as you can see, all possible values in the column, that is all the publisher names, are ticked. The first task is to click on *Clear* to remove these selections and then type the name we want into the search box:

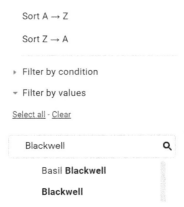

Sort A → Z

Sort Z → A

▸ Filter by condition

▾ Filter by values

Select all - Clear

| Blackwell   🔍 |

Basil **Blackwell**

Blackwell

All the options now appear, anything containing our search string, as we can see by scrolling down:

Blackwell

Blackwell Publishing

Blackwell Science

Wiley-**Blackwell**

If we now tick on *Select all* and then *OK*, all these entries, and these entries only, are visible:

	A	B	C	D	E
1	**Place**	**Publisher**	**Year**	**Title**	**List Pri**
72	Malden Mass.	Blackwell	2000	The handbook of linguistics	$74.95
92	Chichester West	Wiley-Blackwell	2012	Research Methods in Second Language Acquisition: A Practical Guide	$43.32
116	Malden (Massac	Blackwell Publishing	2008	A Companion to Greek Tragedy	$64.50
148	Oxford	Basil Blackwell	1985	An introduction to contemporary epistemology	$90.68
214	Oxford	Blackwell Science	2000	Ecological economics : an Introduction	$171.50
333	Oxford	Blackwell	1998	Art in theory 1815-1900: An anthology of changing ideas	$45.38

As you can see from the row numbers to the left, a selection has been made from the much larger set of data. If we now want to add to the selection all the titles containing the name *Wiley*, we click again on the *Filter* icon in the Header Row and enter it into the search box:

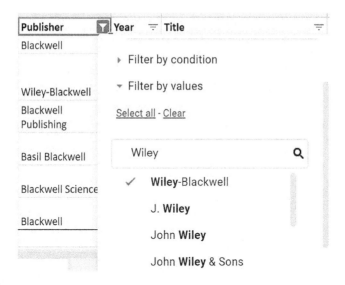

You will see here that the Wiley-Blackwell options are already selected, so we now click on *Select all* to add the other Wiley iterations:

More rows have now become visible:

	A	B	C	D	E
1	Place	Publisher	Year	Title	List Pri
4	Milton Qld.	John Wiley & Sons Australia, Ltd	2002	Managing Organisational Change	$127.66
5	Hoboken N.J.	Wiley	2010	Becoming a Master Manager: A Competing Values Approach	$93.43
17	Hoboken NJ	Wiley	2011	The world food economy	$79.58
19	Chichester	Wiley	1997	Applied Fluvial Geomorphology for River Engineering and Management	$102.45
72	Malden Mass.	Blackwell	2000	The handbook of linguistics	$74.95
74	Hoboken N.J.	John Wiley & Sons	2004	Essentials of WISC-IV Assessment	$20.43
92	Chichester West	Wiley-Blackwell	2012	Research Methods in Second Language Acquisition: A Practical Guide	$43.32

The result of a filtering operation is known as a *View*—this is because nothing has actually changed with the worksheet, but what we can *see* has altered.

This operation is very similar in Excel. When we click on the *Filter* icon, drop-down arrows appear in each of the Header cells, and when we click on *Publisher,* all the publisher names are presented. We click *Select all* to remove the ticks and enter the publisher name, then click on *OK:*

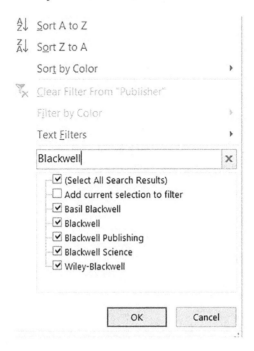

When we come to add the second option, we select *Add current selection* to the filter before clicking *OK:*

Having filtered on the *Publisher* column, we could add a second filter on *Place* to see only those rows where the place of publication was New York or Oxford. Because the process is identical, it is not necessary to repeat it, but our filtered spreadsheet now looks like this:

	A	B	C	D	E
1	**Place**	**Publisher**	**Year**	**Title**	**List Price**
107	New York	John Wiley & Sons	2003	Early Childhood Assessment	$76.09
108	New York N.Y.	John Wiley & Sons	1997	Handbook of human factors and ergonomics	$184.61
121	New York	Wiley	2001	Handbook of the psychology of women and gender	$90.00
124	New York	John Wiley & Sons	2003	Media training 101: A guide to meeting the press	$62.32
148	Oxford	Basil Blackwell	1985	An introduction to contemporary epistemology	$90.68

Those of you familiar with Boolean logic might notice that this *View* corresponds to the search formulation

(Blackwell OR Wiley) AND (New York OR Oxford)

When you have a very large data set, filtering can be a useful method of searching it for relevant information.

Value filters give us direct access to all the entries in the column, and we can select or unselect as many as we wish. If we decided, for example, that we did not wish to see the rows relating to John Wiley & Sons Australia, we could simply remove the tick for that entry. By using the search function, we are also able to include multiple variations in our *View* without having to scan through our data visually to find them. However, there will be times when the search feature will not be useful in defining exactly what it is we are trying to filter by. We might want, for example, to identify books published in the English city of York, only to discover that the search pulls up everything published in New York. Not helpful! In this case we would need to specify that the name of the place of publication had to begin with *York*. This is known as a *condition* rather than a value, and the filter will be a *Conditional filter* rather than a *Value filter*. Conditional filters are particularly useful for nontext values such as numbers and dates.

To illustrate this, we can add a third filter to our earlier selection that will limit our *View* to titles to costing $80 or less. In Sheets we filter the *List Price* column and choose the condition *Less than or equal to:*

The value is entered and we click on *OK:*

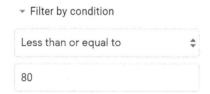

The sheet is now filtered accordingly:

1	Place	⧩	Publisher	⧩	Year	⧩	Title	⧩	List Pri⧩
107	New York		John Wiley & Sons		2003		Early Childhood Assessment		$76.09
124	New York		John Wiley & Sons		2003		Media training 101: A guide to meeting the press		$62.32
168	New York		Wiley		1978		Principles of sedimentology		$33.95
212	New York		J. Wiley		1997		Dangerous earth: An introduction to geologic hazards		$54.63
333	Oxford		Blackwell		1998		Art in theory 1815-1900: An anthology of changing ideas		$45.38

Because there are filters in place for the *Place, Publisher,* and *List Price* columns, a *Filter* icon now appears in the row headers, and you can click on this to identify what the filter is based on:

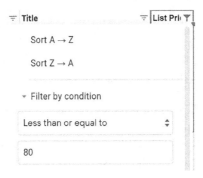

The process in Excel is more or less identical:

You will notice that Excel does not use the term "Conditional filter," because it recognizes that the *List Price* column contains numbers we are offered a range of Number Filters. The *Less Than Or Equal To* option is chosen:

Once it is in place, a simple mouseover will reveal detail about the filter:

Conditional Filtering by Text

A conditional filter can also be created by a text string. If we wanted to see only those rows in which the publisher name was simply *Wiley*, this can only be done with difficulty by using the search function in a Value filter because you would have to scroll through all the other options and tick only the one selection. In Sheets we will clear all the filtering and begin again, this time using the *Filter by condition* option on the *Publisher* column:

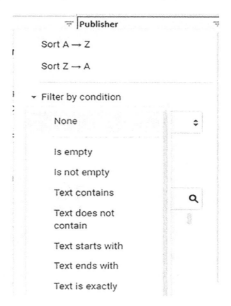

Choosing *Text is exactly* we enter our term and click *OK:*

▼ Filter by condition
Text is exactly ⬍
Wiley

Here is the result:

Publisher	Year	Title	List Price
Wiley	2010	Becoming a Master Manager: A Competing Values Approach	$93.43
Wiley	2011	The world food economy	$79.58
Wiley	1997	Applied Fluvial Geomorphology for River Engineering and Management	$102.45
Wiley	2001	Handbook of the psychology of women and gender	$90.00
Wiley	1978	Principles of sedimentology	$33.95
Wiley	1976	Ethics and anthropology: dilemmas in fieldwork	$124.10

Once you have done this, however, it would not be possible to add a second condition. The filter could be changed to show only rows with the exact publisher name Blackwell, but you could not create a conditional filter for both exact name Blackwell or exact name Wiley. If you wanted to do this, you would need to return to using a Value filter and selecting only those two options:

Again, the process is similar in Excel, but it detects that the *Publisher* column contains text and accordingly offers Text Filters:

The *Equals* option is chosen, and in this case it is possible to make a second choice:

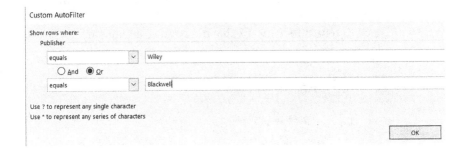

However, if you wish to make a third choice, you would need to revert to selecting the exact values.

Wildcards in Text Filters

We've seen that it is possible to specify phrases like *Blackwell Science* in filters, which opens the possibility of filtering by whole classes of data such as, say, all the titles published by university presses—if we filter the *Publisher* column on the phrase *University Press,* we will capture everything from *Harvard University Press, Oxford University Press, Sydney University Press,* and so on. However, there are a number of university presses, such as *University of Minnesota Press,* that do not conform to this pattern in that the exact phrase *University Press* does not occur in the name. In this case we can use the * wildcard, which stands for any number of characters:

▾ Filter by condition

| Text contains   ⬍ |

| University*press |

One thing to note is that if you enter

University*Press

you will not capture any of the *University Press* publishers because you have accidentally specified that there are at least two spaces between the two words! So although

University*press

may feel wrong, it will always work because the * wildcard stands for any number of characters including one.

EXERCISE

http://bit.ly/2LqnD4U (Sheets)
https://bit.ly/2W2k489 (Excel—download and save)

Open a copy of the spreadsheet and use filters to show the rows corresponding to the following:

- published by a university press
- later than 2011
- costing $90 or less

How many of these were published in New York, and what were the names of the publishers?

Saving Filter Views

When we have finished using a filter, we can clear it by clicking on the *Filter* icon again to return to viewing all rows of data, but if we wish to, we can save this set of criteria as a *Filter view* and return to it at any time. In Sheets, once you have the desired set of filters in place, this is done from the *Data* tab:

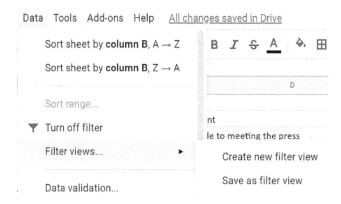

When we click on *Save as filter view*, the screen appears like this:

	A	B	C	D	E
	Place ▼	Publisher ▼	Year ⇒	Title ⇒	List Pri ▼
107	New York	John Wiley & Sons	2003	Early Childhood Assessment	$76.09
124	New York	John Wiley & Sons	2003	Media training 101: A guide to meeting the press	$62.32
168	New York	Wiley	1978	Principles of sedimentology	$33.95
212	New York	J. Wiley	1997	Dangerous earth: An introduction to geologic hazards	$54.63
333	Oxford	Blackwell	1998	Art in theory 1815-1900: An anthology of changing ideas	$45.38

Name: Filter 1   Range: A1:E352

You can see in the Name box at top left of the screen that it has been given the default name *Filter 1*, but we can edit it to something more descriptive:

Name: Blackwell&Wiley<=80

Once this has been done, filtering can be turned off simply by clicking on the *Filter* icon. In the future whenever we wish to use this filter, we simply click on *Data/Filter* views:

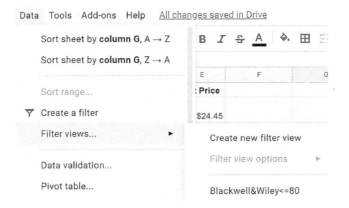

As you can see, the filter *Blackwell&Wiley<=80* is waiting to be used.

A similar process is followed in Excel. Once the filters are in place, click on the *View* tab and then on *Custom Views:*

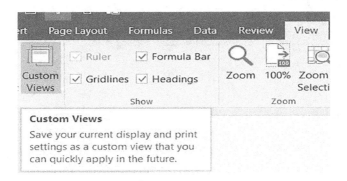

Now the *Custom View* box will appear, and you will be invited to add a permanent *View* based on the current settings of the worksheet, which in this case is a set of filters:

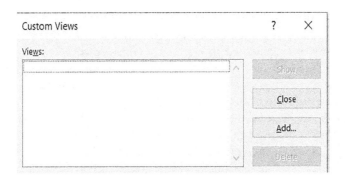

You now enter the name and click on *OK:*

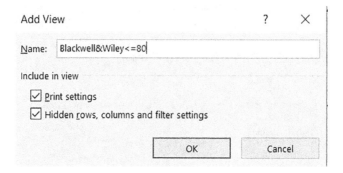

To invoke the filter in the future, simply click on *Data/Custom Views* again, and it will appear as an item to be selected by clicking on *Show:*

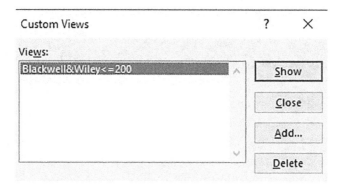

EXERCISE

Save the filter set you created in the previous exercise as a *View.*

There will be times when you want to create a set of rows based on a criterion that is not contained in any of the existing columns. Let's say, for example, that we become aware of the fact that a number of large publishers account for a majority of the items in our list, but we want to look specifically at those titles coming from publishers with only one or two books present in our data. There is no way to use any of the existing columns to create this filter, so instead we need to turn to the idea of a helper column that will provide the information on which a filter could operate. We came across the idea of a helper column in Chapter 7 where it was used to provide a unique identifier for each city/state combination, but this time we will use it to provide a counter for each publisher in column B. To do this we enter the header *Publisher Titles* at the top of column F, and then enter the following formula into cell F2, which is then copied down the whole column:

$$=COUNTIF(B:B,B2)$$

If we then filter on this column to *Less than 3*, this is what our worksheet looks like:

	Place	Publisher	Year	Title	List Price	Publisher Tit
3	Crans-Pres-Celigr	RotoVision	2007	Still Life and Special Effects Photography: A Guide to Professional Lighting Techniques	$50.11	1
4	Milton Qld.	John Wiley & Sons Australia, Ltd	2002	Managing Organisational Change	$127.66	1
6	Cambridge	Polity Press	2007	Media Work	$62.69	2
7	Harlow	Pearson Longman	2008	Language Leader: Upper Intermediate	$35.00	1
9	Edinburgh	Edinburgh University Press	2009	Media audiences: Television, meaning and emotion	$35.95	1
16	San Francisco	Chronicle Books	2000	Coming into focus: a step-by-step guide to alternative photographic printing processes	$44.29	2
18	New York	New York University Press	2003	Female intelligence: Women and espionage in the first world war	$36.24	1
22	North Ryde N.S.V	Law Book Co.	2006	Property valuation and analysis	$202.14	1
23	London	Routledge Classics	2002	The Road to Serfdom	$65.31	1
25	Basingstoke	Palgrave Macmillan Limited	2002	The transformation of cities: Urban theory and urban life	$51.99	1

EXERCISE

Clear all the filters on your spreadsheet on your worksheet and create a new helper column showing the number of titles published in each place of publication. Filter this column to show only items published in cities with 40 or more titles present in the data. If you click on the *Filter* icon at the top of the *Place* column, you will see the names of these cities.

Filtering is a really useful skill to acquire, and it pays to spend time becoming familiar with its operation in Sheets or Excel. It is essentially the same operation in both systems with the difference being that Excel won't offer the numerical options if the column contains text or the text options if it contains numbers. We should be aware, however, that filtering is essentially a "view" operation that does not have an analytical function. It is possible to create a formula that will count the number of books published in *Hoboken*. If column A has the range Name *place*, the formula is

$$=COUNTIF(place,"Hoboken*")$$

This formula returns the result 4, and sure enough if we filter the *Place* column, we will find that there are indeed rows that start with the text string *Hoboken*. Using a formula again, we could calculate the total value of books published in that place:

=SUMIFS(list_price,place,"Hoboken")*

Here the result is 378.54. However, there is no way to perform this operation on filter data—if we put a SUM formula at the bottom of the price column, it will sum all the values in the column, not just the ones we can see. As already noted, the filter is only a *view* that restricts the data that we can see but does not act upon it, anyway. If we wish to combine this sort of *View* with the analytical properties of formulas, we need to turn to our next topic, pivot tables.

Pivot Tables

By now you will have a good sense of the power of spreadsheets to sort and analyze data. Data comes to us in the form of specific "instances"—book titles with publishers and prices, borrowing transactions at a library or across a library system, staff and collection numbers for each library in the country. These instances generally occur as single rows in the spreadsheet, and the formulas we have been using are able to sift through them to count the number of books borrowed by a single person over the course of a year, or the total value of books the library system has purchased from a specific vendor or publisher for a given month or year. To do this we have created deduplicated lists of borrower numbers or publisher names and then used formulas like COUNTIF, COUNTIFS, SUMIF, SUMIFS, AVERAGEIF, and AVERAGEIFS to summarize the data and show us the patterns that we call information. This is vastly more efficient than sifting through masses of paper documents, and it also allows us to adopt an "experimental" approach, delving into the data to test and possibly confirm our intuitions and even to develop future scenarios that would allow us to choose between alternative courses of action. In the course of doing this we have seen the importance of good practice, of dedicating each row and each column to a single purpose, of giving our columns of data clear and explanatory headings, of naming ranges, and of reality-checking our results against the test of common sense.

While these tools are incredibly useful, they can also be complex and cumbersome. By the time we have set three or four conditions on our COUNTIFS, SUMIFS, and AVERAGEIFS formulas (and made sure that exactly the same conditions have been set for each formula), we are looking at a dense and somewhat opaque string of characters started with parentheses, commas, colons, and quote marks. If we decide to change our view of the data, or to create a new scenario, we need to make sure that each of these formulas is changed in an absolutely consistent manner, and the new formulas may need to be copied down every single row of a long worksheet. And then, even if our documenting of our work is exemplary, if we come back to the spreadsheet in six months' time, we will struggle at first to work out what it was all about. In practice, most of us rely on our formulas to document and explain themselves.

If the purpose of spreadsheeting is to automate complex and repetitive data operations, would it be possible for the process of formula creation itself to be automated? Unsurprisingly, the answer to this question is *yes,* and the means through which this is done is the *pivot table.* Many users of spreadsheets avoid pivot tables on the grounds that they are unduly complex and that the concept itself is difficult to understand, but once you have mastered the art of using them, you will take your data analysis to a whole new level of efficiency and effectiveness. Like many of the other skills you have learned so far, becoming fluent with the use of pivot tables requires practice and a willingness to test your ideas, but it will more than repay the effort that you put in. By the time you have finished this chapter, you may be feeling slightly annoyed, thinking "why wasn't I told this before, why did I have to go through all that pain with nesting and commas and parentheses?" Rest assured, however, that the pain was worth it even if only to allow you to appreciate the possibilities that spreadsheeting brings to us. There will also be occasions when a pivot table simply won't be possible, and you will have to fall back on manually created formulas, so the skills that you have acquired so far won't be entirely redundant.

So what is a pivot table? Essentially, it is a summary of data of the type that we have already seen, but it is created by a somewhat different process, not by the writing of formulas but by built-in features of the spreadsheet software that allow header names to be used to define data elements, which are then brought together in new combinations by using your computer mouse rather than your formula-writing skills. Unfortunately, the name "pivot table" is not very descriptive, and words alone only gives a hazy notion of what it's all about. It's easier to get the idea by seeing it in action. Once again, here are the first rows of data in the worksheet *PriceList:*

	Place	Publisher	Year	Title	List Price	Publisher Tit
3	Crans-Pres-Celigr	RotoVision	2007	Still Life and Special Effects Photography: A Guide to Professional Lighting Techniques	$50.11	1
4	Milton Qld.	John Wiley & Sons Australia, Ltd	2002	Managing Organisational Change	$127.66	1
6	Cambridge	Polity Press	2007	Media Work	$62.69	2
7	Harlow	Pearson Longman	2008	Language Leader: Upper Intermediate	$35.00	1
9	Edinburgh	Edinburgh University Press	2009	Media audiences: Television, meaning and emotion	$35.95	1
16	San Francisco	Chronicle Books	2000	Coming into focus: a step-by-step guide to alternative photographic printing processes	$44.29	2
18	New York	New York University Press	2003	Female intelligence: Women and espionage in the first world war	$36.24	1
22	North Ryde N.S.V	Law Book Co.	2006	Property valuation and analysis	$202.14	1
23	London	Routledge Classics	2002	The Road to Serfdom	$65.31	1
25	Basingstoke	Palgrave Macmillan Limited	2002	The transformation of cities: Urban theory and urban life	$51.99	1

Before we begin, here is a useful piece of new terminology—the *Field*. Our data consists of five columns each with a Header and these now become Field names—*Place, Publisher, Year, Title,* and *List Price*. Using good descriptive headers makes the use of pivot tables much easier, and you should note that these are not the same as Range Names—you don't need to have manually named the Range to use it as a Field.

Let's see a pivot table in action. Here is the start of a Google Sheets pivot table based on this data summarizing the entries in the worksheet by *Publisher:*

	A	B	C	D
1	Publisher	COUNTA of Publisher	AVERAGE of List Price	SUM of List Price
2	A. & C. Black	1	$45.00	$45.00
3	Academic Press	1	$47.93	$47.93
4	Aegean Publishing Co	1	$33.33	$33.33
5	Allen & Unwin	12	$40.85	$490.16
6	Allyn & Bacon	1	$70.00	$70.00
7	Allyn and Bacon	4	$108.73	$434.92
8	AltaMira Press	1	$29.80	$29.80

You will notice that four or five distinct operations have been carried out on the raw data:

- A sorted and deduplicated list of publishers has been created (SORT/UNIQUE)
- The number of titles for each publisher has been calculated (really COUNTIF, although it is displayed as COUNTA)
- The average price of each publisher has been calculated (AVERAGEIF)
- The total sum of prices has been calculated for each publisher (SUMIF)

However, all of this has been achieved without the writing of a single formula. Here is how it was done in Sheets:

From the worksheet that you wish to analyze click on *Data/Pivot table*:

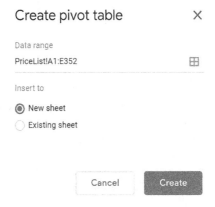

Sheets will automatically select the whole of the worksheet as the range to analyze and will offer to create the pivot table in a *New sheet*. These are the correct options so click on *Create*.

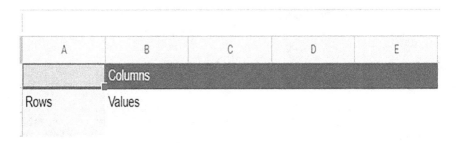

Your empty Pivot table will look like this, but a set of options will be displayed in the *Pivot table editor* to the right of the screen:

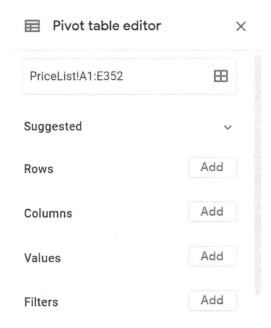

None of the suggested analyses fits what we wish to do, which is to work with the *Publisher* column in our data. We click on the *Add* button for Rows, and the Field names are displayed. Because we wish to have a separate row for each publisher, we select *Publisher:*

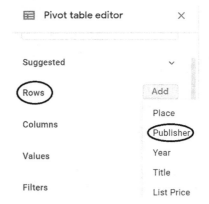

A sorted and deduplicated list of publishers appears in column A of the Pivot table:

	A	B
1	*Publisher*	
2	A. & C. Black	
3	Academic Press	
4	Aegean Publishing Co	
5	Allen & Unwin	
6	Allyn & Bacon	
7	Allyn and Bacon	
8	AltaMira Press	
9	American Society of Agricultural Engineers	

Our next task is to calculate the number of titles for each publisher. This is a *Value*, in other words something not directly contained in the data but calculated from it. (It's worth recognizing at this point that the use of the term "Value" is somewhat confusing here because when we looked at filtering, *Value* referred directly to the items in the column, which could be either text or numbers, whereas here it means something quite different, the *result of the calculation,* which has to be a number.) Anyway, in the *Pivot table editor* we now choose the *Values* option and click *Add*. Once again the Field names are displayed to choose from:

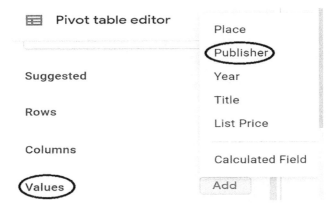

We can choose the *Publisher* option again, because our first task is simply to count how many times each individual publisher name occurs.

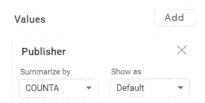

The default is to summarize the data by COUNTA, which is exactly what we want—you might recall that COUNTA is used to count rows containing text in a column. (There are a number of other options in addition to COUNTA, but because *Publisher* is a text Field none of the others produces a meaningful result.) The total number of rows relating to each publisher (i.e., the number of books they have published) appears in the adjacent column, and the pivot table now looks like this:

	Publisher	COUNTA of Publisher
1	*Publisher*	
2	A. & C. Black	1
3	Academic Press	1
4	Aegean Publishing Co	1
5	Allen & Unwin	12
6	Allyn & Bacon	1
7	Allyn and Bacon	4
8	AltaMira Press	1

Now we wish to calculate the average list price for each publisher, so we return to the *Pivot table editor*, click on *Values* again, and this time we select *List Price:*

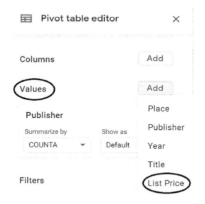

And we choose to summarize by *Average:*

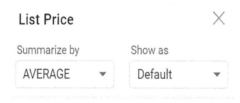

And here is the result:

Publisher	COUNTA of Publisher	AVERAGE of List Price
A. & C. Black	1	$45.00
Academic Press	1	$47.93
Aegean Publishing Co	1	$33.33
Allen & Unwin	12	$40.85
Allyn & Bacon	1	$70.00
Allyn and Bacon	4	$108.73
AltaMira Press	1	$29.80

The final step is to calculate the total cost of all titles from each publisher, and this is done by repeating the previous step with the *Sum* option chosen instead of *Average:*

Publisher	COUNTA of Publisher	AVERAGE of List Price	SUM of List Price
A. & C. Black	1	$45.00	$45.00
Academic Press	1	$47.93	$47.93
Aegean Publishing Co	1	$33.33	$33.33
Allen & Unwin	12	$40.85	$490.16
Allyn & Bacon	1	$70.00	$70.00
Allyn and Bacon	4	$108.73	$434.92
AltaMira Press	1	$29.80	$29.80

And that's our pivot table created without typing in a single character! The Header Row labels have been used to name the data elements, but it has not been necessary to create any Named ranges. At this point it might be useful to recap what has been done:

- Publisher has been selected as a **Row,** and as a result a deduplicated list of all the publisher names in the data has been created in the left-hand column
- Three **Values** have been selected, and each of these performs a mathematical operation on the publishers in the adjacent columns

Our selections can be seen in the *Pivot table editor:*

The next step takes us beyond what could have been done with the formulas we have learned so far—in fact, it would be very difficult to carry out using formulas. We have a list of publishers with numbers of titles, average prices, and the sum total of prices, but our data also contains the year of publication for each title, so the possibility exists of taking an even finer slice of information by breaking down these figures for each publisher in each year. You will have noticed that we used *Rows* for the publishers and *Values* for the other elements, but now we are going to add a second set of *Rows* that will show the year-based level of detail we require. Returning to our *Pivot table editor*, we select this second set by clicking on the *Add* button next to *Rows*. This time we choose *Year*:

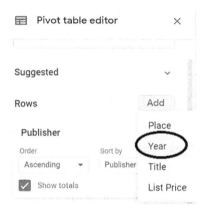

We now have two sets of entries under *Rows:*

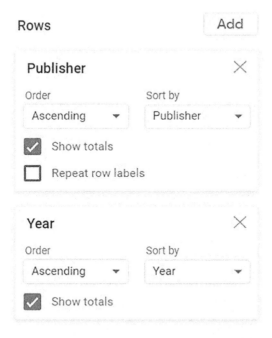

Because *Publisher* is the first entry, it constitutes the primary level, known in fact as the *primary key,* with *Year* being the *secondary key.* The pivot table now looks like this, with subtotals for each year and the full total for the publisher:

Publisher	Year	COUNTA of Publisher	AVERAGE of List Price	SUM of List Price
⊟ A. & C. Black	2002	1	$45.00	$45.00
A. & C. Black Total		1	$45.00	$45.00
⊟ Academic Press	2011	1	$47.93	$47.93
Academic Press Total		1	$47.93	$47.93
⊟ Aegean Publishing Cc	1993	1	$33.33	$33.33
Aegean Publishing Co Total		1	$33.33	$33.33
⊟ Allen & Unwin	1938	1	$18.95	$18.95
	1977	1	$59.95	$59.95
	2004	2	$29.91	$59.81
	2005	1	$59.62	$59.62
	2007	1	$53.95	$53.95
	2009	1	$45.00	$45.00
	2010	1	$39.95	$39.95
	2011	1	$21.95	$21.95
	2012	1	$39.95	$39.95
	2014	1	$49.66	$49.66
	2015	1	$41.37	$41.37
Allen & Unwin Total		12	$40.85	$490.16

And now, if we wish to make *Year* the primary element of analysis, we can simply drag *Year* above *Publisher* in the *Pivot table editor*:

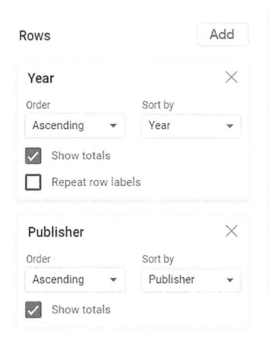

And this is what we get:

Year	Publisher	COUNTA of Publisher	AVERAGE of List Price	SUM of List Price
⊟	1938 Allen & Unwin	1	$18.95	$18.95
1938 Total		1	$18.95	$18.95
⊟	1952 Cohen & West	1	$55.42	$55.42
1952 Total		1	$55.42	$55.42
⊟	1959 Doubleday	1	$13.53	$13.53
1959 Total		1	$13.53	$13.53
⊟	1963 Princeton Univer	1	$39.95	$39.95
1963 Total		1	$39.95	$39.95
⊟	1969 Bodley Head	1	$156.34	$156.34
	Schocken Books	1	$16.94	$16.94
1969 Total		2	$86.64	$173.28

In Excel, the process is similar but not identical. Rather than initiating the pivot table from the worksheet containing the data you wish to analyze, you can create a new worksheet and insert a pivot table there. It is also necessary to specify the range of data to be included the table. This is done from the *Insert* tab where there is a *Pivot Table* option:

The range is then specified by clicking on the worksheet containing the data and using the mouse to select the columns to be included (or pressing Ctrl-A to select all):

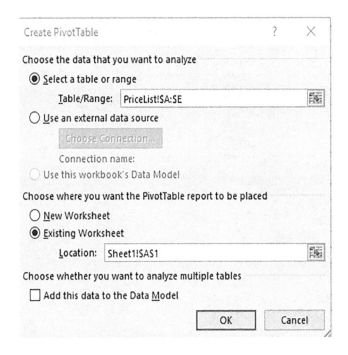

The *PivotTable Fields* box appears to the right of the screen, with the Fields listed at the top:

Adding *Rows* and *Values* to the Pivot table is very similar to what we have seen with Google Sheets, but even simpler. To create a row for *Publisher,* all that is needed is to tick the box.

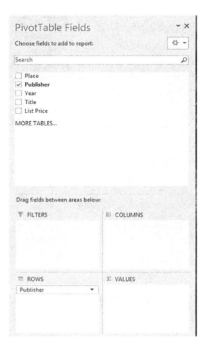

If we wish to know the number of titles for each publisher, we drag *Publisher* down to the *Values* area:

In fact, this would work for whichever Field we placed on the *Values* area, because it is simply counting the number of rows there are in the data for each publisher:

Row Labels	Count of Publisher
A. & C. Black	1
Academic Press	1
Aegean Publishing Co	1
Allen & Unwin	12
Allyn & Bacon	1
Allyn and Bacon	4
AltaMira Press	1

Rather than taking the Field name, the left-hand column is given the somewhat unappealing title of *Row Labels*—later we will look at changing this.

If we now wished to calculate the average list price for each publisher, we simply drag *List Price* down to the *Values* area and click on the drop-down arrow to change the *Value Field Settings* from the default of *Count:*

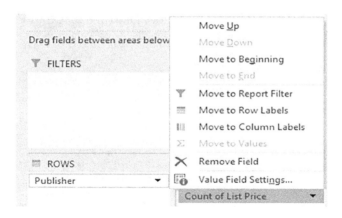

Obviously, the value we choose is *Average:*

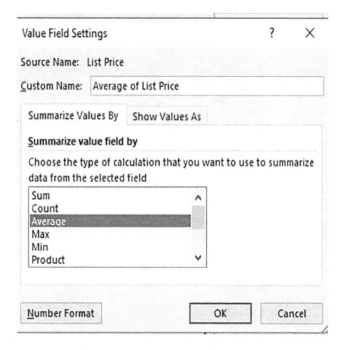

And our Pivot table now looks like this:

Row Labels	Count of Publisher	Average of List Price
A. & C. Black	1	45
Academic Press	1	47.93
Aegean Publishing Co	1	33.33
Allen & Unwin	12	40.846667
Allyn & Bacon	1	70
Allyn and Bacon	4	108.73
AltaMira Press	1	29.8

To get the total of prices for each publisher, we drag *List Price* to the *Values* area again and choose the *Sum* option:

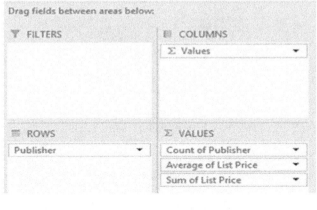

Row Labels	Count of Publisher	Average of List Price	Sum of List Price
A. & C. Black	1	45	45
Academic Press	1	47.93	47.93
Aegean Publishing Co	1	33.33	33.33
Allen & Unwin	12	40.846667	490.16
Allyn & Bacon	1	70	70
Allyn and Bacon	4	108.73	434.92
AltaMira Press	1	29.8	29.8

This looks better when we reformat the columns containing money values to *Currency:*

Row Labels	Count of Publisher	Average of List Price	Sum of List Price
A. & C. Black	1	$45.00	$45.00
Academic Press	1	$47.93	$47.93
Aegean Publishing Co	1	$33.33	$33.33
Allen & Unwin	12	$40.85	$490.16
Allyn & Bacon	1	$70.00	$70.00
Allyn and Bacon	4	$108.73	$434.92
AltaMira Press	1	$29.80	$29.80

Because we have done things in a slightly different order this time, the columns are ordered differently as well, but we can alter the arrangement by changing the order of the items in the *Values* area by dragging them:

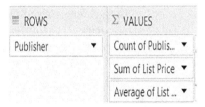

And the Pivot table changes accordingly:

Row Labels	Count of Publisher	Sum of List Price	Average of List Price
A. & C. Black	1	$45.00	$45.00
Academic Press	1	$47.93	$47.93
Aegean Publishing Co	1	$33.33	$33.33
Allen & Unwin	12	$490.16	$40.85
Allyn & Bacon	1	$70.00	$70.00
Allyn and Bacon	4	$434.92	$108.73
AltaMira Press	1	$29.80	$29.80

We might now decide to add *Year* as a secondary set of rows:

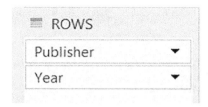

Our Pivot table now looks like this:

Row Labels	Count of Publisher	Sum of List Price	Average of List Price
⊟A. & C. Black	1	$45.00	$45.00
2002	1	$45.00	$45.00
⊟Academic Press	1	$47.93	$47.93
2011	1	$47.93	$47.93
⊟Aegean Publishing Co	1	$33.33	$33.33
1993	1	$33.33	$33.33
⊟Allen & Unwin	12	$490.16	$40.85
1938	1	$18.95	$18.95
1977	1	$59.95	$59.95
2004	2	$59.81	$29.91
2005	1	$59.62	$59.62

When you become fluent with the use of these tables, you will find that they can often provide a quick and easy alternative to writing formulas. For example, if we simply want to summarize the number of titles in the worksheet, their average price, and total value, this can be done simply by leaving the *Rows* area blank and specifying the calculations we want in the *Values* area:

Here is what this looks like in Sheets:

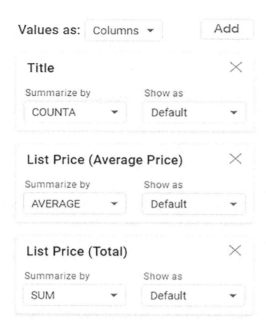

And in Excel:

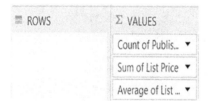

And the result is a simple summary of all the values in the worksheet:

Count of Publisher	Sum of List Price	Average of List Price
351	$24,614.17	$70.13

Here, *Count of Publisher* simply refers to the number of rows in the spreadsheet, or in other words the total number of books.

EXERCISE

http://bit.ly/2LqnD4U (Sheets)
https://bit.ly/2W2k489 (Excel—download and save)

Open a copy of the spreadsheet in Google Sheets or Excel.

Go to the *Pivot table 1* worksheet and add *Year* as a secondary row using the *Pivot table editor* (Sheets) or *PivotTable Fields* box (Excel).

How many 2013 titles from Cambridge University Press appear in the data, and what is their average price?

Go back to the *PriceList* worksheet, and click on *Data/Pivot table* to create a new one. This time select *Place* as the primary data element for Rows and *Year* as the secondary element. Use COUNTA (of Place), AVERAGE, and SUM (of List Price) as the *Values*.

What is the average price of books in the data published in London in 2002?

Filtering Pivot Tables

We have seen the ability of spreadsheets to count, sum, and average data in a fast and flexible manner without the need to write complex formulas, but so far we have been working with *all* the data in a specific sheet. If we had been using formulas, we would have chosen COUNT, COUNTA, SUM, and AVERAGE, but what about COUNTIF, SUMIF, and AVERAGEIF? These are conditional functions that allow us to analyze particular slices of the data—is it possible to use this approach when working with pivot tables? The answer is, obviously, *yes,* and this is done through filtering our pivot tables. Where the filtering of columns in a normal worksheet, which we have already seen, only affects our *view* of the data, when we filter pivot tables we are actually *restricting* the data on which they work, so that any calculations carried out by the pivot table will be governed by what is in the filter.

As we have already seen, when it comes to filtering, Sheets and Excel work in rather different ways, and switching between the two can be confusing. Neither of them is perfect, and each has different strengths and capabilities, so sometimes it might be necessary to test out your analysis on both systems to see which is going to give you the answers that you want. An easy starting point is to be aware of the fact that Sheets can only filter on Fields, while Excel is able to filter on the additional pivot table columns created by the *Values* area as well—that is, on the number of titles per publisher, average price, and total cost. This means that we can filter an Excel pivot table to include only titles from those publishers with more than, say, five titles, but because this is a calculated value it is not possible to do this in Sheets, without creating an additional helper column that makes this number explicit—the value in the helper column is then used to create the filter. As we will see, however, the advantage does not run all in Excel's favor, and there is at least one instance in which we will have to do use a helper column to filter a pivot table in that system as well. If you are serious about using pivot tables, it would be a good idea to become familiar with the functioning of both Excel and Sheets.

Looking first at Sheets, our data fields are *Place of publication, Publisher, Title, Year,* and *Price,* and our Pivot table is organized in rows by *Publisher* showing the numbers of titles for each publisher, the average price, and the total cost:

Row Labels	Count of Publisher	Average of List Price	Sum of List Price
A. & C. Black	1	$45.00	$45.00
Academic Press	1	$47.93	$47.93
Aegean Publishing Co	1	$33.33	$33.33
Allen & Unwin	12	$40.85	$490.16
Allyn & Bacon	1	$70.00	$70.00
Allyn and Bacon	4	$108.73	$434.92
AltaMira Press	1	$29.80	$29.80

We know that Melbourne, Australia, is the place of publication for some of these books, so we want to know these same details for those titles only. This is different from using Place as a *Row* value, because we wish to maintain the existing structure of the pivot table, and we suspect that some publishers have more than one place of publication. What we do then is to filter the table so that only titles with Melbourne as the place of publication are included in the analysis. This is done from the *Pivot table editor* by adding a filter in exactly the same manner we used for filtering columns in a worksheet:

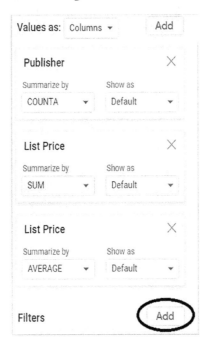

When we click on *Add*, the list of Fields is displayed and we choose *Place:*

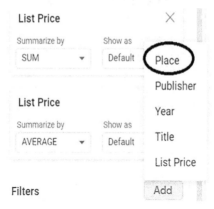

As before, we *Clear* the existing values, enter Melbourne into the search box, and click on *Select all,* then *OK:*

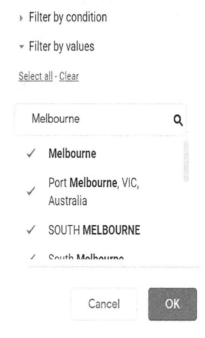

And here is the result:

Publisher	COUNTA of Publisher	SUM of List Price	AVERAGE of List Price
Cengage Learning	2	$214.00	$107.00
Nelson Cengage Learning New Zealand	1	$175.11	$175.11
Oxford University Press	13	$844.06	$64.93
Thomson	2	$204.72	$102.36
Grand Total	**19**	**$1,535.88**	**$80.84**

To complete our picture of Australian publishing, we can add Sydney, Crows Nest, and North Ryde:

Publisher	COUNTA of Publisher	SUM of List Price	AVERAGE of List Price
Cambridge University Press	1	$97.99	$97.99
Cengage Learning	2	$214.00	$107.00
Law Book Co.	1	$202.14	$202.14
McGraw-Hill Education	1	$114.91	$114.91
Murdoch Books	1	$24.63	$24.63
Nelson Cengage Learning New Zealand	1	$175.11	$175.11
New Holland	1	$87.63	$87.63
Oxford University Press	13	$844.06	$64.93
Sydney University Press	2	$58.00	$29.00
Thomson	2	$204.72	$102.36
Grand Total	**35**	**$2,434.45**	**$69.56**

The *Pivot table editor* alerts us to the presence of multiple items in the filter:

Filters	Add
Place	X
Status	
Showing 16 items	▼

If we add *Place* as a secondary row, we see again that there is some work to do on tidying up the entries in this field:

Publisher	Place	COUNTA of Publisher	SUM of List Price	AVERAGE of List Price
Allen & Unwin	Crows Nest	1	$21.95	$21.95
	Crows Nest Australia	1	$41.37	$41.37
	Crows Nest N.S.W.	5	$204.38	$40.88
	Crows Nest NSW	1	$39.95	$39.95
	Sydney	2	$103.61	$51.81
Allen & Unwin Total		10	$411.26	$41.13
Cambridge University Press	Port Melbourne, VIC, Australia	1	$97.99	$97.99
Cambridge University Press Total		1	$97.99	$97.99
Cengage Learning	South Melbourne Vic.	1	$99.00	$99.00
	South Melbourne, Vic.	1	$115.00	$115.00
Cengage Learning Total		2	$214.00	$107.00
Law Book Co.	North Ryde N.S.W.	1	$202.14	$202.14
Law Book Co. Total		1	$202.14	$202.14
McGraw-Hill Education	North Ryde	1	$114.91	$114.91
McGraw-Hill Education Total		1	$114.91	$114.91
Murdoch Books	Sydney	1	$24.63	$24.63
Murdoch Books Total		1	$24.63	$24.63

As we have already seen, pivot tables in Excel have a similar, although not identical, functionality to those in Sheets with a rather different look and feel. To begin with, there is an important distinction between filters placed on *Rows* and those placed on *Values*. To recap, it's useful to look at the *Pivot-Table Fields* box to get this distinction clear in our minds:

In this case, *Publisher* is the row and the *Values* are the numbers of titles, the average price, and total price for each publisher. If we wish to filter by *Publisher*, then we can do this directly in the Pivot table as it stands, simply by clicking on the drop-down arrow in the *Row Labels* header:

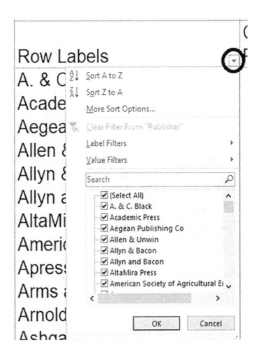

You will notice that we are given the option of *Label Filters* and *Value Filters*, which we will come back to shortly. At the moment we simply want to filter to those publishers with the word *Wiley* in their name, so we can enter this into the search box and click on *OK* to confirm the selection:

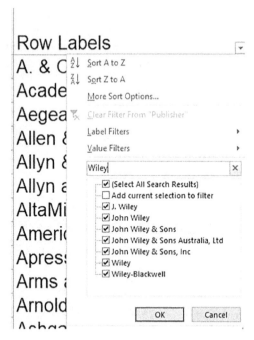

As already seen in filtering columns, we could add further publishers to this selection by entering them into the search box and ticking *Add current selection to filter.*

When it comes to filtering on Fields that are not *Rows*, such as *Place*, we drag them into the *Filters* area of the *PivotTable Fields* box:

In the pivot table this now appears as a separate row above the main table:

Place	(All)
	Count of
Row Labels	Publisher
A. & C. Black	1

The filtering is initially sent to *(All)*, but we use the drop-down arrow to access the choices. Again we use the search box to specify the places that we want and tick *Select Multiple Items* to confirm:

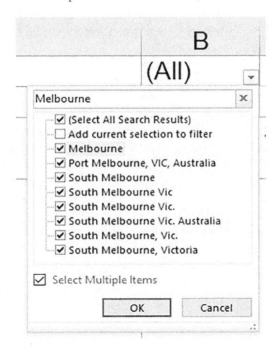

> Now select *Publisher* as a secondary Row to show which publishers relate to which cities. In this data, how many books with Wiley imprints were published in New York?
>
> You will notice that there is more than one variation of *New York—* how would you go about fixing this?

Filtering Pivot Tables by Condition

So far, we have created filters by selecting particular values in the Field on which we are filtering, but as we saw when filtering columns it is also possible to set Conditional filters for, say, publishers with the exact name Wiley or prices under $250. Once again, there are differences between the look-and-feel and functioning of Sheets and Excel.

In the examples above, we have seen that it is relatively easy to use a combination of search and select functions to create filters on the names of publishers or places, but there will be circumstances in which we will need to be a bit more specific in setting out the criteria. In the data we have been examining there are a large number of titles published in New York, but in addition to these there are a smaller number published in York in England and a few others published in North York in Ontario. To see only those published in York would be possible using filtering by Value, but it would not be as easy as specifying that we want only those places of publication beginning with the character string *York*. In Sheets this is a Conditional filter, which we have already encountered when filtering columns, and when we choose Conditional filtering on the *Place* Field, we have two potential choices, *Text starts with* and *Text is exactly:*

Text starts with

Text ends with

Text is exactly

We could start with *Text is exactly:*

With the *Row* value set to *Publisher* here is the result:

Publisher	COUNTA of Publisher	AVERAGE of List Price	SUM of List Price
York Medieval Press	2	$66.31	$132.62
Grand Total	**2**	**$66.31**	**$132.62**

But if we change to *Text starts with,* we get a more accurate result:

	A	B	C	D
	Publisher	COUNTA of Publisher	AVERAGE of List Price	SUM of List Price
	The Borthwick Institute, University of York	1	$175.00	$175.00
	York Medieval Press	3	$55.86	$167.57
	Grand Total	**4**	**$85.64**	**$342.57**

If we add *Place* as a secondary row, the reason for this is obvious:

Publisher	Place	COUNTA of Publisher	AVERAGE of List Price	SUM of List Price
⊟ The Borthwick Institute, University of York	York [England]	1	$175.00	$175.00
The Borthwick Institute, University of York Total		1	$175.00	$175.00
⊟ York Medieval Press	York	2	$66.31	$132.62
	York, UK	1	$34.95	$34.95
York Medieval Press Total		3	$55.86	$167.57
Grand Total		**4**	**$85.64**	**$342.57**

This sort of experimentation and testing is an important means of ensuring that our pivot tables provide an accurate summary of the data.

While Sheets has been able to create a Conditional filter on the *Place* Field even though *Place* is not itself a *Row* in the pivot table, this is not possible in Excel. With our primary Row Field set to *Publisher,* when we drag *Place* into the Filter area and click on the drop-down arrow, these are the choices:

The Label Filters and Number Filters options that we saw in the earlier example, when we were filtering by *Publisher*, are missing. In order to make them appear, it is necessary to make *Place* a secondary *Row*:

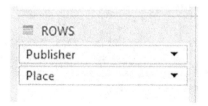

The left-hand column of the pivot table now looks like this:

Row Labels	Count of Publisher
⊟A. & C. Black	1
London	1
⊟Academic Press	1
Amsterdam	1
⊟Aegean Publishing Co	1
Santa Barbara	1
⊟Allen & Unwin	12
Crows Nest	1
Crows Nest Australia	1
Crows Nest N.S.W.	5
Crows Nest NSW	1
London	2
Sydney	2

When we click on the drop-down arrow in the *Row Labels* box, we now select *Place* as the filtering option:

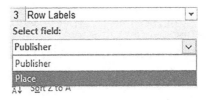

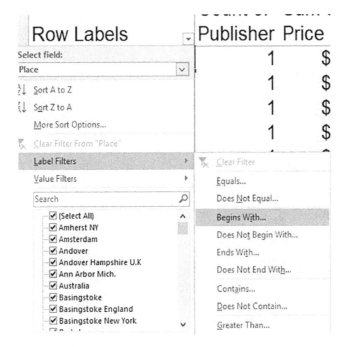

And then we make our selection

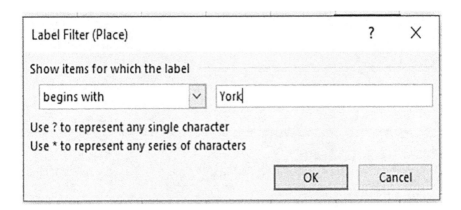

And here is the result:

Row Labels	Count of Publisher	Sum of List Price	Average of List Price
⊟York Medieval Press	3	$167.57	$55.86
York	1	$70.42	$70.42
York, England	1	$62.20	$62.20
York, UK	1	$34.95	$34.95
⊟The Borthwick Institute, University of York	1	$175.00	$175.00
York [England]	1	$175.00	$175.00
Grand Total	4	$342.57	$85.64

Conditional Filtering by Number

When we filter by number rather than by text, we use the *Greater Than, Greater Than Or Equal To, Less Than, Less Than Or Equal To, Equals,* or *Does Not Equal* options. In this case we will filter the pivot table to summarize only titles with a list price of $80 or less. In Sheets we go to the *Pivot table editor,* add a filter, and select *List Price*:

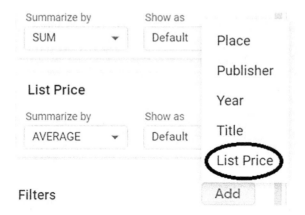

Again we choose *Filter by condition* and select the *Less than or equal to* option:

> ▾ Filter by condition
>
> | Less than or equal to | ⇕ |
> |---|---|
>
> | 80 |

Prices of more than $80 are now excluded from the summarizing options of the pivot table:

Publisher	COUNTA of Publisher	SUM of List Price	AVERAGE of List Price
A. & C. Black	1	$45.00	$45.00
Academic Press	1	$47.93	$47.93
Aegean Publishing Co	1	$33.33	$33.33
Allen & Unwin	12	$490.16	$40.85
Allyn & Bacon	1	$70.00	$70.00
Allyn and Bacon	2	$149.56	$74.78
AltaMira Press	1	$29.80	$29.80

As we have already seen, Excel does not offer *Label Filters* and *Number Filters* on Fields that are not *Rows*, so if we drag *List Price* into the Filter area, we are only offered selection by individual prices:

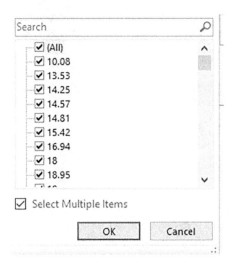

Obviously, having to select only prices under $80 would be very laborious, so one option is to make *List Price* a secondary Row:

Row Labels	Count of Publisher
⊟A. & C. Black	1
$45.00	1
⊟Academic Press	1
$47.93	1
⊟Aegean Publishing Co	1
$33.33	1
⊟Allen & Unwin	12
$14.81	1
$18.95	1
$21.95	1

In order to force the table to work on the *List Price* Field rather than *Publisher*, it is necessary to select one of the *List Price* cells (by clicking on it) before choosing the *Label Filters* option:

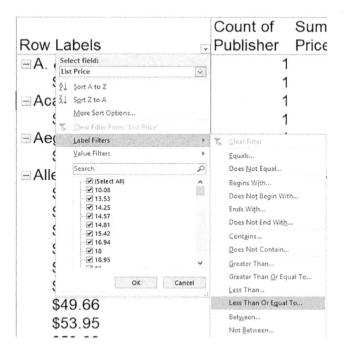

The value is then entered:

Label Filter (List Price)   ?   X

Show items for which the label

| is less than or equal to | ∨ | 80 |

Use ? to represent any single character
Use * to represent any series of characters

OK   Cancel

Our pivot table is now filtered to summarize only those titles costing $80 or less:

Row Labels	Count of Publisher	Sum of List Price	Average of List Price
⊟A. & C. Black	1	$45.00	$45.00
$45.00			5.00
⊟Academic Press			7.93
$47.93	1	$47.93	$47.93
⊟Aegean Publishing Co	1	$33.33	$33.33
$33.33	1	$33.33	$33.33
⊟Allen & Unwin	12	$490.16	$40.85
$14.81	1	$14.81	$14.81
$18.95	1	$18.95	$18.95
$21.95	1	$21.95	$21.95

Label Filters
List Price: is less than or equal to 80

Because it has been necessary to include *List Price* as a *Row*, the pivot table is very cluttered, so the next step is to suppress display of the secondary rows. When any cell within the pivot table is selected, you will notice that two Pivot Table tools appear at the top of the screen, *Analyze* and *Design:*

Click on *Analyze.* There are lots of really helpful features here that are beyond the scope of this chapter, but the one we are going to use is *Collapse Field:*

When you click on this, only the primary *Row* values are visible, although the plus sign to the left indicates the presence of hidden secondary rows:

Row Labels	Count of Publisher	Sum of List Price	Average of List Price
⊞ A. & C. Black	1	$45.00	$45.00
⊞ Academic Press			7.93
⊞ Aegean Publishing Co			.33
⊞ Allen & Unwin	12	$490.16	$40.85
⊞ Allyn & Bacon	1	$70.00	$70.00
⊞ Allyn and Bacon	2	$149.56	$74.78
⊞ AltaMira Press	1	$29.80	$29.80

(overlaid: Label Filters — List Price: is less than or equal to 80)

There is a further Conditional filter by *Number Labels* that can be done in Excel. The Pivot table has three *Values* attached to the *Publisher* Row—*Count of Publisher, Average of List Price,* and *Sum of List Price*—and these appear in the three columns to the right of *Publisher.* If we wish to filter the pivot table to include only items from those publishers with four or more titles in the list, this is simply done by clicking on the *Row Labels* drop-down arrow:

We choose *Value Filters* and *Greater Than Or Equal To,* but note that we could have used any of the other Values on which to filter:

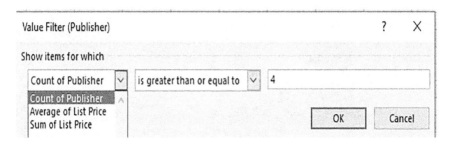

And the pivot table is adjusted accordingly:

Row Labels ⟱	Count of Publisher	Sum of List Price	Average of List Price
⊞ Allen & Unwin	12	$490.16	$40.85
⊞ Allyn and Bacon	4	$434.92	$108.73
⊞ Cambridge University Press	18	$1,216.37	$67.58
⊞ Cengage Learning	6	$424.43	$70.74
⊞ Human Kinetics	5	$199.76	$39.95
⊞ John Wiley & Sons	5	$403.59	$80.72
⊞ Longman	4	$221.43	$55.36
⊞ McGraw-Hill	4	$324.63	$81.16
⊞ MIT Press	5	$199.48	$39.90
⊞ Open University Press	5	$240.81	$48.16
⊞ Oxford University Press	27	$1,827.25	$67.68
⊞ Palgrave Macmillan	13	$865.39	$66.57
⊞ Pearson	5	$615.39	$123.08
⊞ Routledge	33	$1,975.19	$59.85
⊞ Sage	18	$1,577.18	$87.62
⊞ Sage Publications	5	$426.60	$85.32
⊞ Wiley	6	$523.51	$87.25
Grand Total	175	$11,966.09	$68.38

The total at the end of the table also adjusts down to $11,969 from $24,614 as it is no longer calculated on all the data, but only on prices from the larger publishers.

This operation is not possible in Sheets because, as already noted, Sheets is only able to filter on *Rows* and, although the count of titles for each publisher is part of the pivot table, it is a *Value*. Fortunately, it is a relatively simple matter to turn this number into a *Row* by adding a helper column to the original data. Again, here is what the data in the worksheet *PriceList* looks like:

Place ⊽	Publisher ⊽	Year ⊽	Title ⊽	List Price ⊽
New York	Longman	1998	An Introduction to Human Factors Engineering	$24.45
Crans-Pres-Celigny	RotoVision	2007	Still Life and Special Effects Photography: A Guide to Professional Lighting Techniques	$50.11
Milton Qld.	John Wiley & Sons Australia, Ltd	2002	Managing Organisational Change	$127.66
Hoboken N.J.	Wiley	2010	Becoming a Master Manager: A Competing Values Approach	$93.43
Cambridge	Polity Press	2007	Media Work	$62.69
Harlow	Pearson Longman	2008	Language Leader: Upper Intermediate	$35.00
London	Routledge	1999	The discourse reader	$66.16
Edinburgh	Edinburgh University Press	2009	Media audiences: Television, meaning and emotion	$35.95
Champaign Ill.	Human Kinetics	2008	Teaching Physical Activity: Change, Challenge, and Choice	$34.00
Oxford	Oxford University Press	2007	New Headway Academic Skills: Reading, Writing, and Study Skills. Level 3	$24.00

In cell B2 we have the name *Longman,* and we know that this name must occur at given number of times in column B. What we do then is to give column F the header *Publisher Titles* and then enter the following formula into cell F2:

$$=COUNTIF(B:B,B2)$$

This returns the result *12,* which tells us that Longman occurs 12 times in column B, so that when we copy the formula down column F every Row in which that name occurs will show the value *12.* What we then do is to add column F (*Publisher Titles*) to the pivot table and then filter on it to restrict the calculation to publishers with four or more titles.

So here is our data with the helper column added:

Place	Publisher	Year	Title	List Price	Publisher Titles
New York	Longman	1998	An Introduction to Human Factors Engineering	$24.45	4
Crans-Pres-Celigny	RotoVision	2007	Still Life and Special Effects Photography: A Guide to Professional Lighting Techniques	$50.11	1
Milton Qld.	John Wiley & Sons Australia, Ltd	2002	Managing Organisational Change	$127.66	1
Hoboken N.J.	Wiley	2010	Becoming a Master Manager: A Competing Values Approach	$93.43	6
Cambridge	Polity Press	2007	Media Work	$62.69	2
Harlow	Pearson Longman	2008	Language Leader: Upper Intermediate	$35.00	1
London	Routledge	1999	The discourse reader	$66.16	33
Edinburgh	Edinburgh University Press	2009	Media audiences: Television, meaning and emotion	$35.95	1
Champaign Ill.	Human Kinetics	2008	Teaching Physical Activity: Change, Challenge, and Choice	$34.00	5
Oxford	Oxford University Press	2007	New Headway Academic Skills: Reading, Writing, and Study Skills. Level 3	$24.00	27

Returning to the pivot table we first need to edit its top row to include the additional column from this:

▦ **Pivot table editor**　　　✕

PriceList!A1:E352　　　⊞

to this:

Now when we add the filter, column F has become a *Field*, and we can select it:

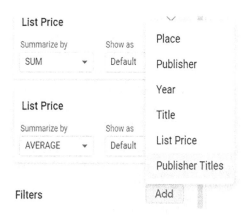

The Conditional filter *Greater Than Equal Or To* is now used:

The result is identical to that found by using Excel:

Publisher	COUNTA of Publisher	SUM of List Price	AVERAGE of List Price
Allen & Unwin	12	$490.16	$40.85
Allyn and Bacon	4	$434.92	$108.73
Cambridge University Press	18	$1,216.37	$67.58
Cengage Learning	6	$424.43	$70.74
Human Kinetics	5	$199.76	$39.95
John Wiley & Sons	5	$403.59	$80.72
Longman	4	$221.43	$55.36
McGraw-Hill	4	$324.63	$81.16
MIT Press	5	$199.48	$39.90
Open University Press	5	$240.81	$48.16
Oxford University Press	27	$1,827.25	$67.68
Palgrave Macmillan	13	$865.39	$66.57
Pearson	5	$615.39	$123.08
Routledge	33	$1,975.19	$59.85
Sage	18	$1,577.18	$87.62
Sage Publications	5	$426.60	$85.32
Wiley	6	$523.51	$87.25
Grand Total	**175**	**$11,966.09**	**$68.38**

EXERCISE

Clear any existing filters from your pivot table, and then filter it to calculate only rows where the place of publication is responsible for more than 15 titles.

Showing Values as Percentages

While the raw numbers calculated by pivot tables are useful, they are often not very revealing, so we might wish to express them as percentages. Let's start with a simple example in Sheets, with a pivot table showing only the number of titles for each publisher and the total cost:

Publisher	COUNTA of Publisher	SUM of List Price
A. & C. Black	1	$45.00
Academic Press	1	$47.93
Aegean Publishing Co	1	$33.33
Allen & Unwin	12	$490.16
Allyn & Bacon	1	$70.00
Allyn and Bacon	4	$434.92
AltaMira Press	1	$29.80

If we want to express COUNTA of *Publisher* as a percentage of the total number of titles in the data, we could simply alter its setting in the *Pivot table editor*:

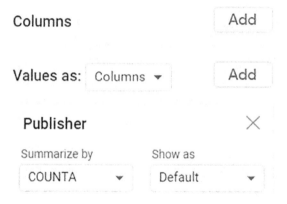

Currently, it is said to *Show as Default*, which simply means that a simple number will be generated. However, if we click on the drop-down arrow, we see a number of choices:

As there are 351 titles in the data, if we choose *% of grand total,* each publisher's number of titles will be expressed as a percentage of this number:

Publisher	COUNTA of Publisher
A. & C. Black	0.28%
Academic Press	0.28%
Aegean Publishing Co	0.28%
Allen & Unwin	3.42%
Allyn & Bacon	0.28%
Allyn and Bacon	1.14%
AltaMira Press	0.28%

It might make sense at this point to include the *Publisher* Field as a *Value* twice, the first showing the raw number and the second the percentage:

Publisher	COUNTA of Publisher	COUNTA of Publisher
A. & C. Black	1	0.28%
Academic Press	1	0.28%
Aegean Publishing Co	1	0.28%
Allen & Unwin	12	3.42%
Allyn & Bacon	1	0.28%
Allyn and Bacon	4	1.14%
AltaMira Press	1	0.28%

And we can repeat this with the total cost for each publisher:

Publisher	COUNTA of Publisher	COUNTA of Publisher	SUM of List Price	SUM of List Price
A. & C. Black	1	0.28%	$45.00	0.18%
Academic Press	1	0.28%	$47.93	0.19%
Aegean Publishing Co	1	0.28%	$33.33	0.14%
Allen & Unwin	12	3.42%	$490.16	1.99%
Allyn & Bacon	1	0.28%	$70.00	0.28%
Allyn and Bacon	4	1.14%	$434.92	1.77%
AltaMira Press	1	0.28%	$29.80	0.12%

What becomes really interesting is when we alter the values to show the average *List Price* for each publisher:

Publisher	AVERAGE of List Price
A. & C. Black	$45.00
Academic Press	$47.93
Aegean Publishing Co	$33.33
Allen & Unwin	$40.85
Allyn & Bacon	$70.00
Allyn and Bacon	$108.73
AltaMira Press	$29.80

If we go to the bottom of the table, we see the average for all titles in the data:

Yale University Press	$59.00
York Medieval Press	$55.86
YYZ Books	$288.00
Grand Total	**$70.13**

So the average cost of a book is $70.13. If we now add a second average *List Price* value and set it to show the percentage of the grand total, we can see whether the books of a given publisher cost more or less than the average:

Publisher	AVERAGE of List Price	AVERAGE of List Price
A. & C. Black	$45.00	64.17%
Academic Press	$47.93	68.35%
Aegean Publishing Co	$33.33	47.53%
Allen & Unwin	$40.85	58.25%
Allyn & Bacon	$70.00	99.82%
Allyn and Bacon	$108.73	155.05%
AltaMira Press	$29.80	42.50%

In Excel, the process is similar. *Publisher* is dragged to the *Values* area twice and by default appears as a *Count:*

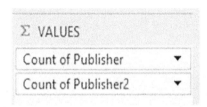

The drop-down arrow for the second iteration is clicked on and then *Value Field Settings* selected:

Summarize Values By is left on *Count,* and we click on *Show Values As:*

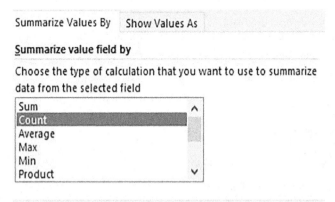

From the drop-down *% of Grand Total* is selected:

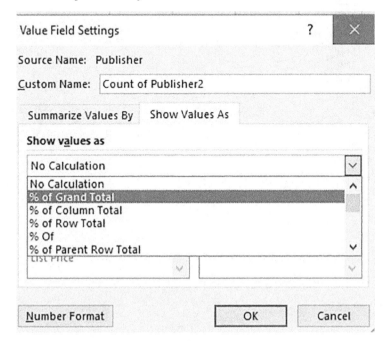

And here is the result:

Row Labels	Count of Publisher	Count of Publisher2
A. & C. Black	1	0.28%
Academic Press	1	0.28%
Aegean Publishing Co	1	0.28%
Allen & Unwin	12	3.42%
Allyn & Bacon	1	0.28%
Allyn and Bacon	4	1.14%
AltaMira Press	1	0.28%

The same process is followed to get the average of the *List Price:*

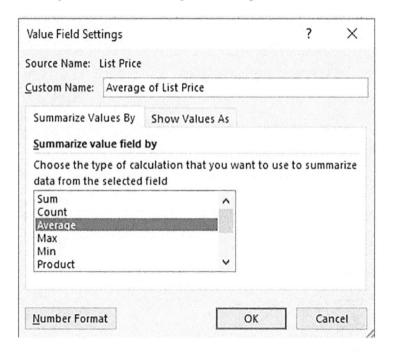

And to repeat this value as a percentage:

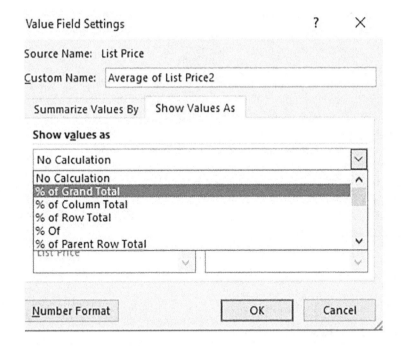

with this result in the pivot table:

Row Labels	Average of List Price	Average of List Price2
A. & C. Black	$45.00	64.17%
Academic Press	$47.93	68.35%
Aegean Publishing Co	$33.33	47.53%
Allen & Unwin	$40.85	58.25%
Allyn & Bacon	$70.00	99.82%
Allyn and Bacon	$108.73	155.05%
AltaMira Press	$29.80	42.50%

Changing Pivot Table Labels

So far we have been using the default pivot table labels provided by Sheets and Excel—*Average of List Price, Count of Publisher* or *COUNTA of Publisher,* and so on. This is convenient while we are creating the pivot tables because it is completely transparent to us as owners of the spreadsheet. We are familiar with the Field names and the pivot table functions, and it makes the process of editing and experimentation very easy, but one of the great values of a pivot table is that it can be used to summarize a large amount data for inclusion in a report or even a PowerPoint aimed at people who don't have access to the data itself. Unless we are able to use rather more descriptive labels, these summaries could be difficult for others to understand. For example, we know that *Count of Publisher* refers to the number of rows of the data in which the publisher name occurs, and from that we are able to infer the number of individual titles that the publisher is responsible for, but the label itself conveys none of this meaning—*Number of Titles* would make far more sense. The label *Row Labels* is particularly uninformative to anyone but a spreadsheet expert!

Fortunately, there is a simple way to change these labels in both Sheets and Excel, although Excel also provides a second alternative. Once you have got your pivot table as you want it, simply click on the individual cells in the first row of the table and you can edit them directly.

In Excel the label can be customized when the *Value Field Settings* are being created, from this:

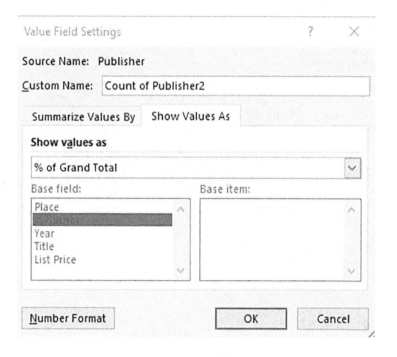

to this:

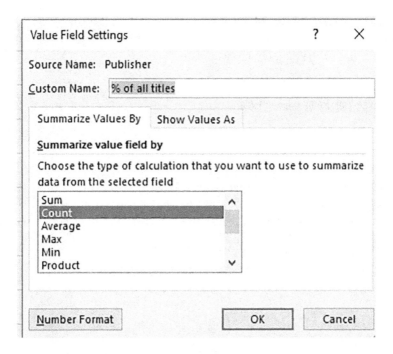

In Sheets, when you click on a label cell, the label itself appears in the *Formula* bar where it can be edited from this:

to this:

You should note that these are the only cells in a pivot table that can be edited. If you decide that the table is not showing *exactly* what you would like in a particular cell, you can't edit the cell to "correct" it—the cell, and the whole table, has been generated from the data by the specifications you have set, and you are not allowed to cheat, or at least not in this way. If you want a different outcome, you need to change the specifications (which would not be cheating) or the data (which would).

Refreshing Your Pivot Table in Excel

If you are using Sheets, your pivot table will automatically update if any of the values in the data are changed. For example, we have a variant name for the publisher *Allyn and Bacon* in the form of *Allyn & Bacon* so that our pivot tables have separate lines for these two versions, but if we remove the ampersand from the second version so that it becomes *Allyn and Bacon,* then the additional line disappears from the pivot table and the totals and averages are adjusted according. This does not happen automatically in Excel, but if you right-click on any cell within the pivot table, you are able to Refresh the table:

	Copy
	Format Cells...
	Refresh
	PivotTable Options...
	Hide Field List

Pivot Charts

The Pivot Chart feature allows us to make a quick and easy visualization of the data we have summarized in our pivot table. Here, for example, we have a table showing the number of titles for each publisher, filtered to university presses with three or more titles in the data:

Publisher	Titles
Cambridge University Press	18
Open University Press	5
Oxford University Press	27
Princeton University Press	3
University of California Press	3
Grand Total	56

If we click on the *Analyze* tab, there is a Pivot Chart icon to the right:

Clicking on this gives us a number of options for creating charts:

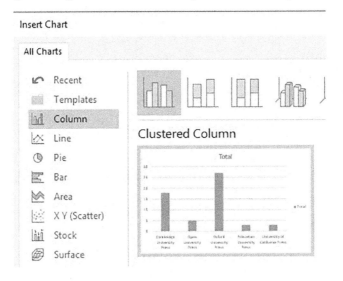

The *Clustered Column* option gives us this:

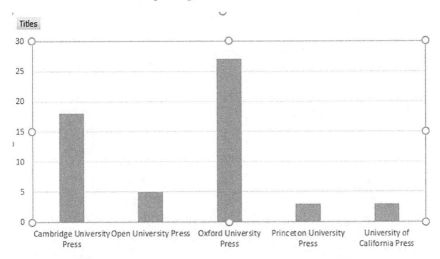

We will take a closer look at graphs and charts in Chapter 9.

Using Helper Columns to Categorize Data

Sometimes we might want to place our data into broad categories and then use pivot tables to make comparisons between these groupings. To a certain extent we can use filtering—for example, we could filter our table to exclude titles published after 2007 and then change the filter to exclude those published before 2008. However, unless we make two pivot tables, it is difficult to compare them side by side, so a useful trick is to create a helper column that will label our data in a way that can easily be picked up by a filter table. Let's say we want to create three classes of publishers:

- University presses
- Society publishers
- All others

To do this we could write a formula in column G:

=IF(ISNUMBER(FIND("University",B2)),"University Press",IF(OR(ISNUMBER (FIND("Society",B2)),ISNUMBER(FIND("Association",B2))),"Society","Other"))

We give column G the header *Type* and then create a pivot table showing the numbers of titles for each category and the average prices:

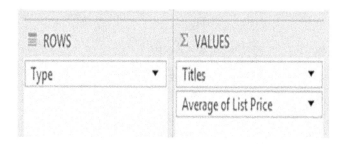

And here is a very neat summary of our data:

Publisher	Titles	Average of List Price
Other	263	$72.11
Society	3	$46.11
University Press	85	$64.84
Grand Total	351	$70.13

Summing It All Up

By now you will have become aware that pivot tables have the potential to save you a great deal of time and effort, both by removing the necessity for writing complex formulas and also by giving you the ability to interact with your data and to interrogate it. You will also be aware that the successful operation of pivot tables relies on well-structured data and clear labels in the Header Row. The data that we have been using in our examples and exercises contains a number of inconsistencies that the pivot tables have brought to light, so if nothing else we have some useful guidance on where additional housekeeping is needed, but the real power of the pivot table lies in its ability to draw out patterns that we might not otherwise have recognized. Are the titles from university presses more expensive than the average title in our data (*No*); are titles from New York more expensive than those from London (*Yes*)?

While answers to some of these questions could be found through the careful writing of formulas, this would be a tedious and time-consuming process and in some cases impossible. If you are using spreadsheets to analyze any but the simplest data, then becoming fluent in the creation and use of pivot tables will be essential. This chapter may have seemed dense at times, but it has really only scratched the surface, although I hope it has given you some sense of the excitement that comes from complex data analysis. Don't be afraid to try things out, and always remember that a pivot table is only a *view* of the data and that anything you do should not affect the data itself. As you practice, try out all the features and see if you can work out what they are doing. If some of the results you get seem odd, go back to the data and give it a reality check. It is usually possible to recreate the workings of a table by filtering the raw data, and doing so will give you a more hands-on sense of how your analysis has arrived at its results. As you become more familiar with this aspect of spreadsheeting, it will become second nature, and you will begin to think and see your data in filters and pivot tables. By which time you will have become a fully-fledged data analyst!

CHAPTER NINE

Looking at Graphs and Charts

Words and numbers are a great way of describing information, but when it comes to communicating what you have found, they can require an effort of understanding on the part of your audience. For example, if I say that 8% of the titles your library acquired cost nothing, that a further 7% cost less than $10, 32% cost between $10 and $50, and the rest cost more than $50, you need to think a little about what this means. We could place the information in a table:

Cost	%
Nothing	8%
Less than $10	7%
$10 to $50	32%
More than $50	53%

But it really comes into its own as a pie chart:

Cost of books

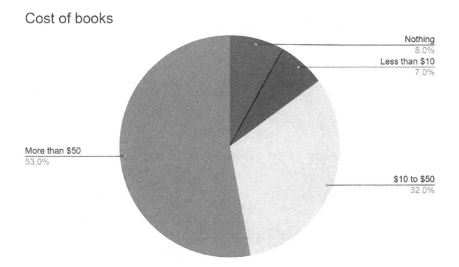

Nothing
8.0%

Less than $10
7.0%

More than $50
53.0%

$10 to $50
32.0%

Even for those of us who consider ourselves mathematically literate, the scale of the difference between 7% and 53% is much more obvious in graphic form—we don't really stop to say to ourselves that 53% is more than seven times greater than 7%, whereas our eye is able to pick this out immediately. By turning the numbers into areas and assigning colors to the categories, we have made the contrast physical and "real" as opposed to abstract and notional.

This becomes really important when your task is to convey to someone else the significance of what your spreadsheet has revealed. You have probably become very familiar with your numbers and their meaning, but for somebody coming to them fresh you need to really spell out in the simplest terms what it is that the numbers are saying. A well-constructed graph or chart allows the viewer to grasp its meaning and significance without the need for further mental processing, and it is for this reason that spreadsheeting software includes a suite of sophisticated tools for the visualization of data. If you wish to take full advantage of these capabilities, it would be a good idea to get hold of a book on the subject, but this chapter will take you through some of the major types of graphs and charts and should give you some idea of their different uses and potentials.

A Simple Line Graph of Time Series Data

When you create a graph or chart, it is always to compare something with something else, and those somethings are going to have to be numbers. In theory, you could create a graph of the number 5 or one that showed that 100% of students received an A, but it wouldn't convey any useful formation.

Let's start with a simple example taken from our spreadsheet of visits to a library for each month the years 2017 and 2018.

http://bit.ly/30Zh9yv

Here is the data stored in range *A1:B14* of the worksheet *Visits*.

	A	B	C
1	Month	Visits 2017	Visits 2018
2	January	4654	4832
3	February	4139	4244
4	March	4475	4086
5	April	4251	4518
6	May	3972	4614
7	June	4011	4644
8	July	3872	3819
9	August	3794	4011
10	September	4421	4914
11	October	4219	4588
12	November	4587	4936
13	December	4531	5096
14	Total	50926	54302

You will note that each column is clearly labeled in the Header Row, and that the names of the months are listed in column A—both of these facts will be important when we come to create graphs and charts. The totals for each year appear in row 14. Let's start by creating a line graph in Sheets for the months of 2017 and 2018. We begin by using the mouse to select the range *A1:C13*, and then click on *Insert/Chart*. Sheets comes back with some options and recommends that I use a *Column chart,* but I'm going to opt for a *Line chart* instead:

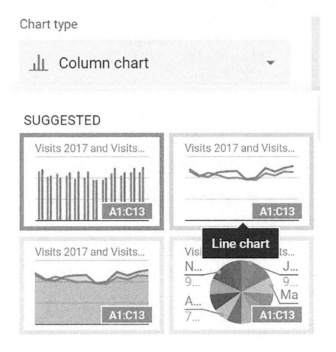

And here is the result:

Visits 2017 and Visits 2018

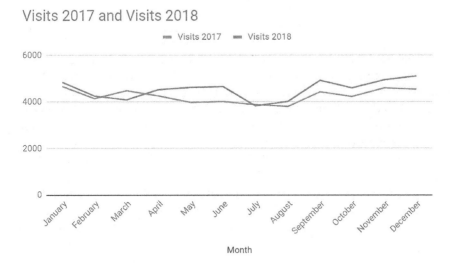

You may have noticed that row 14 was not included in the selection. This is because it contains the *total* for the year, which would be nearly 12 times the size of the largest month—it's always important to make sure that everything within the graph can be usefully compared with everything else.

If we click on the three dots in the top right-hand corner of the graphic and click on *Edit chart,* we are given a useful insight into how the graph is created using the Header Row labels and the software's ability to detect the type of data it is dealing with.

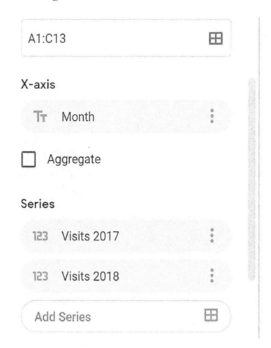

The X-axis represents the horizontal line at the bottom of the graph, and this is where the individual months are listed. The Y-axis is the vertical line on the left, which shows the numbers of visits each month. The data in columns B and C each make up a *Series,* and in future years we would be able to add additional columns to appear as further *Series.* The Headers from these columns have been used as *Series* labels and also to create the title of the chart, *Visits 2017 and Visits 2018.* The chart title can be changed on the *Customize* tab.

The procedure in Excel is very similar. The range *A1:C13* is highlighted and the *Insert* tab clicked on. At this point you are given the choice of looking at the *Recommended Charts* for this data or selecting the type of chart you wish to use directly:

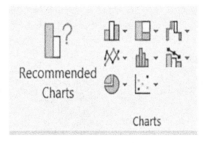

Clicking on *Recommended Charts* will allow you to inspect a number of options:

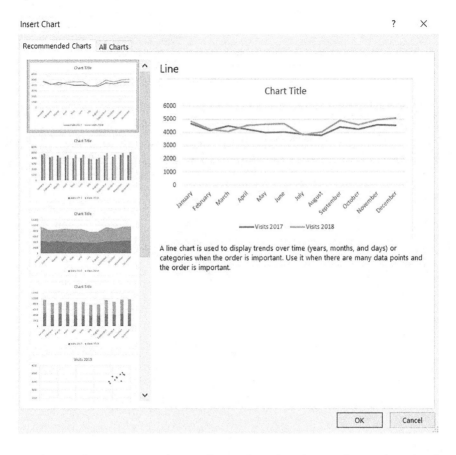

The result is very similar to Sheets, but the chart title can be edited directly:

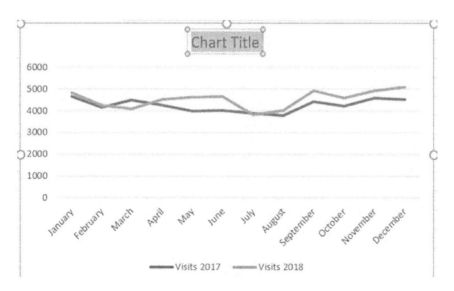

Line graphs are particularly useful for sequential data like this, where we are trying to plot trends—are the numbers going up or down? They can also accommodate large numbers of *Series*, so that when we extend our coverage of library visits back in time the different years can still be shown on the same graph:

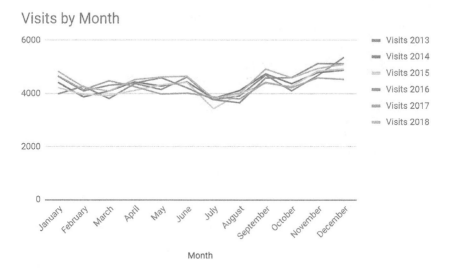

By now this is beginning to look rather like spaghetti, but the graph tells us at a glance that December and January are the busiest months while the number of visits has never reached 4,000 in July.

Column Charts

Column charts are really useful for conveying a sense of quantity and making comparisons between quantities. Here's some data we have already seen on the book titles and prices of a group of publishers:

	A	B	C	D
1	**Publisher**	**Titles**	**Price>$50**	**Price<=$50**
2	Routledge	33	23	10
3	Oxford University Press	27	20	7
4	Sage	23	19	4
5	Cambridge University Press	18	9	9
6	Palgrave Macmillan	13	7	6
7	Allen & Unwin	12	3	9
8	Wiley	11	9	2

Column B shows the total number of titles, while columns C and D split them into those costing more than $50 and those costing $50 or less. Working first in Sheets, we select the range *A1:B8* to create a visualization of the total number of titles published, click on *Insert/Chart,* and this time select *Column chart.*

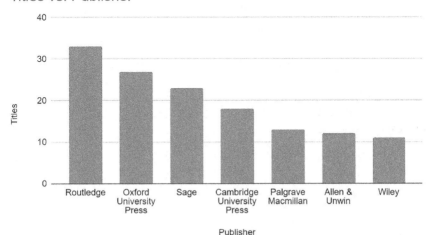

Things become more interesting, however, when we extend the selection to *A1:D8*:

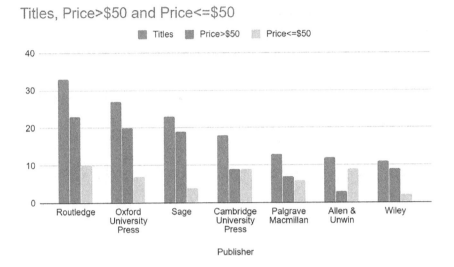

We now have three columns for each publisher, and at a glance we can see that a much higher proportion of the Cambridge and Allen & Unwin titles cost $50 or less compared to the other publishers. We might notice at this point that the column for Titles is really redundant because it is simply the result of adding together the other two columns so we can return to the Chart editor and remove the *Titles* Series:

Series

    123   Titles   ⋮

    123   Price>$50   Edit

                          Remove

We then change the Chart type to *Stacked column*, and our chart now looks like this:

As a final step we might want to compare the average performance of these publishers regardless of the number of titles, in which case we could choose a *100% stacked column chart*:

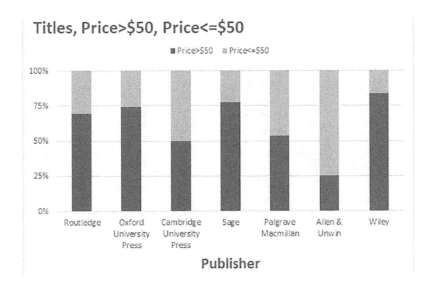

The differences are, we might say, pretty graphic, although please bear in mind that these figures are based on a very small and random sample from the publishers in question and are not intended to stand as a survey of their actual prices!

The process is very similar in Excel. Once the chart has been created, you can right-click and choose the *Select Data* option to remove the *Titles* Series:

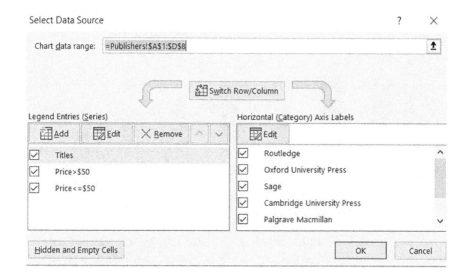

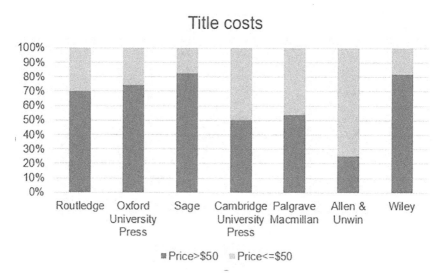

Slicing the Pie Chart

As we saw at the beginning of this chapter, the pie chart is an excellent way of presenting information in graphic form, in particular the sort of information that is generally shown as percentages. With the examples above, we chose a selection of publishers, but there was no suggestion that these were all the publishers that existed or even that the data relating to these publishers was all the data in our spreadsheet—we were only really comparing the performance of the top seven publishers. However, there will be many occasions in which there are a finite set of classes to compare. A good example comes from politics when generally between two and five major parties will account for virtually all the votes cast in a national election, so that it is possible to show their proportions of the vote as segments of the pie. Here is an example from close to home:

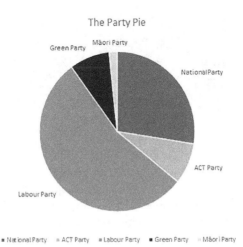

However, this graphic simplicity falls down when we want to include a further dimension of the data, by looking at voters in different age groups or income sectors, for example. It would be possible to do this with column charts, but pie charts are strictly one-dimensional. Having said that, they do what they do very effectively, so here is a library-based example. We have a set of journal articles with different access statuses:

	A	B
1	**Access Status**	**Status count**
2	diamond	15
3	green	77
4	gold	110
5	closed	344
6	hybrid	98
7		644

They total 644 articles in all, but they are spread over only five statuses, so it is easily possible to create a pie chart showing the proportions that fall into each status:

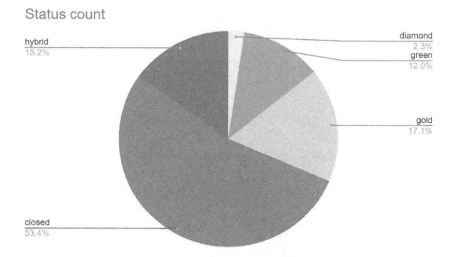

Status count

From this, it is immediately obvious that the closed papers slice consists of more than half the pie, that gold and hybrid are roughly equal in numbers and somewhat ahead of green, while diamond status accounts for very few papers.

Charts and Data Analysis

As we saw in Chapter 8, pivot tables represent the high point of spreadsheet data analysis. Their ability to create sophisticated views of the data, and in doing so to create real information and insight out of a seemingly random collection of words and numbers, gives the data analyst a set of tools that are not readily available through other means. It is also possible to create charts out of pivot tables, and this will often be the first port of call when it is necessary to present data graphically. However, it is definitely worth your while becoming familiar with the complexities of graphs and charts, particularly if the end product of your work is to be a report or publication. Let's face it, tables are an efficient way of communicating data to the reader, but most of us will have had the experience of reading a report and skipping over the tables while searching the written text to gain a sense of their significance. Charts and graphs, on the other hand, attract the eye and draw attention to the "big point" being made.

Unlike a pivot table, a chart doesn't "do anything"; it just gives graphic form to what is already there. However, it is able to give visual expression to whatever you can make the spreadsheet do. For example, if you place a filter on a range of data and then use it in a graphic, the chart or graph will show the data as filtered and will change as the filter changes or is removed. As with much spreadsheet activity, experimentation and trial and error are necessary for you to take full advantage of the capacity of graphics. Unless your job is graphic design, try not to get carried away with all of the wonderful variety of visual expressions available through Excel, but do start with an optimistic frame of mind. If there is some way in which you would like to express your data visually, start from the assumption that it is possible and then work out how to do it! You may not find exactly what you wanted, but you will probably end up in a better place than where you started.

CHAPTER TEN

Flat Files and Data Imports

So far, we have treated Excel as a "desktop" system using software and files, with Sheets, by contrast, being a cloud-based system accessed from a Google Drive through a browser and not maintaining separate files external to Google. This is not entirely true as there is also a web-based version of Excel, accessible through Microsoft's office.com (free version) and Office 365, which can be used for collaborative work. However, for the present, we will maintain this distinction as we examine the relationship between spreadsheets and files.

If you are using an Excel spreadsheet and you click on *File/Save As,* you will be presented with a bewildering choice of options of which the first will be *Excel Workbook.* Generally speaking, this format will be all that you need in order to use all of the features of Excel that we have examined so far. A fully configured Excel file has the extension XLSX or, if it has been produced under an older version of the software, XLS. This format allows you to use all of the following features:

- Multiple worksheets
- Formulas
- Formatting—bold, italics, currency, date, and so on
- Pivot tables
- Graphs

XLSX has been the Excel standard since 2007 and can be used by a wide range of spreadsheet software. If you wish to use XLSX spreadsheets in Sheets, you will need to upload them, and they will be stored in Google Drive. Spreadsheets created in Sheets can also be downloaded and saved as XLSX files external to Google Drive. The important point to understand is that Google Drive operates quite separately from whatever other file structure you are using, so that if you have an Excel spreadsheet saved on your computer, you can upload it to Google Drive and work on it using Sheets, but you cannot use Sheets to work on the spreadsheet in its original location.

Opening an XLSX File in Sheets

If you wish to use Sheets to work on a spreadsheet that has been created as an XLXS file, this can be done from any open spreadsheet. If you are not already working in a spreadsheet, go to Sheets and choose *Start a new spreadsheet.* Then click on *File/Open* and choose the *Upload* option. This will give you the chance to select the file you wish to import using either *Drag* or *Select a file from your device.* The entire spreadsheet, with the name of the original Excel file and with all its worksheets, formulas, tables, and graphs will now be open in Sheets and available for you to work on. However, there are differences and incompatibilities between Sheets and Excel that make it preferable to recreate advanced functions such as pivot tables directly in Sheets.

If you wish to add an XLSX spreadsheet to an existing spreadsheet in Sheets, choose *File/Import* and follow the same *Upload* procedure and then choose the *Insert new sheet(s)* option. All the worksheets of the imported spreadsheet will be added to the existing one.

Downloading XLSX Files from Sheets

There will be occasions on which it is necessary to save your Sheets spreadsheet as an XLSX file that can be opened by Excel or another desktop application. This is a very simple operation—just click on *File/Download as* and choose the *Microsoft Excel (.xlsx)* option. Where the file is saved will depend on the Download settings for your browser, which will designate a specific location as the default. Although you will be able to open it from this location, it's generally not a great idea to keep it there, so consider saving it to a different location or moving the file. Once again, advanced features like the pivot tables and graphs downloaded from Sheets will probably not operate very successfully in other systems. While it is possible to move spreadsheets between systems, using Sheets and Excel interchangeably may lead to problems. If you are collaborating, Sheets is probably a better option, or else use the web-based version of Excel. In particular, emailing spreadsheets back and forth could result in versioning issues!

Importing Data from External Sources

As already mentioned, spreadsheets consist of many different elements, including cells containing character strings, formulas, graphs, and pivot tables, not to mention the formatting that determines the appearance of the contents of cells and ranges. They can also be made up of multiple work-sheets and links between cells in these worksheets. Apart from the pure character strings, which is known as "data," all of these features are what we might call *artifacts* of the spreadsheet software, reflecting the outcomes of data manipulation processes determined by the software. So what do we mean by the term *data* that is different from these things? Put simply, data consists of characters or character strings arranged in cells, rows, and columns. If cell A2 contains the number 4 and cell B2 contains =A2*4, then A2 is data and B2 is a formula based on that data and displaying an output. The equals sign is necessary to instruct the spreadsheet that cell B2 is a formula, and if we remove it then B2 will simply contain the character string A2*4, which will be a piece of (rather meaningless) data.

So how does data come into existence? There are number of possible routes—

- It could be entered from the keyboard
- It could be the output of an information system, such as a database or library catalog
- It could be the output of a computer program which has been written to produce data in a format that allows it to be imported into a spreadsheet
- It could be imported directly from a data store on the Internet or received as an email attachment

Apart from direct keyboard entry, external data has to be brought into a spreadsheet via an import process using "delimiters" that are used to arrange the various character strings into their appropriate columns and cells. The most common of these is the comma-delimited file format known as CSV, which stands for *comma-separated values*.

To illustrate what we mean by this, here is an example of some lines from a CSV file:

issn,journal_title,oa_mode,apc,year
1745–7270,Acta Biochimica et Biophysica Sinica,Hybrid,3040,2019
1755–0645,Adaptation,Hybrid,2814,2019
2161–8313,Advances in Nutrition,Hybrid,5000,2019
1090–820X,Aesthetic Surgery Journal,Hybrid,3360,2019
0001–9909,African Affairs,Hybrid,3260,2019

This is the beginning of 330 lines telling us a number of basic facts about some journals—the ISSN, the title of the journal, the Open Access "mode," the Article Processing Charge in U.S. dollars, and the year to which the data relates. These five elements are indicated in the first row of the data, and they are separated by four commas—there is no need for a comma after the final element, but instead there is a "hard return" indicating the end of the line.

Then each subsequent line contains four commas and five elements, each of which corresponds to the description in the first row. When the file is imported, the spreadsheet places the delimited elements into columns so that it looks like this:

issn	journal_title	oa_mode	apc	year
1745–7270	Acta Biochimica et Biophysica Sinica	Hybrid	3040	2019
1755–0645	Adaptation	Hybrid	2814	2019
2161–8313	Advances in Nutrition	Hybrid	5000	2019

Let's walk through this process. You can access the data here:

http://bit.ly/2yD1pEA

This link will take you to a preview of the spreadsheet, and if you click on *Open with* and choose Google Sheets, it will open as a full spreadsheet saved in your Google Drive in a new tab. You can examine this new spreadsheet, but once you've done this return to the preview tab and click on the *Download* icon. When the file has downloaded, go to the location on your computer where it is stored (for Windows users your *Downloads* folder), right-click on it and open it with a text editor, perhaps *Notepad* or *Notepad++*. This allows you to see the "raw" file before it has been subject to processing by Sheets or Excel. If you are using Excel, double-clicking on the file will now open it, although it is a good idea to move the file to a more permanent location before you do this. Looking at the file in the text editor (rather than Excel or Sheets), the first line looks like this:

issn,journal_title,oa_mode,apc,year

while here is the first row of the spreadsheet in Sheets or Excel:

issn	journal_title	oa_mode	apc	year

It's pretty easy to see what has happened—every time the spreadsheet software has encountered a comma it has started a new column. We can now use this data in formulas, format it, add additional worksheets, and generally treat this as any other spreadsheet. An obvious first step would be to format column D as *Currency*. Because CSV files are "pure" data and contain no formatting of any kind, this is an important step in making a spreadsheet more comprehensible. Our spreadsheet now looks like this:

issn	journal_title	oa_mode	apc	year
1745–7270	Acta Biochimica et Biophysica Sinica	Hybrid	$3,040.00	2019
1755–0645	Adaptation	Hybrid	$2,814.00	2019
2161–8313	Advances in Nutrition	Hybrid	$5,000.00	2019
1090–820X	Aesthetic Surgery Journal	Hybrid	$3,360.00	2019
0001–9909	African Affairs	Hybrid	$3,260.00	2019

We need to save the file after we have made changes and, because we opened it as a CSV file, the default is also to save it as a CSV, in which case the reformatting and any other changes that we made, such as formulas and separate worksheets, will be lost. We are therefore prompted to save it in a different format:

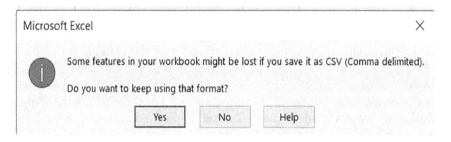

Click on *No* and choose the *Excel Workbook* option:

Excel Workbook
Excel Macro-Enabled Workbook
Excel Binary Workbook
Excel 97-2003 Workbook
XML Data
Single File Web Page
Web Page
Excel Template
Excel Macro-Enabled Template
Excel 97-2003 Template
Text (Tab delimited)
Unicode Text
XML Spreadsheet 2003
Microsoft Excel 5.0/95 Workbook
CSV (Comma delimited)

The imported data is now available for all spreadsheet operations.

The Problem with Commas

Now, this would seem very simple, but if you scroll down to row 45 in the spreadsheet, you will see this entry for *Cambridge Journal of Regions, Economy and Society*:

1752–1378	Cambridge Journal of Regions, Economy and Society	Hybrid	2812	2019

Now you have a small puzzle as the title of this journal contains a comma—why wasn't the text immediately following the comma placed in a new column? You can find the answer to this puzzle if you go to the file in the text editor and scroll down to find the original input for this row, which looks like this:

1752–1378,"Cambridge Journal of Regions, Economy and Society",Hybrid, 2812,2019

Because the title of the journal is enclosed in double quotation marks, Sheets and Excel will treat it as a single unit and will not place the text following the comma into a new column. There are a total of seven titles in this data containing commas, and you can see them by filtering column B.

If you were processing purely numerical data none of this would matter, but as librarians we will frequently be handling textual data in the form of book and journal titles, personal names, subject headings, and other metadata, all of which are likely to contain commas. If the data we are using does not take account of this, then we will run into real problems with placing all the elements of our input into their correct columns. To avoid this problem, most library systems that export comma-delimited files will generally place double quotes around *all* fields like this:

"issn","journal_title","oa_mode","apc","year"
"1745–7270","Acta Biochimica et Biophysica Sinica","Hybrid","3040","2019"

Even that may result in occasional problems, as it is not unknown for authors to use double quotation marks and commas in the titles of books and articles! If you experience real problems with this, you may be able to specify that your system exports data using another form of delimiter such as the tilde (~), which is highly unlikely to occur in any data. We will now proceed to look at the use of other delimiters in CSV files.

Semicolon-Delimited CSV Files

Here is a file that uses the semicolon as a delimiter—http://bit.ly/2oquVLD.

issn;journal_title;oa_mode;apc;year
1745–7270;Acta Biochimica et Biophysica Sinica;Hybrid;3040;2019
1755–0645;Adaptation;Hybrid;2814;2019

2161–8313;Advances in Nutrition;Hybrid;5000;2019
1090–820X;Aesthetic Surgery Journal;Hybrid;3360;2019
0001–9909;African Affairs;Hybrid;3260;2019

If you choose the *Open with Google Sheets* option, the file will automatically save to your Google Drive. You will notice that all of the data, rather than being placed in separate columns, sits in column A looking like this:

	A	B	C	D
1	issn;journal_title;oa_mode;apc;year			
2	1745-7270;Acta Biochimica et Biophysica Sinica;Hybrid;3040;2019			
3	1755-0645;Adaptation;Hybrid;2814;2019			
4	2161-8313;Advances in Nutrition;Hybrid;5000;2019			
5	1090-820X;Aesthetic Surgery Journal;Hybrid;3360;2019			
6	0001-9909;African Affairs;Hybrid;3260;2019			
7	0002-0729;Age and Ageing;Hybrid;3570;2019			
8	0735-0414;Alcohol and Alcoholism;Hybrid;3749;2019			
9	0002-9092;American Journal of Agricultural Economics;Hybrid;3308;2019			

Our task now is to use the semicolons to split each row, including the Header Row, across five columns, and we do this by selecting the whole of column A and then using the *Data* tab. In Sheets the command is *Split text to columns*.

The semicolon option is chosen:

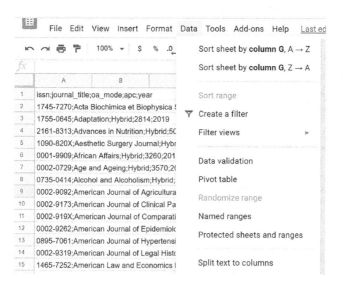

Detect automatically

Comma

Semicolon

Period

Space

Custom

If you are using Excel, you first need to download the CSV file by clicking on the *Download* icon. It will be saved to whichever location on your computer is used as the download default, and it is a good idea to move or copy the file to a more permanent location before opening it. As we saw with Sheets, all the data will be located in column A, and the command to split it is *Data/Text to Columns*. First specify that the data is *Delimited,* and then select *Semicolon*. You will be given a preview of the data arranged in columns, and if this is satisfactory click *Finish*.

Our data is now separated into columns and ready for use as a spreadsheet:

issn	journal_title	oa_mode	apc	year
1745–7270	Acta Biochimica et Biophysica Sinica	Hybrid	3040	2019
1755–0645	Adaptation	Hybrid	2814	2019
2161–8313	Advances in Nutrition	Hybrid	5000	2019
1090–820X	Aesthetic Surgery Journal	Hybrid	3360	2019
0001–9909	African Affairs	Hybrid	3260	2019

You might think that because we are using a semicolon-delimited file that the problem we earlier experienced with commas would not occur, but this is not the case. Excel will always default to using commas as delimiters, and it is necessary to use double quotation marks to avoid this. If you open the original CSV file in *Notepad* or *Notepad++,* you will see that it is necessary to use a different format for semicolon-delimited files and that lines containing commas look like this:

"1752–1378;""Cambridge Journal of Regions, Economy and Society"""; Hybrid;2812;2019"

The whole line is enclosed in double quotation marks, and the field containing the comma sits within two sets of double quotes.

If the CSV file has not been formatted like this, you will get a warning when you attempt to split the text into columns—*There's already data here. Do you want to replace it?* If you click on *OK,* the rows already divided into columns will be damaged, so it would be better to open the CSV file in a text editor and edit the offending lines. Again, *Notepad* or *Notepad++* are preferable to Word or any other word processing software, although if do use one of these you can save the output as a pure text file.

If the CSV file uses some other character, such as a tilde, as a delimiter, you will need to specify what it is at the point of separating the data into columns. In Excel, choose the *Other* option and enter the character, while in Sheets the option is *Custom.* The same rules for dealing with commas that we used for the semicolon-delimited file will also apply to files using these other delimiters. For example, here is an extract from a tilde-delimited file that will import and format successfully:

```
1050–3293~Communication Theory~Hybrid~3150~2019
"1753–9129~""Communication, Culture and Critique""~Hybrid~3150~2019"
```

Tab-Delimited Files

An alternative to the use of commas and other characters as delimiters is the use of tabs entered from the tab key on the keyboard. A tab is a special character that gives the appearance of either five or eight spaces in a file and is commonly used for indenting text, but you need to be aware that a tab *is not the same thing* as five or eight spaces even though it may appear to be. Here is what a tab-delimited file looks like in *Notepad++* with the tab symbols displayed:

```
issn      journal_title     oa_mode apc year
1745-7270   Acta Biochimica et Biophysica Sinica      Hybrid   3040    2019
1755-0645   Adaptation   Hybrid   2814     2019
2161-8313   Advances in Nutrition   Hybrid   5000    2019
1090-820X   Aesthetic Surgery Journal   Hybrid   3360    2019
```

And here is the same content using spaces:

```
issn    journal_title    oa_mode    apc    year
1745-7270   Acta Biochimica et Biophysica Sinica    Hybrid    3040    2019
1755-0645   Adaptation    Hybrid    2814    2019
2161-8313   Advances in Nutrition    Hybrid    5000    2019
1090-820X   Aesthetic Surgery Journal    Hybrid    3360    2019
```

The first example will import successfully into a spreadsheet, while the second will not.

In order to open in Sheets a tab-delimited file needs to have the extension TSV as in *oup_apcs.tsv*, rather than TXT. A TSV file will open automatically in Excel once the association has been made on your computer. If a tab-delimited file has a TXT extension, it can be opened in Excel by right-clicking, but if it has a CSV extension it can be opened by direct clicking—you will then need to carry out a *Text to Columns* operation with the *Tab* option set. Generally speaking, it is not advisable to use a CSV extension for a tab-delimited file as you are quite likely to run into problems with commas.

Saving Spreadsheets as CSV Files

There will be times when you wish to make your work available to others as raw data in the form of comma-delimited or tab-delimited files. There are two ways of performing this operation in Excel:

* File/Save as and choose CSV format
* File/Export and choose CSV format

In either case you will receive the warning that "Features of your workbook may be lost," and at this point you need to be aware of two limitations:

* CSV files consist of a single worksheet only. They are sometimes known as "flat files" because they consist of two dimensions only, rows and columns.
* They consist of "pure text" or character strings with no special formatting.

If your spreadsheet consists of multiple worksheets, you can save only a single worksheet as a CSV file—if you wish to save multiple worksheets, they will need to be done as separate CSVs.

This second point is particularly important. In a spreadsheet cell formatted to show currency as dollars and cents, if the contents of the cell are 45, then what we see will be $45.00. If it is formatted to show dollars only, then we will see $45. The dollar sign, the period, and the zeros are products of the formatting operation and are not part of the cell contents.

Here's part of a spreadsheet with prices formatted as currency:

Title	Publication Date	Publisher	USD
A dictionary of animal behaviour	2014	Oxford University Press	$18.00
Adam's nose, and the making of humankind	2015	Imperial College Press	$38.00

An introduction to animal behavior	2012	Cambridge University Press	$145.00
Animal behavior	2018	Storytellers, Inc	$80.00
Animal behavior: an evolutionary approach	2011	Apple Academic Press	$26.00
Animal nature and human nature	2018	Taylor and Francis	$103.00

The actual content of cell D2 is simply *18*, but what is displayed is *$18.00*. However, if we save the file as a CSV and then open it in *Notepad*, we find that what we have actually saved is this:

Title,Publication Date,Publisher,USD
A dictionary of animal behaviour,2014,Oxford University Press,$18.00
"Adam's nose, and the making of humankind",2015,Imperial College Press,
$38.00
An introduction to animal behavior,2012,Cambridge University Press,
$145.00
Animal behavior,2018,"Storytellers, Inc",$80.00

Now, this is where things begin to get interesting. If we subsequently open the CSV file in Excel, we find that the content in cell D2 has reverted to plain *18* but that the cells in column D are now formatted as *Currency*. This is because Excel has done some smart work with interpreting the CSV file and has recognized that these entries relate to money—it has automatically stripped out the dollar sign, the period, and the zeros and has altered the cell format accordingly. However, we have to bear in mind that cell formatting is a function of Excel and not of the CSV file itself, which consists only of characters and punctuation, and if we now save the CSV file from Excel, we find that it continues to look like this:

A dictionary of animal behaviour,2014,Oxford University Press,$18.00

Excel's smart saving of CSV files to include formatting can lead us into complexities when we want to use them in other systems, in our case Sheets. We have already seen that it is possible to upload a CSV file to Google Drive and open it in Sheets, but when this is done with a CSV file that has "borrowed" formatting from Excel this will carry over into Sheets, and some readjustment of formats will be needed if all the standard numerical functions like SUM are to work. If you are planning to save a worksheet as a CSV, it is a good idea to format all the cells as *General* before this is done, and then they can be reformatted to currency when the file is converted to a full spreadsheet.

Non-Latin Characters in Imported Files

In Chapter 5 we looked at the issues raised by nonstandard characters, such as those with diacritics or accents such as ā or è. While it's not possible to give more than a brief explanation of the complexities raised by the use of different character sets in the data that librarians are likely to be using, because much of our work relates to textual information we do need to be aware of these issues and have some idea of how to deal with them.

Here's the first line of Homer's *Odyssey* in Greek script:

Ἄνδρα μοι ἔννεπε, Μοῦσα, πολύτροπον, ὅς μάλα πολλὰ

Both Excel and Sheets are capable of storing this text and carrying out the normal textual functions on it, such as determining its length using the LEN function or giving us 10 characters to the left using the LEFT function. We run into problems, however, if we use Excel to open a CSV file containing this script. Here's an example of a simple CSV file:

Author,Line
Homer,"Ἄνδρα μοι ἔννεπε, Μοῦσα, πολύτροπον, ὅς μάλα πολλὰ"

However, when it is opened directly in Excel it can appear like this:

Author	Line
Homer	á¼ŒÎ½Î´ÏÎ± Î¼Î¿Î¹ á¼"Î½Î½ÎµÏ€Îµ, ÎœÎ¿á¿¦ÏƒÎ±, Î€Î¿Î»á¿»Ï„Î¿Ï€Î¿Î½, á½… . . . Ï, Î¼Î¬Î»Î± Ï€Î¿Î»Î»á½°

This is because the Greek script falls outside the range of characters that Excel is set to handle by default. This is known as the ANSI character set, and although it includes most of the variations used in the standard characters of the Latin alphabet used in languages such as English, French, Italian, and German, it does not include non-Latin alphabets such as Greek, Russian, Arabic, Hindi, Chinese, Japanese, Korean, and so on. Often Excel will recognize that the CSV file contains non-Latin characters, but if it does not, then you will need to do a special import.

Rather than opening the CSV file by double-clicking, we instead open a new spreadsheet, place our cursor in cell A1, and click on the tab, then on the *From Text* option.

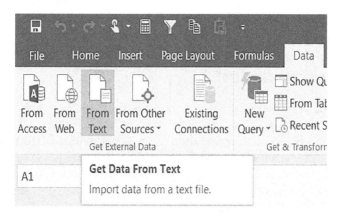

The file is selected and we click on *Import*:

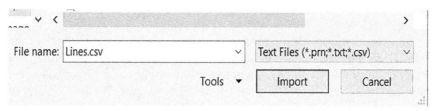

Fortunately, in this case Excel has now detected that there are non-Latin characters in the file and has selected Unicode UTF-8 as the appropriate character set:

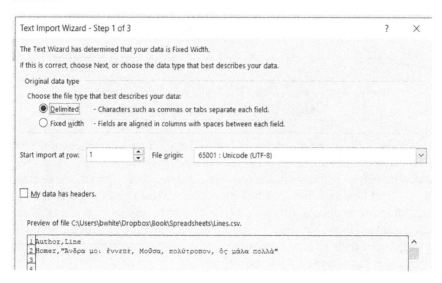

If this does not happen automatically, you need to choose UTF-8 manually. This character set has been designed to encompass all possible script-derived characters, and sure enough the imported file is now displayed correctly:

Author	Line
Homer	Ἄνδρα μοι ἔννεπε, Μοῦσα, πολύτροπον, ὅς μάλα πολλὰ

There is one final step. In importing the CSV as a text file, we have simply created a link between our new spreadsheet and the original file. If we right-click on cell A1, we see an option called *Data Range Properties*:

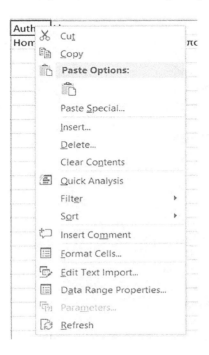

Remove the tick from *Save query definition* and click on *OK*.

External Data Range Properties ? ✕

Name: Lines

Query definition

☑ Save query definition

The link to the original CSV file is now broken, and the imported characters are now incorporated into your spreadsheet.

There is no need to follow a procedure like this in Sheets, which uses UTF-8 as its default.

Problems with CSV Files in Excel

Here's something that will drive you bananas! This is a spreadsheet in Sheets that has been created by importing a CSV file. It consists of journal articles, and column F shows the issue number. The second-to-last row shows a double issue—this is a fairly common occurrence—and consists of the two numbers joined by a hyphen.

Authors	Title	Year	Source title	Volume	Issue
Chilvers, B. L.	Variability of little blue penguin (Eudyptula minor) diving behaviour across New Zealand	2019	New Zealand Journal of Ecology	43	2
Shamsi, S., Briand, M. J., Justine, J.-L.	Occurrence of Anisakis (Nematoda: Anisakidae) larvae in unusual hosts in Southern hemisphere	2017	Parasitology International	66	6
Chilvers, B. L.	Comparison of New Zealand's little blue penguins, Eudyptula minor, diving behaviour	2017	Polar Biology	40	10
Chilvers, B. L., Finlayson, G., Candy, E. J., Sriram, A., Morgan, K. J., Cockrem, J. F.	Corticosterone stress hormone responses in oil rehabilitated and non-rehabilitated little penguins	2016	Marine Pollution Bulletin	113	1–2
Tavecchia, G., Sanz-Aguilar, A., Cannell, B.	Modelling survival and breeding dispersal to unobservable nest sites	2016	Wildlife Research	43	5

The CSV file is comma-delimited and the entry for this row looks like this:

"Chilvers, B. L., Finlayson, G., Candy, E. J., Sriram, A., Morgan, K. J., Cockrem, J. F.",Corticosterone stress hormone responses in oil rehabilitated and non-rehabilitated little penguins,2016,Marine Pollution Bulletin, 113,1-2

However, when I open the file in Excel, what I see is this:

Authors	Title	Year	Source title	Volume	Issue
Chilvers, B. L.	Variability of little blue penguin (Eudyptula minor) diving behaviour across New Zealand	2019	New Zealand Journal of Ecology	43	2
Shamsi, S., Briand, M. J., Justine, J.-L.	Occurrence of Anisakis (Nematoda: Anisakidae) larvae in unusual hosts in Southern hemisphere	2017	Parasitology International	66	6
Chilvers, B. L.	Comparison of New Zealand's little blue penguins, Eudyptula minor, diving behaviour	2017	Polar Biology	40	10
Chilvers, B. L., Finlayson, G., Candy, E. J., Sriram, A., Morgan, K. J., Cockrem, J. F.	Corticosterone stress hormone responses in oil rehabilitated and non-rehabilitated little penguins	2016	Marine Pollution Bulletin	113	1-Feb
Tavecchia, G., Sanz-Aguilar, A., Cannell, B.	Modelling survival and breeding dispersal to unobservable nest sites	2016	Wildlife Research	43	5

Rather than showing the issue number in cell F5 as *1–2*, it is instead displayed as a date, *1-Feb*! What is worse, when I look at the actual contents of the cell, I see this—*1/02/2019*. Where did *2019* come from? Oh, it just happens to be the year in which I'm writing this!! But how did it end up in cell F5 when all we wanted to do was to record the double issue of a journal?

A closer look at the cell formats gives me a clue—all the cells have a *General* format whereas cell F5 has a *Custom* format. Now, CSV files are supposed to be pure text with no formatting, so obviously something strange is going on here, but at least I could expect that if I saved the spreadsheet in CSV format that the underlying data, which we have seen above, would remain unchanged.

Not so. After saving the file, I close it and then open it in *Notepad*. The line in question now looks like this:

"Chilvers, B. L., Finlayson, G., Candy, E. J., Sriram, A., Morgan, K. J., Cockrem, J. F.",Corticosterone stress hormone responses in oil rehabilitated and non-rehabilitated little penguins,2016,Marine Pollution Bulletin, 113,1-Feb

The number of the double issue has been permanently altered to look like a date! And what is worse, if I now open the saved CSV file in Sheets, the error has now spread to there as well and it shows as 1-Feb.

What's going on here? Unfortunately, this is a bad case of "not a bug but a feature," and it is one that has persistently annoyed Excel users over many years. What Excel is doing is taking any combination of two numbers joined by a hyphen that *could* be interpreted as a date, and doing just that, even though nobody asked it to. If the second of the numbers is greater than 12, then there's no problem, but if there's any possibility of interpreting the number as a date, then this will be done. This is particularly bad news for librarians because data describing publications will regularly include page ranges, such as *35–107* or *1–10*. With the first of these there will not be a problem, but the second will inevitably, and unhelpfully, become a date.

Excel is probably the most widely used spreadsheet software in existence, so it is possibly for this reason, to avoid inflicting this annoyance on librarians everywhere, that library systems such as Scopus export CSV files of journal articles with *Page start* and *Page end* as separate fields rather than simply giving a single page range. However, there is no simple solution for double issues of journals, so CSV files containing bibliographic data must always be carefully checked if they have been opened in Excel.

So what can we do about this? Well, an obvious answer is to reformat the cell as *General* rather than *Custom* to make it conform with all the other cells, but this just makes the problem worse as it now changes to the serial number of the date, *43497*, and if the file is saved, this is now transferred to the raw data. The only way to permanently fix an individual cell is to delete the contents, format the cell as *Text*, and then enter the page numbers.

Clearly, however, this is an unsatisfactory solution and relies on persistent awareness of the problem and a willingness to manually fix these system-created errors. One solution is to avoid using Excel entirely if you are using data that is likely to generate these problems. Many librarians prefer to use Sheets or other packages such as LibreOffice in order to avoid this issue. If, however, you are committed to Excel, then there is a solution that will produce correctly formatted spreadsheets.

Rather than opening the CSV file directly in Excel by double-clicking, open a new blank spreadsheet, select cell A1, and then open the *Data* tab. We now follow the same routine that we earlier used to import non-Latin characters, except that there are some added complexities.

Choose the *From Text* option:

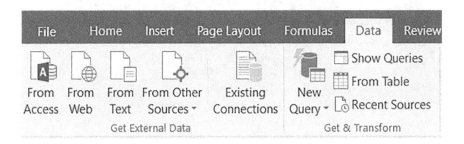

Choose your file and click on *Import:*

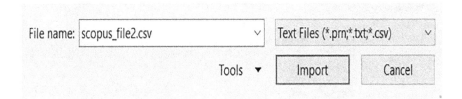

As before, choose the comma-delimited option (*.csv*), and then click on *Next* as there is still more work to do. The Text Import Wizard now opens:

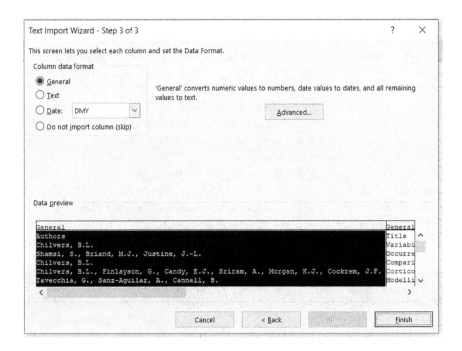

Column A (Authors) is highlighted, and *General* format is the default. Navigate across to column F (Issue) and highlight it. You will notice that it is also formatted as *General:*

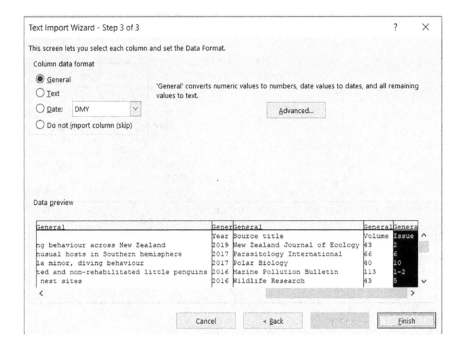

Change this to *Text:*

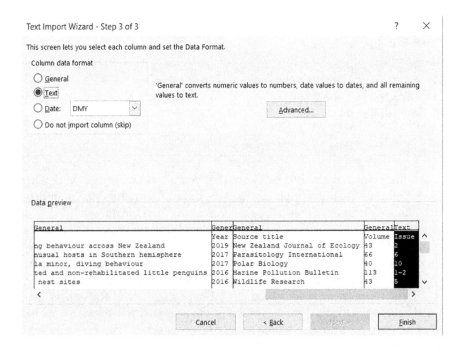

Now click on *Finish,* and the *Issue* column is now properly formatted:

Authors	Title	Year	Source title	Volume	Issue
Chilvers, B. L.	Variability of little blue penguin (Eudyptula minor) diving behaviour across New Zealand	2019	New Zealand Journal of Ecology	43	43
Shamsi, S., Briand, M. J., Justine, J.-L.	Occurrence of Anisakis (Nematoda: Anisakidae) larvae in unusual hosts in Southern hemisphere	2017	Parasitology International	66	66
Chilvers, B. L.	Comparison of New Zealand's little blue penguins, Eudyptula minor, diving behaviour	2017	Polar Biology	40	40

Chilvers, B. L., Finlayson, G., Candy, E. J., Sriram, A., Morgan, K. J., Cockrem, J. F.	Corticosterone stress hormone responses in oil rehabilitated and non-rehabilitated little penguins	2016	Marine Pollution Bulletin	113	113
Tavecchia, G., Sanz-Aguilar, A., Cannell, B.	Modelling survival and breeding dispersal to unobservable nest sites	2016	Wildlife Research	43	43

At this point you need to be aware that you are no longer working with the original CSV file and that instead you have imported its data to a new XLSX file, which now needs to be saved under its own file name.

Once you have done this, you need to delink the imported data from its original source. Go to cell A1, which is where you began the process, and write-click. *Select Data Range Properties* and remove the tick from *Save query definition*. Once this has been done, there is no further linkage to the original CSV file.

A final word on this topic—although I have highlighted the danger that Excel poses to raw data files, this problem can also arise when you are manually inputting page ranges, double issues and other similar pieces of information. Cells in Excel automatically set to *General* format and need to be changed to *Text* format *before* the data is entered. Try opening a new Excel spreadsheet and entering 1–2 into a cell to see what I mean. I can only hope that by the time you're reading this the problem will have been fixed, but it has persisted for many years, so I am not optimistic!

Displaying ISBN Numbers in Excel

Another example of Excel being less than helpful in a way that proves particularly annoying to librarians is its handling of ISBNs, numbers with 10 or 13 characters. Now, we know that these are not *real* numbers but simply identifiers. The character string 9781552388655 does *not* represent the number 9,781,552,388,655, which would be 9 trillion, 781 billion, 552 million, 388 thousand, 655. Instead, it is simply a string of digits with no numerical or quantitative significance and intended only to provide unique identification of a specific edition of a book. However, because Excel detects it to be a number, it displays it in scientific notation:

Title	ISBN
Animal Metropolis: Histories of Human-Animal Relations in Urban Canada	9.78155E+12

The answer to this problem is surprisingly simple. As we saw when importing page sequences that Excel turned into dates, it is necessary to format the cell as *Text* prior to typing and or pasting a long number. If a column is to be used to store ISBNs, it can be formatted as text before any data entry is done.

Conclusion

By now you may be wondering whether it is all worth it! What seemed like a sensible way of storing information and doing a few calculations has instead turned into a complex nightmare of unexpected and incomprehensible textual and numerical oddities that need to be solved by arcane workarounds and fixes. Sometimes, indeed, it seems as if spreadsheets have given us the power to work on all sorts of problems that we could understand but not solve, but at the cost of giving us another set of problems that we couldn't even understand. While on the one hand, modern organizations are able to carry out stunning feats of data manipulation, this has often been at the cost of having to employ highly skilled specialists to sort through the problems that their information systems create. This is sometimes known as the "productivity paradox," the idea that the gains achieved by automated information systems are frequently less than those promised or expected and that this loss of productivity is down to the slippage caused by system imperfections.

Clearly, however, libraries and librarians do not have the luxury of simply opting out of the modern electronic information environment. We were among the earliest pioneers of automated information, and library systems in general lend themselves to digital solutions. One way in which we can avoid becoming victims of the productivity paradox is to recognize the dangers that exist and to equip ourselves properly to deal with them. It is part of the purpose of this book to support you in doing this.

In defense of spreadsheets, it might be said that they have been the victims of their own success. Some of the problems we have seen with Excel are embedded deep within its code and go back several decades—things that must have seemed like a good idea at the time have turned out to cause all sorts of headaches. At the time these systems were being developed, nobody really envisaged that they would be universally used and would need to adapt themselves to all the world's languages and scripts, to a variety of date and time systems, and to the complex demands of modern organizations wanting to integrate all their operations into a single information entity, and to reach out beyond their own boundaries and engage in global information sharing. If this sounds a lot like the traditional mission of libraries, then that is intentional—by dealing with words in all their variety we ourselves place very heavy demands on the bits and bytes that we so much take for granted.

Which brings us neatly back to the importance of CSV files. Although they are highly imperfect packages, and although we might wish that they had originally been created to use less common delimiters than commas, quotation marks, and tabs, the fact that they are an international standard means that they can act as a point of interchange between widely different systems. One of the recurring nightmares of the computer age has been the discovery that data produced by proprietary systems can become completely obsolete when those systems, or the machinery used to run them, cease to function. The simple flat file structure of the CSV allows it to operate as a sort of universal language that is future-proof as well as being able to cross boundaries of language. If librarians are to lay credible claim to the status of data and information specialists and facilitators of information sharing, then we need to be able to operate fluently with information at this level. By reading this chapter carefully, you will be able to anticipate and avoid problems, find solutions, and make efficient use of the universe of data that is available to you in this simple format.

CHAPTER ELEVEN

Multiple Spreadsheets and Data Ecosystems

Linking Between Spreadsheets

We have looked at spreadsheets largely as independent entities, although in Chapter 10 we saw that it is possible to import flat files created by other users and systems and also to export individual worksheets in the same formats. It is highly likely that over time you will accumulate a number of spreadsheets, and some of these will relate to the same operations or activities. Rather than keeping one massive spreadsheet or duplicating the same operation over a number of different spreadsheets, there will be times when you want to "borrow" information from one spreadsheet to use in another. You may even wish to use data created elsewhere within your organization and stored on its network.

As we have seen, it's an easy matter to create links between different cells in a spreadsheet, even when these are located on separate worksheets. To remind ourselves of how this works, let's look at two simple formulas. The first is

$$=A2$$

which means "repeat the contents of cell A2 in the current cell." If cell A2 contains a number, we could incorporate it into a numerical formula:

$$=A2*5$$

If it contains text, it could be included in a text formula:

$$=UPPER(A2)$$

If the cell is located in a different worksheet, this is incorporated into the formula

$$=VendorList!A2$$

$$=VendorList!A2*2$$

$$=UPPER(VendorList!A2)$$

The next step is to extend this link to an entirely different spreadsheet. Because Excel and Sheets work rather differently, we will start with Excel.

Linking Excel Spreadsheets by Cell

Let's say we have two different spreadsheets called *linkfile1* and *linkfile2,* which are in turn located in separate folders, *S4L_folder1* and *S4L_folder2*. In Windows the full path for *S4L_folder1* is

$$C:\Users\myname\Documents\S4L\_folder1$$

Each of the spreadsheets consists of two worksheets called *data* and *analysis*. Creating a link between a cell of spreadsheet *linkfile1* and another cell of spreadsheet *linkfile2* is exactly the same linking between two worksheets of the same spreadsheet. Simply open both spreadsheets, select the required location in the first spreadsheet, enter an equals sign, and click on the "target" location of the second worksheet. The resulting formula will look like this:

$$=[linkfile2.xlsx]data!\$A\$2$$

This is pretty transparent, incorporating the file name, the worksheet, and the exact cell address. As long as the target spreadsheet is open, it will continue to display in this format, but if *linkfile2* is closed, the formula will display like this:

$$='C:\Users\myname\Documents\S4L\_folder2\[linkfile2.xlsx]data'!\$A\$2$$

Now, you may be wondering what the purpose of this linking is—why not simply incorporate the data from *linkfile2* as a separate worksheet in *linkfile1*? Well, there could be occasions on which you wish to obtain data from a spreadsheet kept by someone else, such as a list of current addresses for library patrons that changes on a daily basis. You wouldn't want to have to keep copying across the new data to your own spreadsheet, so it's much easier simply to create a link. Each time we open *linkfile1* we are prompted to update the links so that any changes that were made to *linkfile2* are incorporated:

Linking between spreadsheets is also a useful way of preventing your own spreadsheets from becoming impossibly large and cumbersome, if you have a large number of separate worksheets or if you have worksheets that are regularly updated with new data. A worksheet with thousands of rows of data might be better stored as a separate spreadsheet. However, you need to keep careful control over spreadsheets that are related to one another in this way. It won't always be apparent that spreadsheet A is linked to from spreadsheet B, so if you delete, move, or rename a spreadsheet, you could be creating problems for yourself.

It is even possible to incorporate data from another spreadsheet into a lookup operation. If *linkfile2* contains borrower numbers in column A and addresses in column B that are updated on a daily basis, the new addresses could be retrieved into *linkfile1* using the following formula based on a borrower number in cell A2:

$$=VLOOKUP(A2,'C:\Users\myname\Documents\S4L\_folder2\[linkfile2.xlsx]$$
$$data'!\$A:\$B,2,FALSE)$$

Because Sheets is web-based, the file location approach used by Excel would not work, so it is not possible to create explicit links between cells in different spreadsheets in this way.

Importing Data into Excel

Another way to create links between spreadsheets is to import it using *Data/Import*. We saw this in action in Chapter 10 as a means of avoiding Excel's tendency to reformat number ranges as dates, but this time we will use it to create permanent updatable links between a spreadsheet and a CSV file. This is done by clicking on *Data/Import* and selecting the *From Text/CSV* option, then pointing to the file. Select *Load* to import the data. When the original CSV file is updated and saved, you will need to click on Refresh for the changes to be reflected in the linked location. When you import data in this way, two new tabs will appear the top of your spreadsheet—*Query Tools* and *Design Tools*. If you no longer wish to update the spreadsheet with changes to the original source file, click on *Unlink* on the *Design Tools* tab.

Importing Data into Sheets

Sheets uses the IMPORTRANGE functions to import data directly from worksheets of other spreadsheets. If you open a spreadsheet in Sheets, you will notice that the spreadsheet has a unique web address that looks like this:

https://docs.google.com/spreadsheets/d/16yheRGh8qOlnBmfGrcCkwq340m6nmup aiWhQafJ/edit#gid=460227270 (This is not the actual address, so don't try typing it into your browser!)

This spreadsheet happens to contain borrower data including borrower numbers in column A and telephone numbers in column E. Linking is not done at the individual cell level; instead a range is imported. The spreadsheet web address is copied and pasted into the formula between double quotes. The range to be imported, including the worksheet name, also appears between double quotes, and the final result is:

=IMPORTRANGE("https://docs.google.com/spreadsheets/d/16yheRGh8qOlnBmf GrcCkwq340m6nmupaiWhQafJ/edit#gid=460227270","Borrowers!A:E")

This formula appears only in one cell (the top left-hand corner), but all of the contents from the target range appear. We have already seen this done with the UNIQUE function and, as in that case the cells governed by this function cannot be directly edited, but any change to the original data is reflected in the imported data.

Although the IMPORTDATA function in Sheets is designed to import directly from CSV files, in practice this is difficult, and it may be preferable to open the CSV file in Google Sheets and use the web address resulting from that operation using IMPORTRANGE. You will have to remember to manually record any changes to the CSV file in that spreadsheet as well.

Linking to Information on the Web

So far we have brought data into our spreadsheets through the use of flat files in CSV and TSV formats, but now we will look at more direct methods of gathering information. The modern digital information ecosystem is vast and interconnected. As librarians we are used to curating those sections of it that are expressed by formal publications, and we have begun to grapple with the management of research data. In fact, as a profession, we are well placed to understand and manage interconnected information because that is what librarians do—identifying and bringing together books by author and subject, using keywords to locate reports and journal articles, creating bibliographies, using reference management systems, and many other similar activities make up our daily practice. This practice relies on shared and reliable standards, known as metadata, which allow our computers to pass information between one another—MARC and Dublin Core are obvious examples—and on unique identifiers such as ISSNs and DOIs.

Spreadsheets are great for storing and manipulating data, but we can also use them to access information directly on the Internet. Both Excel and Sheets are able to recognize standard HTTP web addresses and open them with a single click. This in itself is not very remarkable, but when we take into account the ability of spreadsheets to create combinations of words and numbers, it becomes apparent that they could be able to save us a good deal of typing, copying and pasting, and other routine activities. Here, for example, is the web address of the homepage of WorldCat:

https://www.worldcat.org/

In its own words, WorldCat "connects you to the collections and services of more than 10,000 libraries worldwide," and it is recognized as the best publicly available source of bibliographic records for library materials of all kinds. One of the useful services of this website is its ability to create links to bibliographic records based on titles, ISBN numbers, authors, and so on. There is a useful description of these links here:

https://www.worldcat.org/links/default.jsp

If web addresses are placed into a spreadsheet cell, we can link to them simply by clicking. There is no need for an equals sign or any other spreadsheet functionality because this is simply a text string that is recognized as a web address. In itself this is not terribly impressive, as the same result could be achieved from almost any word processor so that a list of web addresses automatically becomes a set of hyperlinks. However, there is something that spreadsheets can do that is beyond the capability of word processing systems, and that is to incorporate data from cells into character strings and therefore into web addresses.

Among the instructions on links we notice that it is possible to create a very simple link to a record or set of records simply by using the title in this format:

http://www.worldcat.org/title/catcher-in-the-rye

And, of course, any title can be used, for example:

http://www.worldcat.org/title/introduction-to-human-factors-engineering

It is a short step from here to recognizing that in a spreadsheet containing a list of titles we could use a simple concatenation formula to create a set of links to their WorldCat records. If cell D2 contains the title, then we can use the following to join it to the WorldCat link structure:

=HYPERLINK("https://www.worldcat.org/title/"&D2)

Because this is no longer a pure text string, we have had to use the HYPER-LINK function to indicate that the spreadsheet is to send us somewhere else. Using the title *An Introduction to Human Factors Engineering,* this search produces a moderately good set of results, but there are a number of "false hits" among them. This is because the search created by this formula contains spaces between the title words so that the actual web address for which we searched was

*https://www.worldcat.org/title/An%20Introduction%20to%20Human
%20Factors%20Engineering*

This can be corrected by adding a SUBSTITUTE function to our formula to replace spaces with dashes:

=HYPERLINK("https://www.worldcat.org/title/"&SUBSTITUTE(D2," ","-"))

This produces a web address identical to the WorldCat format:

https://www.worldcat.org/title/An-Introduction-to-Human-Factors-Engineering

This formula works well until we come to a title containing an ampersand (&). One of the titles in our list is *Organizing & Organizations,* and although the web address created by the formula is what we would have expected—https://www.worldcat.org/title/Organizing-&-Organizations—Worldcat does not like ampersands and searches only on the word *Organizing.* With predictable results!

The answer to this problem is to use another substitution to convert the & symbol to the word "and":

*=HYPERLINK("https://www.worldcat.org/title/"&SUBSTITUTE(SUBSTITUTE
(D2,"&","and")," ","-"))*

Obviously, the same substitution process could be used to remove punctuation.

As well as linking to records by title, WorldCat offers the same functionality for ISBNs, and we could use the following formula to link from a spreadsheet containing ISBNs in column E:

=HYPERLINK("http://www.worldcat.org/isbn/"&E2)

Similarly, we could create links for ISSNs and OCLC numbers.

EXERCISE

http://bit.ly/2pu2E7G

You can find the format for an ISSN link to WorldCat here: https://www.worldcat.org/links/default.jsp
Create a formula in column B to link the ISSN numbers in column A.

Sticking with WorldCat, it is possible to go the further step by linking to "topical searches." Here is the recommended format:

http://www.worldcat.org/search?q=Napoleonic+Wars

The *plus* symbol is used to designate spaces between the search terms, and essentially this is an AND search on the words *Napoleonic* and *Wars*. If we place sets of search terms in column A, then we can create linked searches in column B using the following formula:

=HYPERLINK("http://www.worldcat.org/search?q="&SUBSTITUTE(A2," ","+"))

Spaces are substituted with the *plus* (+) symbol. You can test this by typing *data management librarians* into cell A2.

Now that we have grasped the idea of using spreadsheets to hyperlink, we can use it in any number of circumstances where a search produces a stable web address, or where a stable structure or web addresses exists. Looking at the Wikipedia entry for Mark Twain, I see that its web address is

https://en.wikipedia.org/wiki/Mark_Twain

Note that the Wikipedia address uses an underscore to join multiple words together as a phrase, so I can make a reasonable guess that it will work in other cases. My first step is to test my hypothesis that a productive Wikipedia web address could be created for any person likely to have their own entry by creating the following in *Notepad++*:

https://en.wikipedia.org/wiki/William_Shakespeare

And sure enough, this brings up the desired entry. So if I had a list of famous people in column A, I could use the following formula in column B to link to their Wikipedia entries:

=HYPERLINK("https://en.wikipedia.org/wiki/"&SUBSTITUTE(A2," ","_"))

It is also possible to script a keyword search of Wikipedia:

EXERCISE

A search of the Library of Congress website for Mark Twain takes the following format:

https://www.loc.gov/search/?in=&q=mark+twain

On a new spreadsheet create a formula in column B that would search the website for any name in column A. Test it against a variety of likely names.

You will notice that the results page for your search will include the search box that is set to search *Everything*. Change it to search for books and printed material, and examine the new web address. Now create a formula that searches for books and printed material only.

=HYPERLINK("https://en.wikipedia.org/w/index.php?search="&A2)

While it is possible to hyperlink search engine queries in this manner, you need to be aware that repeated searching in this manner may violate their terms of service. With Google Scholar, for example, you may find your searches blocked after a few repetitions, and this could affect other people using the same IP address! One possible exception to this is Google Book Search, which uses a simple web address in the following format:

https://www.google.com/search?tbm=bks&q=sweet+potato+dispersal+pacific

This link will lead me to a useful set of books containing information on the spread of the sweet potato from South America across the Pacific Ocean. As we have seen before, spaces between keywords are indicated by *plus* signs, so a spreadsheet formula that will accept a combination of ANDed keywords could read like this:

=HYPERLINK("https://www.google.com/search?tbm=bks&q
="&SUBSTITUTE(A2," ","+"))

Be warned, however, that there is always the possibility that Google Book Search will use a CAPTCHA to determine whether or not you are a human or a machine—if this happens your spreadsheet may simply report that the website you have requested is not available.

The API: Application Programming Interface

Spreadsheets are really useful for automating repetitive processes, and we have seen the power of hyperlinking to avoid the tedium and waste of time that can be caused by continual copying and pasting of book titles, ISBNs, and so on into search boxes. They are less good, however, at dealing with the results of this process, so that if you click on a link to search for an ISSN in WorldCat, you will still have to manually copy and paste the journal title back into your spreadsheet. For this reason programs such as Python and R are regularly used to interrogate websites and utilities and bring back actual data—which can then be stored in CSV files and opened in spreadsheet software for further analysis.

Librarians and related professionals are pretty good at sharing data, and some of our major bibliographic and information utilities are designed for open use. We have already seen this with WorldCat and Library of Congress, both of which provide a stable web address. Other utilities like Crossref, which oversees the DOI system, provide APIs (application programming interfaces), which specify a format in which a request is to be sent and in return provide highly structured data. As this data is not really intended to be read by humans, it is not particularly user-friendly. Here's a snippet of information on a journal with the two relevant pieces of data highlighted:

{"status":"ok","message-type":"journal","message-version":"1.0.0","message": {"last-status-check-time":1571299270750,"counts":{"total-dois":1064," current-dois":586,"backfile-dois":478},"breakdowns":{"dois-by-issued-year":[[2017,227],[2018,194],[2019,165],[2016,126],[2015,85],[2014,77], [2013,74],[2012,69],[2011,47]]},"**publisher":"Springer (Biomed Central Ltd.)**","coverage":{"affiliations-current":0.0,"similarity-checking-current": 1.0,"funders-backfile":0.26359832286834717,"licenses-backfile": 0.5794979333877563,"funders-current":0.7610921263694763," affiliations-backfile":0.0,"resource-links-backfile":0.5794979333877563," orcids-backfile":0.04393305256962776,"update-policies-current":1.0," open-references-backfile":1.0,"orcids-current":0.4317406117916107," similarity-checking-backfile":0.5878661274909973,"references-backfile": 0.9623430967330933,"award-numbers-backfile":0.20502091944217682," update-policies-backfile":0.560669481754303,"licenses-current":1.0," award-numbers-current":0.7184300422668457,"abstracts-backfile":0.0," resource-links-current":1.0,"abstracts-current":0.0,"open-references- current":1.0,"references-current":1.0},**"title":"AMB Express"**

However, the link to this record is a very simple one:

https://api.crossref.org/journals/2191-0855

It consists of a base web address—https://api.crossref.org/journals/—plus an ISSN, so that if the ISSNs are stored in column A, the formula in column B is very simple:

=HYPERLINK("https://api.crossref.org/journals/"&A2))

If you wished to know the title and publisher of the journal represented by this ISSN, then it would be simple enough to click on the link and copy and paste the data from the web page that opened back to the spreadsheet. Although this would be tedious if information were to be retrieved for more than a few ISSNs, it would certainly be quicker and more efficient than searching for each number on a website. However, APIs are not intended to be used in this way, and we will now proceed to look at a more efficient and scalable method of retrieving the data that we want and importing it to a CSV file, which can then be used for further analysis in a spreadsheet.

The Power of Python

Python is a (relatively) simple and intuitive programming language that has a feature which allows us to send requests out to the Internet and receive information back. If the snippet of data that we have just seen that was captured by our simple API appears confusing, that's because it wasn't designed to be read by us but by a computer program. Looking more closely at the snippet, we can see that the two important pieces of information are both preceded by distinctive tags—*publisher*": and *title*":. What is more, in both cases the relevant information is followed immediately after by a double quotation mark so that the whole entry reads:

publisher":"Springer (Biomed Central Ltd.)"
title":"AMB Express"

What this allows us to do is to specify to our Python program that the piece of information we want sits between the initial tag and the double quote. Because of this consistent structure, the program is able to capture both these pieces of data with only the ISSN—delivered through the API—as a starting point.

The real question is how do we deliver the ISSN to the API and how do we receive the journal title and publisher information back, and the answer is through two CSV files, one of which serves as an input and the other as an output. By the use of a specialized module known simply as *csv*, Python is able to read comma-delimited files and also to write them. A second module (*requests*) sends the API out onto the web and receives the data back. Here is a short program that reads ISSNs and journal titles from a CSV file, sends them to Crossref via an API, and identifies the publisher relating to each one. It then writes all this information—ISSN, journal title, and publisher—back to a second CSV file.

```
import csv
import requests

headers=['ISSN','Journal','Publisher']
with open('issn_with_publisher.csv', 'w', newline='') as outputfile:
    writer = csv.writer(outputfile)
    writer.writerow(headers)

with open('issnlist.csv') as inputfile:
    reader = csv.DictReader(inputfile)

for line in reader:

    journal = line['Journal']
    issn = line['ISSN']

    crossrefget = requests.get('https://api.crossref.org/journals/'+issn)
    crossrefdata = str(crossrefget.content)

    startpublisher = crossrefdata.find('publisher":"')+12
    endpublisher = crossrefdata.find('"',startpublisher)
    publisher = crossrefdata[startpublisher:endpublisher]
    row=[issn,journal,publisher]

    with open('issn_with_publisher.csv', 'a', newline='') as outputfile:
        writer = csv.writer(outputfile)
        writer.writerow(row)
```

The first element involves importing two Python modules, *csv* and *requests*, into the program. The *csv* module allows the program to read and write CSV files, while the *requests* module allows it to access the Internet and retrieve content from web pages.

The next section creates an output file called *issn_with_publisher.csv* and writes three column headings to it using the csv module.

Then the input file called *issnlist.csv* is opened. It is comma-delimited and looks like this when opened in a text editor:

```
Journal,ISSN
AMB Express,2191-0855
Applied Microbiology and Biotechnology,1432-0614
"Applied Physiology, Nutrition, and Metabolism",1715-5320
"Asia-Pacific Journal of Health, Sport and Physical Education",1837-7130
```

The first row consists of the column headings. You will notice that when the journal titles contain commas they are surrounded by double quotes.

DictReader is a specialized function of the *csv* module, which uses the first row of the input file to detect the column headings and to mark them as field values. The input file itself is converted to a virtual file called *reader,* and the program now works through this file line by line. First of all, it reads the journal and ISSN data and assigns them to values with the same names—in fact, we could call them anything, but it's always a good idea to keep your program transparent and easy to understand. Although there were only two columns in our input file, the real power of the *DictReader* function becomes apparent when you are using an extensive CSV file with many columns for input. Rather than having to delete unwanted columns, you simply use the names in the Header Row to specify which data elements are to be used in the program.

The next section uses the *requests* module to send an API query incorporating the ISSN to Crossref. The response that is received back (in other words the snippet above plus a good deal more) is stored temporarily in a long string of text string called *crossrefdata.* The program then searches within this text string to find the character string *publisher":"*, which indicates that what follows is the name of the publisher. As each individual character in *crossrefdata* has a location number, the exact starting location of the string *publisher":"* is also a number. Then, as this string is 12 characters in length, the exact starting location of the actual publisher name is given by the formulation

crossrefdata.find('publisher":")+12

This in turn is stored as a numeric value called *startpublisher,* which is used in the next line:

endpublisher = crossrefdata.find('"',startpublisher)

This creates a second numeric value (*endpublisher*) based on the first double quote found after *startpublisher.* These two values are then used to tell Python that we want the text in between them, which in our example is *Informa UK (Taylor & Francis).* This is stored to a value named *publisher.*

publisher = crossrefdata[startpublisher:endpublisher]

The next step is to place the three data elements—the ISSN and the journal title which we had read from the input file, plus the publisher name retrieved from Crossref—into a single list called *row:*

row=[issn,journal,publisher]

Finally, the output file (*issn_with_publisher.csv*) is opened again, and the csv module appends the row in comma-delimited format. Where a comma occurs in a journal title, the title is surrounded by double quotes. When this is done, the program cycles back to process the next line.

When the last line is completed, the final result looks like this:

ISSN,Journal,Publisher
2191-0855,AMB Express,Springer (Biomed Central Ltd.)
1432-0614,Applied Microbiology and Biotechnology,Springer-Verlag
1715-5320,"Applied Physiology, Nutrition, and Metabolism",Canadian Science Publishing
1837-7130,"Asia-Pacific Journal of Health, Sport and Physical Education", Informa UK (Taylor & Francis)

You will notice that the order of the fields was determined by the order in which they were specified in the statement that created *row,* which was different from their order in the input file.

This is a pretty simple program, only 20 lines in length, but it would allow us to capture publisher data for many thousands of ISSNs. A similar Crossref API gives access to information about individual journal articles with DOIs, including how often they have been cited by other articles within Crossref. For example, the API link *https://api.crossref.org/works/10.1371/journal.pone.0209600* accesses the Crossref data for the article *Assignment of a dubious gene cluster to melanin biosynthesis in the tomato fungal pathogen Cladosporium fulvum* published in the journal *PLOS One,* and if the character string *is-referenced-by-count"* is used as a "start marker," then the number of citations can be extracted in exactly the same way the publisher name was extracted in the earlier example. The journal title can also be extracted so that if, for example, all the DOIs for publications from a particular institution, or set of institutions, were submitted, then a substantial CSV file could be created that would then allow for these sorts of spreadsheet-based data analysis that we have seen in earlier chapters.

Crossref is a good example for us to use because it is particularly open, with the API not requiring users to register to obtain a "key"—rather than requiring special registration, they rely on the politeness of users. Most APIs will require you to sign up for a key, and you should read the terms and conditions of the provider carefully. An example of an API that does require registration comes from the Sherpa/Romeo website that provides access to information on the Open Access provisions of journals. The API incorporates the journal ISSN and takes the following format:

http://www.sherpa.ac.uk/romeo/api29.php?issn='+issn+'&'key'

Here is a snippet from its output for the *Accounting, Auditing and Accountability Journal*:

<condition>
Published source must be acknowledged with citation
</condition>
<condition>Publisher's version/PDF cannot be used</condition>
Closed deposit is permitted upon acceptance

The very clear (XML) structuring of the data makes it easy for a program like Python to extract these conditions and export them to a CSV file.

Library proprietary databases, such as Scopus and Web of Science, also provide APIs to eligible registered users. The following API string would allow us to search Scopus to find the number of items in the database that included within their references the book *Bully for Brontosaurus*:

https://api.elsevier.com/content/search/scopus?query=ref(bully-for
-brontosaurus)&apiKEY=key

The output for this includes the following:

<opensearch:totalResults>391</opensearch:totalResults>

From this we are able to extract the number of citations of this book, which is 391! Because the book itself is not included in the database and this citation number is the result of a search process, it was not directly accessible in Scopus.

Putting All of This Together

With this set of tools we can begin to take on some major projects. Here's an example of how we could use bibliographic and circulation data on books exported from a library management system (LMS), submit titles to a data-base in order to extract citation numbers, and then recombine the data into a new CSV file.

http://bit.ly/2IzjEjw

From the LMS bibliographic data classification numbers, titles, authors, publishers, publication years, and editions have been exported as a CSV file which has been incorporated as a worksheet (*Bib_list*) within a spreadsheet (*Circulation_data*). Each book has a unique record number by which the bibliographic data has been sorted—this sits in column A to act as a key to the circulation data.

Record_No.	b10177711	b1017946x	b1018224x
Classification_No.	591 Top	591.012 Cla	591.0182 Gil
Author	Topsell		Gill
Alt_Author	Gesner		
Title	The history of four-footed beasts and serpents and insects	Classification of the animal kingdom: an illustrated guide	Design and analysis of experiments in the animal and medical sciences
Publisher	Da Capo Press	English Universities Press	Iowa State University Press
Year	1967	1972	1978
Edition			1st Ed.

From the circulation system three CSV files are exported for the same titles and copied into the spreadsheet as separate worksheets. Once again the unique record number is placed in column A of each worksheet:

- The worksheet *Locations* contains the location codes for each individual copy relating to the record number, each in a separate column

RECORD NO.	LOC		
b10177711	mbk55	mbk55	mbk09
b1017946x	mbk55		
b1018224x	mbk55		

- The worksheet *Checkouts* contains the checkout numbers for each of these copies in separate columns

RECORD NO.	TOT CHKOUT		
b10177711	5	2	5
b1017946x	6		
b1018224x	7		

- The worksheet *Last_Checkin* contains the date number for the last time each of these copies was checked in

RECORD NO.	LCHKIN		
b10177711	34918	38960	37361
b1017946x	37511		
b1018224x	40133		

If the worksheets are not already sorted by *Record Number*, this should be done now so that the same row for each sheet will relate to the same title. For example, row 7 of each of these sheets contains data for the record number b10186189, and there will be three entries in the row relating to the three copies.

The worksheet *Bib_list* contains the bibliographic data in columns B to H and then three additional columns based on the circulation data from the other worksheets. Cell I2 contains the following formula:

$$=COUNTA(Locations!B2:J2)$$

This formula counts the number of cells in each row of the *Locations* worksheet that contain data in order to calculate the number of copies. If we later wish to use the accumulated data to help us decide on deselecting or weeding copies from the collection, this could be very relevant.

Column J gives a total sum of checkouts for all these copies:

$$=SUM(Checkouts!B2:J2)$$

Column K uses the MAX function to determine which of the date numbers on the *Last_Checkin* worksheet is the highest:

$$=MAX(Last\_Checkin!B2:J2)$$

This will tell us the *latest* returned date of any copy of the book. You will notice that on the *Last_Checkin* worksheet the cells are formatted as *General* and the dates displayed as serial numbers, while on the *Bib_list* worksheet they are formatted as dates in MM/DD/YYYY style.

This aggregation of data tells us a good deal more about the use of the book within the library's circulation system than we would previously have known. A book may have been borrowed frequently in the first few years after purchase but then fallen out of favor as more recent publications have superseded it, or as interest in the subject has declined. On the other hand, an older title may continue to be of current interest because of its "classic" status. Our next step is to obtain further data on the book's standing in its subject area by determining how often it is cited in the literature.

The first step is to save the *Bib_list* worksheet as a CSV file. In Sheets this is done by clicking on *File/Download* and choosing the CSV option. In Excel click on *File/Save As CSV* and choose *OK* to save only the active sheet. In either case, you will have created and saved a file called *Bib_list.csv* as input for the Python program, which will retrieve citation numbers for each of the books from the Scopus database. To begin with, the Python program will create a second CSV file to record its output and will duplicate all the column headers as well as adding an additional one for citations. It will then use the *DictReader* function of the csv module to open the input file and process it line by line, first of all storing the content of each column as a separate data element like this:

```
recordno = line[Record_No.]
classification = line[Classification_No.]
title = line[Title]
```

Note again that *DictReader* uses the headers of the input file to identify these elements. Most of them are stored only for the purposes of copying across to the output file, except for title which becomes input for our query of Scopus. This uses the *requests* module and the title is incorporated into the *requests.get* statement using the API, which we have already looked at:

https://api.elsevier.com/content/search/scopus?query=ref(bully-for
-brontosaurus)&apiKEY=key

Using the title data from our input file, the full statement looks like this in Python code:

```
scopusget=requests.get('https://api.elsevier.com/content/search/scopus
?query=ref('+title+')&apiKEY=key')
scopusdata = str(scopusget.content)
```

As already noted, the tagging in the retrieved data makes it very easy to identify and extract the number of citations:

<opensearch:totalResults>391</opensearch:totalResults>

By using these tags, we can easily snip out the number between them:

citations=scopusdata[startcitations:endcitations]

The output row for each title looks like this:

row=[recordno,classification,author,alt_author,title,publisher,year, edition,copies,total_checkout,last_checkin,citations]

Apart from the citations, all these elements have been read in from the input file.

. This is not a book about Python, and the brief description above is intended simply to give you a view of the potential of extending your use of spreadsheets and CSV files in order to take advantage of the wealth of data that is available to you from external sources. Although the Internet holds a mass of raw data in the form of CSV and TSV files, there may come a time when you want to move beyond the work being done by others and undertake your own research. Personally, I'm a user of Python (because that's what I know!), but there are a number of other programming languages that also empower us to use APIs and other outward-facing tools. Perhaps the best way to take advantage of this capability is to find someone within your organization who already possesses programming skills and who is willing and able to help. If that assistance is not available, then you need to think carefully before setting out to become a programmer yourself—it could be time-consuming, and you need to invest a reasonable amount of time before you can expect any return. However, if you do choose to follow this path, you will benefit from the autonomy that comes from being able to make your own research data-gathering decisions.

The important point in this context, however, is that spreadsheets and programs like Python exist within the same information ecosystem with the common linkage between them being the CSV and TSV file. The power of the spreadsheet lies in its ability to store and analyze data with a set of formulas and functions that allow you to carry out a wide variety of information management activities while programming skills give you almost infinite flexibility in gathering and manipulating text and numbers. The existence of the *csv* module within Python creates a simple and flexible link between the two.

Conclusion

This chapter and Chapter 10 have tried to give you a sense of the spreadsheet as part of a bigger overall system, sometimes known as the "information ecosystem." Those of us who work with spreadsheets a lot generally spend time typing in words and numbers, but more time trying and testing formulas and pivot tables, interacting with the data to find and test new insights, and finding ways in which to express these to colleagues, management, or readers of our published research. However, without data spreadsheets literally do not exist, so finding the best data to "feed" them with is a critical function—as with people, the better the diet the better the performance. Data may come from existing spreadsheets of your own (hold onto them and keep track of where they are), from other spreadsheets within your organization, or from CSV files created by library management systems, downloaded from the web or generated by programs using APIs. Before you go to the effort of generating your own data, you should use your search skills to make sure that it doesn't really exist and that you are not reinventing the wheel, but you should not let your imagination be limited by what already exists. I'm not a huge fan of the idea that if you can think it you can do it, but on the other hand if you don't think and ask questions, then forward progress will not happen. If you do occasionally reinvent the wheel, that will not be time entirely wasted either as you will have an existing data set to test yours against.

As you move forward and develop new skills, your spreadsheets will grow in complexity and sophistication. As this happens you need to make sure that your skills are fully up to the tasks that you are undertaking and also that you are carefully documenting what you do so that others (including your future self) are able to pick up the work and understand what you are doing. I'm not always good at this myself, which is why I'm sharing it with you as a piece of sound advice. Remember that a spreadsheet consists of a number of worksheets and that one of these can be used for documentation. You should explain the overall "system" that the spreadsheet is using, the data sources used, and perhaps an explanation of the more complex formulas. These are all aspects of sound data management, and the best place to acquire good data management skills is your own work!

CHAPTER TWELVE

Conclusion

This book will by no means have told you everything you will ever need to know about spreadsheets, but I hope that those of you who have read this far will now have a good sense of their potential and some enthusiasm for continuing under your own steam. If you do wish to know everything, there will be better books than this for taking you deep into the complexities, but what I have tried to do is to suggest *why* you might want to do this and to point out some of the main directions in which you might want to direct your efforts. I have tried, within the limits of my own knowledge and imagination, to make it relevant to your work as a practicing librarian and to introduce you to some tips and tricks that will make you more effective and productive. I have done my level best to make sure that everything I have told you "works" and every formula in this book has been tested on an actual spreadsheet, but from time to time some of you may have been shaking your heads and saying "I wouldn't have done it that way!" Part of the joy, as well as the frustration, of any IT project is that there are always several ways of achieving the same result. Sometimes I have gone back to spreadsheets that I've done in the past and have been amused to see the roundabout route that I took to get from point A to point B, but that's all part of the learning process. And, in fact, having more than one way of arriving at a result can often be useful—if the two methods don't give you the same outcome, then you need to do some closer examination!

If you have read a significant portion of this book and carried out some of the exercises, you are clearly prepared to invest some of your time in getting to know spreadsheets properly. Like any tool they are best and most efficiently used by those who know what they are doing. You may, if you are like me, have come to enjoy the challenge of testing your methods against your data and seeing words, numbers, tables, and charts appear as if by magic. However, don't lose sight of the fact that they are, first and foremost, supposed to be a productivity enhancement tool and not a sort of mental gymnasium where the challenge is to test yourself on all the equipment. In the end, spreadsheets are there to provide answers to questions that already exist, so you need to be able to clearly describe what it is that you are wanting to know before you start a new spreadsheet. On the other hand, however, there are times when an exploratory or experimental mind-set can be helpful, and you can begin asking other questions about the data in front of you. Imagination is an important part of any research methodology, and it is my hope that this book has given you the tools and techniques that will allow you to begin looking at columns of rows and numbers and seeing real shapes emerge from them, like a statue out of a block of marble.

The bad news is that you will need more books, but I hope that as librarians we all understand this better than most people! You can never have too much information, and although I have gone into considerable detail in some places, in others it has been very much a once-over lightly approach. I have tried to explain the various formulas and functions we have encountered in simple nontechnical language, but there will be subtleties and complexities that are not well served by this approach. And sometimes we just need to have things explained more than once before the lightbulb moment occurs. Make sure you have access to a proper reference guide, and don't be afraid to use it. Excel is rather better served in this regard than Sheets, but most of the formulas and functions we have dealt with work in pretty much the same way in both systems. A short list of books follows this chapter.

Likewise the Internet is a great source of information, and I have included a list of useful websites. I have done a fair amount of googling for information, perhaps more than I would have wanted to, and have found answers to some of my more difficult questions in this way. Be aware though that you will need to apply your full set of information literacy skills when using this approach. Although I haven't found any out-and-out fake news, I have encountered a certain amount of bad advice, some highly abstruse technical discussion, a fair few attempts to sell me add-ons, and one or two WTFs.

When I embarked on the writing of this book, I was largely an Excel user who had made occasional use of Sheets and other systems like LibreOffice. It was at the publisher's request that I extended my coverage to Sheets, and I have been very glad that this was the case, being now something of the convert and more likely to reach for Sheets when I just want to do some quick calculations. Writing about two very similar systems has been a challenge at times, and I'm aware that it may make certain parts of the book rather repetitive. I've occasionally remarked to friends that it's been rather like setting out to write a book on conversational Italian and then having to include conversational Spanish as well—there's a fair amount of "the same but different" throughout these pages. I would encourage you to look at both systems and think carefully about them before making your choice. However, you also need to take into account the practice within your own organization and the advice of your IT department. If everybody is using Excel, then go with the flow. Nobody will thank you after you have moved on from your job to find out that all the spreadsheets you have created will need converting! My advice is to avoid becoming too hung up on this—there are a number of good spread-sheeting systems that all do a fairly similar job, and your primary concern should be doing your job as a librarian, not being a software advocate. However, if you really want to become a software warrior, go right ahead—you don't need my permission.

You will notice that I have not hesitated to identify shortcomings as I have come across them (as well as areas of specific strength) and, without being too negative, I have tried to give a fair and balanced account of the spread-sheeting universe. I would like to say that I was optimistic that some of these long-standing glitches would be solved in the near future, but it is in the nature of long-standing glitches not to be sorted out—that's how they achieve this distinction. Spreadsheeting is a relatively mature technology, and Excel has been around since the 1980s. While it is glaringly obvious to me, and probably to you, what should be done to sort out some of its annoyances, we should probably assume that they are very much baked in and not suscepti-ble to easy fixes. I'm still hoping that if you are reading these words in a few years time, you will be wondering what I'm talking about, but I'm not going to lay any money on it.

Looking back, writing this book has given me a great deal of pleasure and has also been an enormous learning experience. At times I have been asking myself why I ever volunteered for the task as the extent of my own ignorance became clear to me. I don't claim to be a fully-fledged expert, but over the years I have approached whatever spreadsheeting tasks came my way with a spirit of exploration and open inquiry. Technical knowledge is a great thing, and you should acquire as much of it as you can, but it is really only useful if it is powered by imagination and curiosity. I hope that by showing you the operation of spreadsheets in real-life library situations, I will have been able to open your eyes to a world of possibilities. If you now go away and begin asking questions of your data and trying different ways of arriving at answers, then my job has been done.

Suggested Readings

Books

Greiner, T., & Cooper, B. (2007). *Analyzing library collection use with Excel*. Chicago, IL: American Library Association.

Held, B., Moriarty, B., & Richardson, T. (2018). *Microsoft Excel functions and formulas* (4th ed.). Dulles, VA: Mercury Learning & Information.

Jelen, B. (2019). *Microsoft Excel 2019 inside out*. Redmond, WA: Microsoft Press.

Jelen, B., & Alexander, M. (2019). *Microsoft Excel 2019: Pivot table data crunching*. Hoboken, NJ: Pearson Education.

Walkenbach, J. (2016). *Microsoft Excel 2016 Bible: The comprehensive tutorial resource*. Indianapolis, IN: John Wiley & Sons.

Articles Relating to Excel

Bangani, S., Chizwina, S., & Moyo, M. (2018). An analysis of interlibrary loan services: A case study of a university in South Africa. *Information Discovery and Delivery*, 46(1), 26–37. https://doi.org/10.1108/IDD-08-2017-0059

Brennan, D. (2016). Simple export of journal citation data to Excel using any reference manager. *Journal of the Medical Library Association: JMLA*, 104(1), 72–75. https://doi.org/10.3163/1536-5050.104.1.012

Coyle, A. (2011). Interior library GIS. *Library Hi Tech*, 29(3), 529–549. https://doi.org/10.1108/07378831111174468

Herrera, G. (2015). Testing the patron-driven model: Availability analysis of first-time use books. *Collection Management*, 40(1), 3–16. https://doi.org/10.1080/01462679.2014.965863

Kimball, R. (2016). Journal overlap analysis of the GeoRef and Web of Science databases. *Science and Technology Libraries*, 35(1), 91–98. https://doi.org/10.1080/0194262X.2015.1128374

Marshall, S. P., & Kawasaki, J. L. (2005). The master serial list at Montana State University—A simple, easy to use approach. *Serials Librarian*, 47(4), 3–15. https://doi.org/10.1300/J123v47n04_02

Meyer, J. (2015). Monitoring the pulse: Data-driven collection management. *Computers in Libraries, 35*(6), 16–21.

Miller, A. (2014). Application of Excel pivot tables and pivot charts for efficient library data analysis and illustration. *Journal of Library Administration, 54*(3), 169–186. https://doi.org/10.1080/01930826.2014.915162

Miller, A. (2014). Introduction to using Excel pivot tables and pivot charts to increase efficiency in library data analysis and illustration. *Journal of Library Administration, 54*(2), 94–106. https://doi.org/10.1080/01930826 .2014.903365

Oliphant, T., & Shiri, A. (2017). The long tail of search and topical queries in public libraries. *Library Review, 66*(6/7), 430–441. https://doi.org/10.1108 /LR-11-2016-0097

Pouchard, L., & Bracke, M. S. (2016). An analysis of selected data practices: A case study of the Purdue College of Agriculture. *Issues in Science and Technology Librarianship.* https://doi.org/10.5062/F4057CX4

Spratt, S. J. (2018). Datavi$: Negotiate resource pricing using data visualization. *The Serials Librarian, 74*(1–4), 1–5. https://doi.org/10.1080/0361526X.2018 .1428002

Velasquez, D. L., & Evans, N. (2018). Public library websites as electronic branches: A multi-country quantitative evaluation. *Information Research, 23*(1). Retrieved from http://www.informationr.net/ir/23-1/paper786.html

Articles Relating to Google Sheets

Bartczak, J., & Glendon, I. (2017). Python, Google Sheets, and the Thesaurus for Graphic Materials for Efficient Metadata Project workflows. *Code4Lib Journal,* (35), 1. Retrieved from https://journal.code4lib.org/articles/12182

Boman, C., & Voelker, R. (2017). Between the sheets: A library-wide inventory with Google. *Code4Lib Journal* (38), 1. Retrieved from https://journal .code4lib.org/articles/12783

Knight, R. C., Rodrigues, E., & Ciota, R. (2017). Collaborating for metadata creation on digital projects: Using Google Forms and Sheets. *Library Hi Tech News, 34*(8), 20–23. Retrieved from http://10.0.4.84/LHTN-08-2017-0056

Laskowski, L. (2016). Google Forms and Sheets for library gate counts. *Journal of Access Services, 13*(3), 151–158. https://doi.org/10.0.4.56/15367967.2016 .1184577

Lindsay, B. D. (2016). Using Google Forms to track library space usage. *Journal of Access Services, 13*(3), 159–165. https://doi.org/10.0.4.56/15367967.2016 .1184578

Luo, J. (2018). Using Google apps to manage embargo records: Automating institutional repository reminders. *College & Research Libraries News, 79*(3), 137–140. Retrieved from http://10.0.22.228/crln.79.3.137

Suon, E. B. (2019). DIY data dashboards in Google Sheets. *Computers in Libraries, 39*(7), 16–19.

Useful Websites

500 Excel formula examples. (2019). Retrieved November 14, 2019, from https://exceljet.net/formulas

Google Sheets function list. (n.d.). Retrieved November 14, 2019, from https://support.google.com/docs/table/25273?hl=en&ref_topic=1361471

Google Sheets 101: The beginner's guide to online spreadsheets. (2016). Retrieved November 14, 2019, from https://zapier.com/learn/google-sheets/google-sheets-tutorial

Working with data: Essential spreadsheets. (n.d.). Retrieved November 14, 2019, from https://sites.google.com/a/york.ac.uk/workingwithdata/spreadsheets

Index